The Dark Side of Reform

The Dark Side of Reform

Exploring the Impact of Public Policy on Racial Equity

Edited by
Tyrell Connor and Daphne M. Penn

LEXINGTON BOOKS
Lanham • Boulder • New York • London

Chapter 2 was initially published in Volume 48, Book 3, of the Fordham Urban Law Journal and is republished with permission. Jefferson-Bullock, J and Jefferson Exum, J. (2021). That is Enough Punishment: Situating Defund the Police Within Antiracist Sentencing Reform. The Fordham Urban Law Journal, 48(3), 625.

Published by Lexington Books
An imprint of The Rowman & Littlefield Publishing Group, Inc.
4501 Forbes Boulevard, Suite 200, Lanham, Maryland 20706

www.rowman.com

6 Tinworth Street, London SE11 5AL, United Kingdom

Copyright © 2022 The Rowman & Littlefield Publishing Group, Inc.

All rights reserved. No part of this book may be reproduced in any form or by any electronic or mechanical means, including information storage and retrieval systems, without written permission from the publisher, except by a reviewer who may quote passages in a review.

British Library Cataloguing in Publication Information Available

Library of Congress Cataloging-in-Publication Data

Names: Connor, Tyrell, 1987- editor. | Penn, Daphne M., 1986- editor.
Title: The dark side of reform : exploring the impact of public policy on racial equity / edited by Tyrell Connor and Daphne M. Penn.
Description: Lanham : Lexington Books, [2022] | Includes bibliographical references and index. | Summary: "The Dark Side of Reform contains nine chapters on the development of social policies with the potential to advance racial equity. The volume also offers recommendations for implementing policies that address the unique concerns of structurally disadvantaged communities-with particular emphasis on Black and Latinx people"—Provided by publisher.
Identifiers: LCCN 2021053175 (print) | LCCN 2021053176 (ebook) | ISBN 9781793643759 (cloth) | ISBN 9781793643773 (paperback) | ISBN 9781793643766 (ebook)
Subjects: LCSH: United States—Race relations—Political aspects. | Racial justice—United States. | Civil rights—United States. | United States—Social policy.
Classification: LCC E184.A1 D2685 2022 (print) | LCC E184.A1 (ebook) | DDC 305.800973—dc23/eng/20211203
LC record available at https://lccn.loc.gov/2021053175
LC ebook record available at https://lccn.loc.gov/2021053176

Contents

Preface   vii

Introduction: Advancing Racial Equity through Public Policy   1
Daphne M. Penn and Tyrell Connor

1   The Gun Control Debate and Its Policy Implications for Reducing Firearm Violence in Communities of Color   15
Daniel Semenza and Brian Wade

2   Policing Is Punishment: Defunding the Police as Sentencing Reform   33
Jalila Jefferson-Bullock and Jelani Jefferson Exum

3   Four Racial Justice Principles for Policy Response to Carceral Technology   49
Emily Tucker

4   Marijuana Legalization   67
Angela S. Murolo

5   American Dream into Nightmare: Immigration, Systemic Structural Racism, and Health Inequity in the United States   87
Jay Pearson

6   #StopAsianHate: Examining Rising Levels of Anti-Asian Hate Crimes in the United States   109
Janice A. Iwama

7   Complexity and Possibility: Black Public Opinion on Immigration   125
Niambi M. Carter

8 Legacy of Good Trouble: The Next Frontier for Voting Rights 141
Candice C. Robinson, LaTeri McFadden, and J. Nicole Johnson

9 Searching for a Racial Justice Agenda in High Poverty Settings: How Title I Reform's Data Blindness Limits Its Educational Effectiveness for Black and Latinx Students 159
Charisse Southwell and Michael Hudson-Vassell

Conclusion 179
Tyrell Connor and Daphne M. Penn

Index 185

About the Authors 195

Preface

The idea for this book originated from conversations between the volume's editors, who are the hosts and founders of the Black and Highly Dangerous (BhD) Podcast—a show dedicated to disseminating scholarly research beyond the academy. The volume reflects a collective effort in which both editors equally engaged in the preparation of the book—from book proposal to final submission. Therefore, the editor order for the book cover and title page follows the conventional practice of listing names alphabetically—not by contribution level. The author order for the introductory chapter, jointly written by both editors, is reversed. Finally, the naming sequence of the closing chapter was decided based on each author's contribution.

This volume would not have been possible without the thoughtful and brilliant authors who dedicated their time and expertise to producing informative, yet accessible, chapters on some of our nation's most pressing policy issues. We are incredibly thankful for their contributions to this effort, especially given that these chapters were drafted, revised, and edited within the context of a global pandemic. We would also like to express appreciation for Lexington Books and our acquisition editors—Courtney Lachapelle Morales and Matthew Valades—for providing us with the opportunity to develop and edit this volume.

DAPHNE'S ACKNOWLEDGMENTS

First and foremost, I would like to thank my spouse, John, for believing in my work, supporting me unconditionally, and encouraging me to remain steadfast in my academic pursuits. I would like to express gratitude to my family, who supported me in all of my endeavors. I feel incredibly blessed to have parents—Irving Penn, Myra Armstrong, and Elgin Armstrong—who encouraged me to "see it through," despite the inevitable obstacles and challenges of life. I also appreciate my siblings, Dywana and DeWayne, for their constant reassurance and well-timed pep talks. For their prayers and inspiring words, I thank Dr. Mike Fonge and Anne Fonge as well as Dr. Takor Arrey-Mbi and Susan Arrey-Mbi. Additionally, I am grateful to the following people for being a source of encouragement, friendship, and laughter while writing and editing a book during a pandemic: Dr. Ashley Custard, Meya (Tidwell) Elijah, Dr. Hardeep Dhillon, Alexis Gaines, Dr. Jonathan Hampton, Valerie Herrera, Garry Mitchell, Valery Parham, Erishika Payne, Dr. Matthew Patrick Shaw, Dr. Renee Rinehart, Dr. Brook Dennard Rosser, and Dr. Andrea White. I am also incredibly grateful to Dr. Rich Furman, who not only helped me change my mindset and habits around writing but also provided me with concrete guidance that enabled us to successfully publish this edited volume. Along those lines, I'm thankful to my editor, Jane, for pushing me as a writer. Additionally, I thank my mentors, Drs. Roberto G. Gonzales and Marty West, for their continued support. Last, but certainly not the least, I would like to thank the "fly lady writers," especially Drs. Sa-kiera T.J. Hudson, Brielle Harbin, and Jamil S. Scott, who motivate me to write, strive, and thrive. I am confident that, with the continued support and wise counsel of my family, friends, mentors, and colleagues, anything is possible. Please note, if I failed to acknowledge anyone, I ask that you charge it to my head—definitely not my heart.

TYRELL'S ACKNOWLEDGMENTS

This volume would not have been possible without the encouragement and support of my wife, Krystin. Her words of affirmation and excitement fueled my desire to complete this volume during a global pandemic. Additionally, my lovely daughter, Maya, provided me with a new sense of purpose and makes everyday special with her infant smiles, giggles, and curious personality. I would like to express deep gratitude to my parents, Cornelius and Francine, for laying the foundation that allowed me to pursue my passions and thrive throughout life. Also, my brothers, Jamaar and Andre, have always been my personal comedians and continue to provide timely laughs and heartfelt joys. Finally, I would like to pay homage to our ancestors who fought and sacrificed so that future generations of Black Americans can live in a world stronger, wiser, and free. We share this volume to continue that mission.

Introduction
Advancing Racial Equity through Public Policy
Daphne M. Penn and Tyrell Connor

Over the past 10 years, there has been a growing appetite among Americans for the government to take active steps to address persistent inequality and improve people's lives through transformative economic and social policy (Jones & Saad, 2019). Indeed, for the first time in nearly three decades, the majority of Americans believe that the government should do more to solve the nation's problems (Brenan, 2020) by increasing the social safety net (Barry et al., 2020) and ensuring basic living standards (Cusick, 2021). Across party lines, voters increasingly support progressive economic and social policies, such as increasing the federal minimum wage, strengthening unemployment benefits, establishing a national medical and paid family leave program, offering higher levels of food assistance to families in need, and developing a universal health insurance program (Barry et al., 2020; Cusick, 2021; Manchester, 2018).

Increased support for "big" government coincides with several unprecedented events that have (a) shed light on contemporary inequality and (b) exacerbated historical inequalities experienced by the most marginalized individuals along ethno-racial divides. In particular, the 2008 global financial crisis, which led to the most severe economic recession in modern history, highlighted vulnerabilities within our capitalist society. Although most Americans were negatively affected by the 2008 economic downturn, the impacts of the recession were not evenly distributed. As the saying goes, when America catches a cold, African Americans—and to an increasing extent Latinxs—catch pneumonia. During the height of the Great Recession, African American and Latinx populations experienced disproportionate rates of unemployment and underemployment. More specifically, the unemployment rate among African Americans, which reached upwards of 16.8 % in March 2010, was nearly double the White unemployment rate during the same period (Cunningham, 2018). Only slightly lower than the African American unemployment rate, the unemployment rate among Latinxs soared to 13 percent during the recession. In addition to adverse labor market outcomes, African Americans and Latinxs also experienced unprecedented declines in wealth (Kochhar et al., 2011).

Along with the Great Recession came the Great American Affordability Crisis, resulting from sharp increases in housing costs and instability. In a 2019 report released by the Joint Center for Housing Studies (JCHS) at Harvard, 47.4 percent of renters are cost-burdened, a term that denotes households which spend more than 30 percent of their income on housing costs. Cost-burdened renters are increasingly facing housing insecurity as natural disasters exert a greater impact on housing affordability and as unsheltered homelessness continues to rise. Unsurprisingly, a greater share of African American and Latinx households are cost-burdened, an issue that was exacerbated by the COVID-19 pandemic.

The most recent event shaping public support for additional social safety net policies is the COVID-19 pandemic, which contributed to both unemployment and adverse health outcomes for millions of Americans. Between February and June 2020, unemployment rates increased by 7.6 percent to reach 11.1 percent unemployment nationwide (Bureau of Labor Statistics, 2020). At one point during the pandemic, more than 20 million US workers filed for unemployment benefits (United States Department of Labor, 2020). Similar to the Great Recession, Black and Latinx people experienced a disproportionate number of negative outcomes related to the pandemic. For example, during this same period, the Black and Latinx unemployment rates rose to 15.4 percent and 14.5 percent, respectively. Beyond employment outcomes, Black and Latinx people disproportionately contracted and subsequently died from COVID-19 when compared to the total population (Ray, 2020). In response to the pandemic fallout, the general public and political leaders, alike, began to have conversations about the role of the government in society.

Overall, the unprecedented events of the past decade have not only highlighted vulnerabilities within our current system, but they have also seemingly sparked interest in progressive public policies. Along with the growing progressive movement, these events have compelled left-leaning political candidates and leaders to articulate a vision for structural change. Not only have progressive policies become key features of the Democratic platform, but they have also increasingly received bipartisan support (Barry et al., 2020; Cusick, 2021; Manchester, 2018). However, given the current extent of racialized inequality, calls for progressive social policies have also been accompanied by conversations about the need to develop and implement public policy that accounts for the various ways that people's identities intersect with systems of power to reproduce inequality. At the heart of these conversations are concerns about the welfare of individuals who occupy the most marginalized positions in society, and whether or not they will receive the full benefit of transformative policies that may emerge in the coming years.

The goal of this volume is to help shape the conversation around what it means to develop inclusive social policies that account for the disparate experiences and outcomes of individuals at different intersections of race, ethnicity, and socioeconomic status. Although this book focuses on contemporary policy proposals, we believe that history has the potential to help us better understand the present and strategize to create a better future. Therefore, in addition to exploring the implications of race within contemporary policy proposals, the chapters in this volume also demonstrate how lessons from the past can be used to inform the direction of current policy discussions. Along those lines, the next sections of this introduction build the case for more inclusive approaches to policy design and implementation by exploring the content of past US social policies and their consequences for persistent racialized inequality.

THE IMPORTANCE OF CENTERING RACE AND HISTORY IN POLICY DISCUSSIONS

The historical roots of racism in the United States have continuously impacted all facets of American life for people of color, particularly within the public policy context. From Reconstruction to the civil rights era to the present moment, the embedded nature of racism within our society has contributed to the development of policies that have reproduced and sustained racial inequality across various domains of life. Specifically, when we reflect on the timeline for major policies in the United States, the most marginalized individuals along ethno-racial divides have not only been excluded from the full benefits of social policies aimed at reducing inequality, but they have also been disproportionately harmed by punitive policies. For instance, the early 20th century was marked by transformative social welfare policies that contributed to wealth accumulation, particularly for White Americans. Although the mid-20th century produced some gains related to civil rights for Black Americans, the 1980s were characterized by a rise in punitive approaches to public policy that disproportionately harmed Black and Brown communities. This pattern, which we further outline below, raises concerns about the extent to which these communities will benefit from this potential new era of transformative policy aimed at reducing inequality and repairing harm.

Who Benefits from Social Policy in the United States?

An examination of major transformative US policies will reveal that the government has done more to promote structural racism than it has for the advancement of all people. Indeed, critical analysis of US social policy indicates that race and racism have and continue to shape access to the full benefit of state-sponsored programs that offer opportunities for social mobility (Brodkin, 1998; Katznelson, 2005; Oliver & Shapiro, 1995). Unsurprisingly, racialized access to seemingly race-neutral policies has contributed to persistent inequality, especially in relation to racial wealth gaps.

In his book, *When Affirmative Action Was White*, Ira Katznelson demonstrates how universalistic policies contributed to the unequal distribution of economic opportunity by race in the United States. He argues that transformative social policies, such as the New Deal and G.I. Bill, were characterized by the systematic exclusion of Black Americans and many immigrant groups. One example of this is the Fair Labor Act, which included provisions related to unionization and minimum wages and excluded domestic and agricultural workers. These provisions negatively impacted the majority of Black female workers—who were often engaged in domestic labor—and upwards of 40 percent of the Black male workforce. The jobs primarily occupied by Black workers were also excluded under the Social Security Act, which denied them benefits despite their years of labor. Furthermore, disparities in homeownership and wealth accumulation can be explained historically because of discriminatory housing and lending practices by the Federal Housing Administration (FHA). Specifically, discriminatory housing practices allowed White Americans to build their suburban dream homes while denying African Americans the same opportunity (Conley, 2001; Oliver & Shapiro, 1995; Rothstein, 2017).

These patterns of exclusion from wealth-generating or -sustaining policies continue into the present day. The most recent example is the Paycheck Protection Program, which aimed to provide relief to small businesses and their employees during the pandemic. Based on early reports, the program's structure, which provided banks with considerable latitude in administering the program, shut out upwards of 90 percent of minority and female business owners (Cerullo, 2020). Subsequent data indicated that among the 14 percent of loans where the race and ethnicity of the business owner were identified, Black- and Latinx-owned businesses received only 2 percent and 6.6 percent of paycheck protection loans, respectively (Kranhold & Zubak-Skees, 2020). Similarly, less than 1 percent of farmers of color received support from a federal grant program designed to provide relief to farmers and producers due to the COVID-19 pandemic (Bustillo, 2021).

The gaps in wealth created by policy exclusions—and/or discriminatory practices by street-level bureaucrats who have discretionary power over the administration of social policy (Weatherley & Lipsky, 1977)—will continue to have a lasting impact given the importance of wealth in a capitalistic society. In total, experts indicate that the racial wealth gap is $10.14 trillion.

From a micro perspective, a typical Black family had a net worth of about $17,100 in 2016 compared to about $170,000 for a typical White family (McIntosh et al., 2020). At the current pace, it would take the average Black household 228 years to achieve wealth parity with White households (Asante-Muhammed et al., 2016). For the typical Latinx family, closing the gap would take 84 years. Given the sobering statistics and outlook related to racialized inequality, we argue that it is important to begin this new era of policy with racial equity in mind.

Who Is Harmed by Social Policy in the United States?

African American and Latinx communities are not only excluded from beneficial policies, but they also bear the burden of punitive legislation. Throughout history, the United States has enacted sweeping policy changes that disproportionately harm people of color. The criminal justice, immigration, and education systems, which we discuss in the following sections, provide useful illustrations.

The War on Crime and, subsequently, the War on Drugs have been the most notable federally supported criminal justice reforms with enforcement outcomes that disproportionately harmed non-White communities. Although research indicates the rate of drug use between White and other communities is not significantly different, the enforcement of the law has not been applied equally (Tonry, 2011). Drug legislation established mandatory minimum jail terms and a sentencing discrepancy between crack cocaine and cocaine. The federal government instituted policies that created a 100-to-1 discrepancy in sentencing patterns; this meant that a person caught with 5 grams of crack cocaine received a mandatory five-year prison sentence, while someone would have to have 500 grams of cocaine to receive the same sentence (Alexander, 2010). Given that crack cocaine—a less expensive form of the drug—was used at higher rates in Black and Brown communities compared to White communities, the laws disproportionately pushed law enforcement into communities of color (Tonry, 2011).

Immigration enforcement is another long-standing policy issue that has disproportionately impacted marginalized groups. Beginning in the 19th century, the United States began the process of creating laws that racialized and criminalized immigrants. For instance, the United States began prohibiting entry into the country for convicted felons in 1875. In 1882, the government placed a moratorium on labor migration from China through the Chinese Exclusion Act. Enforcement efforts continued through the 20th century, including enacting amendments related to immigration marriage fraud, enabling immigration officers to carry firearms, providing judges with the power to order deportation, and, eventually, establishing immigration detention centers (United States Citizenship and Immigration Services, 2019).

The 21st century saw the establishment of the Immigration and Customs Enforcement (ICE) agency as a response to the September 2001 attacks on the Twin Towers. The main goal of ICE was to protect the United States from transnational crime and illegal immigration. Shortly after its founding, scholars noticed an increase in and overlap between immigration and criminalization practices. Law professor Juliet Stumpf coined the term crimmigration to denote the criminalization of immigration law and procedure (Stumpf, 2006). Between 2003 and 2014, there was steady growth in deportations from the United States (Gonzalez-Barrerra & Lopez, 2016). People of color, mainly migrants from Mexico and Central American countries, have been the primary focus of immigration enforcement in the 21st century, with the majority of deportations occurring for noncriminal reasons (Radford, 2019). According to a Pew Research Center Study, 60 % of immigrants who were deported have not been convicted of a crime. In 2010, Arizona passed SB 1070, allowing law enforcement to stop and question suspected undocumented immigrants (Morse, 2011). This law has allowed for greater racial profiling and harassment against communities of color because, although any person has the potential to be undocumented, the Latinx community is often at the center of discussions about this issue.

Like the punitive turn in the criminal justice system, the neoliberal education reform movement has had a disproportionately negative impact on minority-serving schools. Education historians mark *A Nation at Risk*—a 30-page report published by the National Commission on Excellence in Education in 1983—as "the beginning of the standards movement, if not the entire modern school reform movement" (Viteritti, 2012, p. 2091). The report framed the country's "failing schools" as a national crisis and set the stage for an educational policy agenda focused on accountability, expanding market choice, and privatizing education. It also ushered in a new era of reliance on data, an approach that established standardized test scores as a vehicle of racial inequality rather than a tool to attenuate it (Au, 2016; Southwell & Hudson-Vassell, Chapter 9).

The height of this era of reliance on data was the passage of the No Child Left Behind Act (NCLB) of 2001, which was a reauthorization of the Elementary and Secondary Education Act (ESEA) of 1965 under George W. Bush. NCLB required states to create learning standards and annually test children in reading and mathematics. In addition to annual testing, NCLB mandated assessment scores to be disaggregated by different subgroups, such as ethno-racial category, socioeconomic status, English proficiency, and special education needs. Results from these standardized tests have informed decisions such as student placement and retention, school rankings, and school funding (David, 2005; NCLB, 2001). As Southwell and Hudson-Vassell discuss in chapter 9, this policy has disproportionately penalized schools serving Black and Latinx students.

Ultimately, communities of color are the most impacted when policy agendas promote government enforcement. When coupled with their historical exclusion from the full rights and privileges of transformative social policy, the Black and Latinx communities' status as the targets of governmental enforcement efforts has only exacerbated the racial oppression they experience in the United States.

How Do We Design Social Policy to Produce Racial Equity?

Conversations about public policy are beginning to center on more progressive ideas and approaches to solving the nation's problems. In particular, political candidates and leaders are increasingly being compelled to articulate a vision for structural change. In many instances, class inequality—rather than racial inequity—has taken center stage in debates about the best approach to improving the well-being of our nation's most marginalized populations. Although seemingly race-neutral policies have the potential to transform the lives of the majority of Americans, history suggests that policy benefits may not always be equally distributed in the population. Therefore, the inattention to race not only overlooks the cumulative inequality faced by Black Americans and other structurally disadvantaged groups, but it also potentially widens disparities they face across essential domains of social life. Unfortunately, policy-related racial disparities typically surface well after the damage has occurred. Policymakers, then, rush to retroactively address the "unforeseen" racial consequences of past policies. The unequal distribution of benefits and harms associated with policymaking in the United States suggests that we should change the way we discuss and develop social policy moving forward.

This volume emphasizes the need to move beyond universalistic language around social policy that, typically, ignores the racialized nature of inequality in the United States. We argue that race consciousness should be at the heart of every conversation about transformative social policy, especially as the country works to overcome the dual pandemics of racism and COVID-19. Political leaders, candidates, and advocates must begin to recognize and name racial equity as an explicit outcome of public policy. In a political climate where serious conversations about reparations, criminal justice, and wealth inequality are occurring against the backdrop of ongoing police violence and attacks on civil rights, now is the time to prioritize reform initiatives that address race-specific concerns. An approach focused on racial equity allows us to recognize and reduce the inequalities created by both historical and contemporary systemic racism. By focusing on racial equity within the policy design and implementation process, we can work to (a) remedy the harm caused by the racialized nature of policy implementation and enforcement and (b) anticipate some of the unintended consequences of seemingly race-neutral policy initiatives.

Important to note, the fight for racial equity in the United States has been characterized by cycles of oppression, progress, and backlash. For instance, in response to the *Brown v. Board of Education* decision, White politicians and families in the South organized the "massive resistance" campaign to fight integration. Mounting legal challenges in the decades following *Brown* have effectively maintained separate and unequal schooling for children of color and their White counterparts. Affirmative action offers another example. Although affirmative action aims to reduce unlawful discrimination based on legally protected statuses, the practice has generally been associated with quotas—which have been prohibited since 1974—and the notion that women and ethno-racial minorities are provided with an unfair advantage in employment and admissions. As a result of these beliefs among critics of the policy, affirmative action has faced a number of legal challenges. In fact, the Supreme Court has decided on five major affirmative action-related cases over the past forty years. Although current affirmative action policies are generally narrowly defined and use strict scrutiny (e.g., race is not the sole determining factor in achieving the compelling interest of the institution), more challenges—such as *Students for Fair Admissions v. Harvard*, which claims that Harvard's admissions practices discriminate against Asians—are likely on the horizon. As these examples suggest, a policy approach that centers racial equity as an outcome may be met with and limited by the potential backlash.

Despite potential challenges to centering racial equity in the policy process, recent and rising attacks on the rights and freedoms of historically marginalized communities require activists, advocates, and political officials to work proactively to achieve progress and counter backlash. The purpose of this book is to provide information that will allow various stakeholders to think strategically about how to design, evaluate, and implement social policies that address the concerns of structurally disadvantaged communities—with particular emphasis on Black and Latinx people.

AN OVERVIEW OF THE BOOK

The Dark Side of Reform's goal is to be a resource that informs readers about present-day policy ideas using a racial equity lens. Each chapter in this volume addresses a current policy debate or issue, provides insight into the development of the problem, and evaluates potential issues in terms of racial equity. Authors also provide recommendations that could potentially ensure equity in policy design and implementation processes around the various issues addressed. As a note, each contributor is well-versed in and passionate about the topics they cover. They were specially selected because of their extraordinary work and passion within their respective fields. Their knowledge provides a depth of insight that will not only enlighten readers but also motivate them to promote change.

In chapter 1, Daniel Semenza and Brian Wade focus on the ramifications of gun violence in urban, disadvantaged communities as well as potential shortcomings of firearms policy. In addition to discussing racial disparities related to gun violence, the authors also provide policy recommendations and considerations to address the potential pitfalls of widely discussed gun control measures that often fail to address the issue of gun violence in communities of color.

Following the killings of George Floyd and Breonna Taylor by police, many organizers and politicians proposed legislation to defund police departments. Jalila Jefferson-Bullock and Jelani Jefferson Exum, in chapter 2, discuss this growing movement that emerged in response to calls for significant police reform in the wake of ongoing fatal encounters between unarmed Black people and police. This chapter describes what it means to defund police. Additionally, the authors of this chapter highlight how defunding the police may impact communities of color.

Continuing with the topic of policing, chapter 3 explores the intersection between and implications of technology and policing for Black and Latinx people. Specifically, Emily Tucker highlights the need to critically examine how evolving technology shapes racial disparities within the criminal justice context. Although these systems are designed to increase efficiency, recent research suggests that algorithms and facial recognition software reproduce the biases that are already present in society. This chapter will explore the roots of algorithmic bias in criminal justice and offer four policy principles to guide the use of technology within carceral systems. As noted by the author, the principles provide a "heuristic by which those engaged in the longer term fight for racial justice can orient themselves in live policy debates about technology in carceral systems."

Chapter 4, authored by Angela S. Murolo, tackles the widely discussed topic of cannabis legalization. As many states have slowly started the process of legalizing and decriminalizing cannabis use, some advocates and policymakers have suggested that legalization can benefit non-White populations—both economically and within the context of criminal justice. This chapter explicitly addresses these claims by examining the impact of progressive cannabis legalization measures on job creation, entrepreneurship, and criminal justice outcomes for Black and Brown communities. The author concludes by offering a set of recommendations aimed at fostering racial equity within the ongoing cannabis legalization movement.

The COVID-19 pandemic highlighted the long-standing racial disparities related to healthcare access and outcomes. In chapter 5, Jay Pearson explores the role of systemic structural racism (SSR) in racialized health disadvantages. In addition to exploring the roots of racialized health advantage and disadvantage, the author also uses the SSR framework to develop policy recommendations with the potential to produce racial equity for those who are marginalized within the healthcare sector.

With the rise of the COVID-19 global pandemic came a growing wave of anti-immigrant, particularly anti-Asian, rhetoric. Chapters 6 and 7 explore this issue from a public opinion and public policy standpoint. First, Janice A. Iwama provides insight into the history of hate crimes against people of Asian descent in the United States and offers policy recommendations aimed at preventing—and increasing the reporting of—anti-Asian hate crimes. Building on the discussion of anti-Asian violence, Niambi M. Carter reframes the narrative around the growing anti-Asian sentiment—which often centered on potential Black anti-Asian sentiment—by exploring Black political attitudes toward immigration. Based on a review of the literature and available data, the author argues that "Black people do not see immigrants and immigration as enemies to their progress" and expend little political capital on anti-immigration issues. The findings outlined in this chapter have important implications for how we discuss coalition building across communities.

Continuing the conversation on Black political issues, chapter 8—authored by Candice C. Robinson, LaTeri McFadden, and J. Nicole Johnson—explores growing voter suppression efforts and the need for voter reform. Specifically, the authors provide insight into the history of racialized disparities in voting as well as the twenty-first-century fight for voting rights. They conclude by making the call for individual, organizational, and structural efforts to combat voter suppression.

In the final substantive chapter 9, Charisse Southwell and Michael Hudson-Vassell explore the role of colorblindness in exacerbating or reproducing educational inequity, particularly in relation to research planning and data use. Focusing explicitly on Title I of the ESEA, the authors provide historical insight into how race-neutral methodologies have entrenched racial inequity in US schools. The chapter ends with recommendations for revamping Title I research and evaluation practices to ensure that Black and Latinx students are properly served.

The book concludes with the editors drawing on significant themes presented throughout the book to argue for the importance of centering racial equity in policy design and implementation. Overall, the *Dark Side of Reform* will enlighten readers about how current reform proposals may impact communities of color. Recent social movements related to racial inequality in the United States have raised national awareness around the need for systemic change. The contributions from leading experts in this book are meant to be a glimpse into how to think about and evaluate policy through the lens of racial equity. It is with great hope that this volume leaves readers better informed, more empowered, and more motivated to confront oppression and create change.

REFERENCES

Alexander, M. (2010). *The New Jim Crow: Mass incarceration in the age of colorblindness.* The New Press.

Asante-Muhammed, D., Collins, C., Hoxie, J. & Nieves, E. (2016). The ever-growing gap: Without change, African-American and Latino families won't match white wealth for centuries. *Institute for Policy Studies.* https://ips-dc.org/wp-content/uploads/2016 /08/The-Ever-Growing-Gap-CFED_IPS-Final-2.pdf.

Au, W. (2016). Meritocracy 2.0: High-stakes, standardized testing as a racial project of neoliberal multiculturalism. *Educational Policy, 30*(1), 39–62.

Barry, C. L., Han, H., Presskreischer, R., Anderson, K. E., & McGinty, E. E. (2020). Public Support for Social Safety-Net Policies for COVID-19 in the United States, April 2020. *American Journal of Public Health, 110*(12), 1811–1813. doi: 10.2105/AJPH.2020.305919.

Brenan, M. (2020, September 28). New high 54% want government to solve more problems in the U.S. *Gallup.* https://news.gallup.com/poll/321041/new-high-government-solve-problems.aspx.

Brodkin, K. (1998). *How Jews became white folks and what that says about race in America.* New Brunswick, NJ: Rutgers University Press.

Bustillo, X. (2021, July 5). 'Rampant issues': Black farmers are still left out at USDA. *Politico.* https://www.politico.com/news/2021/07/05/black-farmers-left-out-usda-497876.

Cerullo, M. (2020, April 22). Up to 90% of minority and women owners shut out of Paycheck Protection Program, experts fear. *CBS News.* https://www.cbsnews.com/news/women-minority-business-owners-paycheck-protection-program-loans/.

Conley, D. (2001). Decomposing the black-white wealth gap: The role of parental resources, inheritance, and investment dynamics. *Sociological Inquiry, 71*(1), 39–66.

Cunningham, Evan. (2018). Great recession, great recovery? Trends from the current population survey. *Monthly Labor Review.* US Bureau of Labor Statistics.

Cusick, J. (2021, March 10). Release: New polling shows strong bipartisan support for federal aid for people in need. *Center for American Progress.* https://www.americanprogress.org/press/statement/2021/03/10/496969/release-new-polling-shows-strong-bipartisan-support-federal-aid-people-need/.

David, K. (2005). No child left behind? Sociology ignored! *Sociology of Education. 78*(2), 165.

Flynn, A., Homber, S., Warren, D., & Wong, F. (2016). Rewrite the racial rules: Building an inclusive American economy. *Roosevelt Institute: Reimagine the Rules.* https://rooseveltinstitute.org/wp-content/uploads/2016/06/RI-RRT-Race-201606.pdf.

Gonzalez-Barrera, A. & Lopez, M.H. (2016, December 16). *US immigrant deportations fall to lowest level since 2007.* Pew Research Center. https://www.pewresearch.org/fact-tank/2016/12/16/u-s-immigrant-deportations-fall-to-lowest-level-since-2007.

Joint Center for Housing Studies at Harvard University. (2019). *The state of the nation's housing 2019.* Cambridge, MA: Joint Center for Housing Studies. https://www.jchs.harvard.edu/sites/default/files/Harvard_JCHS_State_of_the_Nations_Housing_2019.pdf.

Jones, J. M., & Saad, L. (2019, November 18). U.S. support for more government inches up, but not for socialism. *Gallup.* https://news.gallup.com/poll/268295/support-government-inches-not-socialism.aspx.

Katznelson, I. (2005). *When affirmative action was white: An untold history of racial inequality in twentieth-century America* (1st ed.). New York: W.W. Norton.

Kochhar, R., Fry, R., & Taylor, P. (2011, July 26). *Wealth gaps rise to record highs between whites, blacks and Hispanics.* Pew Research Center. https://www.pewresearch.org/wp-content/uploads/sites/3/2011/07/SDT-Wealth-Report_7-26-11_FINAL.pdf[JH2].

Kranhold, K. & Zubak-Skees, C. (2020, July 6). *Small business loan data includes little about race.* https://publicintegrity.org/health/coronavirus-and-inequality/small-business-loan-data-includes-little-on-owners-race-paycheck-protection-program/.

Manchester, J. (2018). Majority of Republicans supports 'Medicare for all,' poll finds. *The Hill.* https://thehill.com/hilltv/what-americas-thinking/412552-majority-of-republicans-say-the-support-medicare-for-all-poll.

McIntosh, K. Moss, E., Nunn, R. Shambaugh, J. (2020, February 27). Examining the Black-White wealth gap. *Brookings.* https://www.brookings.edu/blog/up-front/2020/02/27/examining-the-black-white-wealth-gap/.

Morse, A. (2011, July 28). *Arizona's immigration enforcement laws. National Conference of State Legislatures.* https://www.ncsl.org/research/immigration/analysis-of-arizonas-immigration-law.aspx.

Oliver, M., & Shapiro, T. (1995). *Black wealth/white wealth: A new perspective on racial inequality.* New York: Routledge.

Pager, D. (2003). The mark of a criminal record. *American Journal of Sociology, 108*(5), 937–975.

Radford, J. (2019, June 17). *Key findings about U.S. immigrants.* Pew Research Center. https://www.pewresearch.org/fact-tank/2019/06/17/key-findings-about-u-s-immigrants/.

Ray, R (2020, April 9). *Why are Blacks dying at higher rates from COVID-19?* Brookings. https://www.brookings.edu/blog/fixgov/2020/04/09/why-are-blacks-dying-at-higher-rates-from-covid-19/.

Rothstein, R. (2017). *The color of law: A forgotten history of how our government segregated America.* Liveright Publishing Corporation, W.W. Norton & Company.

Stumpf, J. P. (2006). The crimmigration crisis: Immigrants, crime, and sovereign power. *American University Law Review, 56,* 367–420.

Tonry, M. (2011). *Punishing race: A continuing American dilemma.* Oxford University Press.

United States Citizenship and Immigration Services. (2019, December 4). *Early American immigration policies.* https://www.uscis.gov/history-and-genealogy/our-history/overview-ins-history/early-american-immigration-policies.

United States Department of Labor. (2020). *Unemployment insurance weekly claims data - report r539cy.* https://oui.doleta.gov/unemploy/claims.asp.

US Bureau of Labor Statistics. (July 2, 2020). *The employment situation—June 2020.* https://www.bls.gov/news.release/empsit.nr0.htm.

Viteritti, J.P. (2012). The federal role in school reform: Obama's "race to the top." (Symposium: Educational Innovation and the Law). *Notre Dame Law Review, 87*(5), 2087.

Weatherley, R., & Lipsky, M. (1977). Street-level bureaucrats and institutional innovation: Implementing special-education reform. *Harvard Educational Review, 47,* 171–197.

Williamson, V. (2020, December 9). Closing the racial wealth gap requires heavy, progressive taxation of wealth. *Brookings.* https://www.brookings.edu/research/closing-the-racial-wealth-gap-requires-heavy-progressive-taxation-of-wealth/.

Chapter 1

The Gun Control Debate and Its Policy Implications for Reducing Firearm Violence in Communities of Color

Daniel Semenza and Brian Wade

In 2020, more than 40,000 people died due to firearm injuries in the United States. Of these deaths, almost two-thirds were suicides while the remaining were largely civilian-involved assaultive homicides (Gun Violence Archive, 2021). Beyond those killed each year, many thousands more are victims of nonfatal shootings, suffering long-term consequences including poorer mental health, physical disability, and substance use (Lee, 2012; Ralph, 2014; Rich, 2009). Even in the face of a precipitous drop in overall crime since the early 1990s, gun violence rates have recently risen in many cities (Giffords, 2021). This rise was particularly stark in the United States alongside the ravages of the COVID-19 pandemic, rendering 2020 one of the most violent years in recent history (Bates, 2020).

Despite these unsettling statistics, the true story of American gun violence is best represented by a nuanced narrative that entails four distinct problems: suicide, urban gun violence, intimate partner violence, and mass shootings (Abt, 2019). Each of these affects communities differently and carries distinct policy implications. Urban gun violence, which disproportionately affects disadvantaged communities of color, is responsible for the greatest burden of assaultive firearm death and injury in the United States. Yet, reducing gun violence among disadvantaged African American communities is often not at the forefront of policy-oriented conversations on gun control. Rather, fleeting solutions to a generalized "gun violence problem" are most often discussed in the wake of a mass shooting. These debates call attention to firearm policies related to background checks, reducing access to guns for those with a history of mental illness, and prohibiting weapons that facilitate mass murder like assault rifles. These are necessary policies to pursue. However, strategies to reduce the "everyday" gun violence that has become normalized in many

African American communities remain largely absent within broader policy discussions.

The focus of this chapter is on the gun violence that occurs in urban, disadvantaged communities of color and the policy ramifications of this violence. We first provide an overview of urban gun violence with particular attention to racial differences in homicide, nonfatal shootings, police-involved shootings, and suicide risk. Following this, we discuss the current state of firearms policy in the United States, which often focuses on strengthening laws for legal firearm purchase, banning high-capacity weapons, and preventing purchase for at-risk individuals. Although these policies are critical for reducing some types of gun violence, they do not equitably address the gun violence that has an outsize effect on communities of color. We argue there is too great a focus on policies to reduce legal firearm access via the primary market rather than regulating secondary and illicit firearm markets and addressing key structural causes of urban gun violence. We conclude by outlining a series of policy considerations to fill these gaps and equitably address gun violence using scientific evidence of effective interventions.

RACIAL DISPARITIES AND GUN VIOLENCE(S) IN AMERICA

Although gun violence affects people of all ages, racial groups, gender identities, and socioeconomic status, the impact is different for certain groups across types of violence. Firearm homicide disproportionately impacts people living in disadvantaged communities of color in US cities. Within cities, gun violence clusters among small groups of individuals living in relatively few neighborhoods or "hot spots" that drive broader homicide and nonfatal shooting rates (Braga et al., 2010; Papachristos et al., 2015). Black men comprise more than half of all gun homicide victims in the United States despite comprising less than 7 percent of the population (Currie, 2020). The homicide rate for Black Americans since the beginning of the twenty-first century has been approximately seven times higher than that of their White counterparts. Young Black men, ages fifteen to twenty-nine, are 16 times more likely to die by homicide than White men of the same age. On the other hand, homicide is the cause of about 5 percent of deaths among young White men. As a result of more than 162,000 homicides between 2000 and 2018, gun violence has contributed to premature mortality among Black American, with an average of 35 years of potential life lost (YPLL) among this population. This represents an average of about nine more years lost by Black than White persons to assaultive gun violence (Currie, 2020).

Although racial disparities in shootings and gun homicides are both enormous and enduring, the demographic group at greatest risk for gun death and injury changes depending on the type of violence. To illustrate, women in the United States are 20 times more likely to be killed with a gun than women in other high-income countries due to high rates of intimate partner homicide (Giffords, 2021). Racial disparities persist here as well such that Black women disproportionately accounted for about 28 percent of all intimate partner homicides between 2003 and 2015 (Currie, 2020). Black Americans, men and women, young and old, are at much greater risk of death and injury at the hands of another civilian than any other group in the country. Despite the fact that Black Americans are also more likely to be the victims of violence and homicide regardless of weapon used, roughly three of every four homicides in America are carried out with a firearm. Thus, the excess risk of violent death for Black Americans is most acutely an issue of gun violence.

It is important to note that racial disparities in gun violence differ drastically between homicide and suicide. Although 82 percent of all gun deaths among Black Americans are homicides, roughly 77 percent of gun deaths among Whites are suicides (Reeves & Holmes, 2015). These figures reflect vastly divergent realities for how guns affect different racial groups in the United States (Metzl, 2019). Yet homicides, shootings, and suicides occur every single day and do little to spur actionable conversations about gun violence reduction among policymakers. Despite their devastating impact on communities and the accompanying national media attention, mass shootings comprise a small number of annual deaths and injuries compared to suicide and homicides in urban communities. Although these rare events are the most influential in generating national discussion on gun violence, the fallout of mass shootings has an outsize impact on the policies regularly considered by lawmakers to reduce gun violence. This represents a fundamental disconnect between the perception and reality of gun violence in America.

THE PRESENT POLICY DISCUSSION: FRACTURED, FLAWED, AND UNFOCUSED

The current firearm policy focus in the United States is largely predicated on restricting access to specific groups or individuals at elevated risk of misusing firearms. Public discourse on firearm policies often centers on reforms that fall broadly into three major categories: (a) licensing policies that place restrictions on who is eligible to purchase, possess, or sell a firearm; (b) policies that regulate firearm transactions at the point of sale; and (c) weapons ban policies that prohibit the sale and purchase of particular firearms and weapon accessories. These policies focus on aspects of "legal" firearm markets rather than illicit weapons dealing. Research on the impact of these reforms on gun violence reduction remains mixed, and questions about their efficacy remain unanswered (Smart et al., 2020). Although these policies may reduce some forms of gun violence, they are unlikely to reduce the burden of death and injury disproportionately experienced among poor urban communities of color.

Licensing Policies

The legal firearm market is divided into a primary market—comprising all transfers of guns by retailers holding federal firearm licenses (FFLs) issued by the Bureau of Alcohol, Tobacco, Firearms, and Explosives (ATF)—and a secondary market that consists of transfers involving individuals not regularly engaged in the business of selling firearms without a license (e.g., private parties, collectors, and unlicensed vendors) (ATF, 2010). More than 63,000 businesses and individuals currently hold an FFL and have a legal right to sell firearms, yet the number of unlicensed individuals who routinely sell weapons through private sales is unknown. Roughly 60 percent of firearms are sold by licensed retailers in the primary market, while the remaining 40 percent are sold by private parties and unlicensed vendors in the secondary market (Braga et al., 2012; Pierce et al., 2012).

Persons prohibited from obtaining firearms legally through the primary market often get them through the informal secondary market (Braga & Hureau, 2015; Braga et al., 2012; Chesnut et al., 2017; Hureau & Braga, 2018). For example, Vittes and colleagues (2013) found that just 13.4 percent of incarcerated respondents obtained firearms from licensed retailers. Moreover, less than 4 percent of respondents who reported being legally prohibited at the time of their purchase received their firearms from FFL retailers. The overwhelming majority of respondents (70 percent) got their firearms from friends, family members, or street sources. More recent studies have uncovered nearly identical findings, suggesting that the secondary "legal" market is a major source of firearm transactions that ultimately lead to criminal usage (Braga et al., 2020; Crifasi et al., 2020; Hureau & Braga, 2018). Currently, only 22 states and the District of Columbia require background checks for secondary market sales, and all secondary market transfers are exempt from federal background checks (Giffords, 2021). Although research remains unclear regarding how many prohibited persons successfully obtain guns without a background check, a 2017 report from the Bureau of Justice Statistics (BJS) found that federal background checks prevented over three million firearm transactions to prohibited persons between 1994 and 2015 (Karberg et al., 2017).

Most policies that propose to reduce gun violence focus on alterations to the legal market. Television pundits and politicians repeatedly call for a closing of the "gun show loophole," creating the perception that gun shows generate the bulk of crime gun transactions. Although some guns used in the course of a crime may indeed be purchased at a gun show, private sales exempted from background checks can take place virtually anywhere (e.g., in the home, on the street, out of the trunk of a car). Any person may sell a firearm to an unlicensed resident of the same state as long as they do not have reasonable cause to believe the purchaser is prohibited from receiving or possessing firearms, yet private sellers are not legally obligated to seek out this information. In recent years, policymakers have sought to tighten restrictions on the secondary legal market, including closing the gun show loophole, though this has not been enacted successfully. Even if this type of legislation were to pass, closing this loophole may not significantly reduce criminal firearm activity since guns are informally exchanged in an array of contexts outside of gun shows.

Universal background checks on the sale or transfer of all firearms are largely supported by Americans (Giffords, 2021). In theory, these checks would regulate both the primary and secondary legal gun market, prevent access to prohibited individuals, and provide administrative transparency into who owns firearms. Although studies have generally found evidence that universal background checks would help to reduce gun violence (Kaufman et al., 2020; Mozaffarian et al., 2013), some scholars argue that the current patchwork nature of federal, state, and local firearm policies would make universal background checks difficult to enforce (Pierce et al., 2004, 2012). Despite these debates, the political will to enact a federal background check system remains inadequate.

Transactional Policies

The second type of gun reform considers firearm access at the point of sale. These policies prohibit high-risk individuals from purchasing firearms (or require a waiting period to do so) to reduce the risk of future violence. Since roughly two-thirds of US gun deaths each year are suicides, the suicide prevention potential of these laws is likely substantial (Anestis et al., 2017). Waiting periods between purchase and handover of a firearm can serve several purposes. First, waiting periods can provide a "cooling-off" period for those seeking a firearm to commit crimes of passion or retaliatory shootings (Roberts, 2009). However, evidence of a homicide reduction effect via cooling-off periods appears to be relatively fleeting (RAND, 2020). Waiting periods are thought to be more effective at reducing suicide since they can provide additional time for individuals considering suicide by gun to reconsider their choice (Lewiecki & Miller, 2013). This is especially important since gun owners have a higher suicide rate than the general population (Anestis et al., 2017). There is no federal waiting period law, and only 10 states currently have mandatory waiting periods, ranging from 1 to 14 days (Elliot & Gebelhoff, 2015).

Red flag laws, also known as extreme risk laws, permit immediate family members and law enforcement to petition a court for an extreme risk protection order (ERPO) to temporarily prohibit individuals from purchasing and possessing guns that are believed to be at-risk of harming themselves or others (Pallin et al., 2020). Additionally, any guns already owned by an individual under an ERPO can be confiscated and held by law enforcement while the order is in effect. While red flag laws have commonly been cited in public discourse as a means of reducing gun violence—mass shootings in particular (Wintemute et al., 2019)—research shows that red flag laws are most effective at reducing suicides (Kivisto & Phalen, 2018). To date, the extant literature on red flag laws is largely silent regarding their effects on gun violence in urban communities of color.

Weapons Ban Policies

The third type of policy centers on banning the manufacture or sale of certain firearms or accessories. Reforms focus on high-capacity assault weapons, with policymakers often noting that these guns are neither useful nor necessary for hunting nor home security (Jacobs, 2015). For instance, the federal government instituted an Assault Weapons Ban (AWB) as part of the Violent Crime Control and Law Enforcement Act of 1994. The ban "prohibited the manufacture, transfer, or possession of semiautomatic assault weapons," identified by make, model, or particular characteristics of the weapon (Koper & Roth, 2002, p. 240). It also prohibited the manufacture of new high-capacity magazines except for sale to law enforcement or military officials. Under the ban, high-capacity magazines included all devices with a capacity for more than 10 rounds of ammunition (Koper & Roth, 2002). However, the AWB and its accompanying prohibition of high-capacity magazines expired in 2004.

In the aftermath of the AWB's expiration, scholars sought to examine its impact on mass shootings and violent crime (Koper & Roth, 2002; Koper et al., 2004). In a 2004 report, Koper and colleagues argued that if the ban was renewed, the effects on gun violence would likely be small because assault weapons are rarely used in gun crimes. Findings from more recent studies on the ban's impact on firearm homicides have been mixed (Lee et al., 2017). While some scholars assert that the AWB had no impact on firearm homicide rates (Fox & DeLateur, 2014; Fox & Fridel, 2016; Gius, 2014), others argue that the ban may have reduced the number of mass shootings or the lethality of shootings that did occur when it was in effect (Gius, 2015). Even though politicians often focus on assault weapons as drivers of mass shootings, the overwhelming majority of mass shootings are committed with handguns (Fox & DeLateur, 2014; Fox & Fridel, 2016). According to a report from Everytown for Gun Safety (2020), roughly 80 percent of all mass shootings between 2009 and 2018 involved a handgun compared to 17 percent that involved an assault weapon. As such, policies that criminalize the possession of assault weapons are likely to be ineffective for broad gun violence reduction (Fox & DeLateur, 2014; Fox & Fridel, 2016).

Despite significant doubts about its efficacy in reducing gun violence, several attempts have been made to revive the AWB. Each of these attempts has been unsuccessful, the most notable of which came during the Obama administration in the aftermath of the 2012 Sandy Hook Elementary School shooting in Newtown, Connecticut. Other policy efforts have focused on limiting the manufacture or sale of high-capacity magazines or accessories that enhance a weapon's firepower. For instance, bump stocks are relatively cheap accessories specially designed to allow semiautomatic rifles to mimic the firing motion of fully automatic rifles (e.g., machine guns). Bump stocks were used in the 2017 Las Vegas mass shooting and could be purchased for around $100 at the time. These accessories were prohibited for civilian possession in 2019 in response to demand for their removal from the public market, but few other firearm accessories have been banned in recent decades.

THE MISSING PIECES: A FLAWED APPROACH TO VIOLENCE REDUCTION IN COMMUNITIES OF COLOR

The dominant public policy discourse—largely focused on legal firearm market reforms, point-of-sale laws, and high-capacity weapons bans—ignores the empirical reality that most gun violence in the United States is committed with illegally obtained or unlicensed handguns. Since the majority of homicides and shootings are conducted with these illegal guns in disadvantaged communities of color, current policies up for discussion will likely find limited success in meaningfully reducing gun violence, if lawmakers can pass the legislation at all. Furthermore, these policies will do little to address major racial inequities in gun violence exposure. The present legislative discourse also creates a false designation wherein gun violence, and policy interventions to reduce it, becomes highly racialized (Walker et al., 2020). Through this racialized lens, for example, the use of assault weapons is thought to be a suburban White problem linked to mass shootings, while illicit handguns are conceptualized as an urban Black problem linked to gang and street violence (McGinty et al., 2013; Walker et al., 2020). In truth, however, handguns account for the overwhelming majority of all types of gun violence across racial groups. Thus, much of the public discussion on reducing gun violence blatantly ignores the complex social problems that disproportionately affect communities of color in favor of much more rudimentary political squabbling about "gun control" versus "gun rights." This section, therefore, focuses on the need to properly address illegal firearms markets and inequities in firearms policing to properly situate gun violence policy and address the ravages of gun violence experienced in disadvantaged communities of color.

Illegal Access: Interstate Trafficking, Scofflaw Dealers, and Underground Markets

There remains limited political discussion devoted to dismantling illegal firearm markets, which are supplied by an intricate web of providers through informal transactions across state lines (Braga et al., 2020, 2012; Cook et al., 2007; Hureau & Braga, 2018). Yet, it is precisely these markets that contribute to the significant gun violence experienced by communities of color. The most notable gun trafficking route, the so-called Iron Pipeline, runs along Interstate 95 (I-95), where guns are trafficked from loosely regulated states in the South—and to a lesser extent the Midwest—into more tightly regulated states in the Northeast (Braga et al., 2020). Despite this known route of illegal firearms, interstate gun trafficking continues to prove frustratingly difficult to prosecute at the federal level (Koper, 2014; Webster et al., 2009). Even within local regions, guns often filter into highly regulated states like Illinois or New Jersey from neighboring states with fewer regulations such as Indiana or Pennsylvania.

In the 30 states without universal background checks, it is legal for individuals to privately transfer firearms anonymously and at any location. Scholars have pointed out that "scofflaw dealers" often exploit the private sale exemption by claiming that they only sell a handful of firearms from private collections (Braga et al., 2002; Pierce et al., 2004; Vernick & Webster, 2013). The ATF has argued that the agency's small size—roughly 1,700 special agents across 25 field divisions—makes it difficult to effectively regulate scofflaw gun dealers' behavior. Moreover, many of the guns trafficked across state lines rely on straw purchasers, legally entitled persons that buy guns on behalf of those prohibited from doing so. Straw purchases are notoriously difficult to prevent since enforcement requires the very same formal paperwork from which the secondary firearm market is largely exempt (Pierce et al., 2012).

Altogether, scofflaw dealers, unregulated private sellers, interstate traffickers, and straw purchasers comprise the major parties governing complex underground gun markets (Pierce et al., 2012). There has been scant policy discussion of approaches to systematically address these illicit markets. In disadvantaged urban neighborhoods nationwide, where many illegally obtained guns are used for both self-defense and the commission of violent crimes, guns are exchanged through bartering, trading, sharing, lending, and gifting within peer networks (Braga et al., 2020; Cook et al., 2007; Crifasi et al., 2020). Policing agencies typically center their enforcement priorities on removing guns from circulation instead of focusing on the higher-up sources of those guns. The focus on "getting guns off the street," however, often exposes residents to disproportionately excessive police contact (Bazelon, 2020). This approach thus fails on two fronts: it is ineffective in addressing the broader structure of illegal firearm markets, and it generates significant collateral damage among communities of color.

Inequitable Policing of Firearms among Communities of Color

Minority residents of high-crime, disadvantaged communities often report feeling estranged from, and cynical of, the criminal justice system due to a prolonged history of both under- and over-policing in communities of color (Bell, 2016; Brunson, 2007; Brunson & Wade, 2019). As a result of this pervasive legal cynicism, some residents turn to protective gun ownership as a means of self-defense (Sierra-Arévalo, 2016). These behaviors are not just cultural pathologies but rather constitute rational responses to the structural exclusion of disadvantaged minorities from what Monica Bell (2016, p. 2054) describes as "the aegis of the law." While scholars and policymakers tend to focus on the most recent instances of police mistreatment of minorities and procedural justice failures, they often ignore larger sociohistorical influences and an extended history of criminal justice system abuses of minority citizens (Bell, 2016; Brunson, 2007; Brunson & Wade, 2019). In this context, the demand for unlicensed guns and instances of defensively motivated violence in urban communities can be conceptualized as a product of the institutional failures of the American criminal justice system (Johnson, 2012).

Mainstream policies to reduce gun violence have largely ignored the broader sociocultural contexts that contribute to violence and the illegal markets that meet the continued demand for firearms. This has resulted in policy recommendations related to legal market reforms that would likely be ineffective in substantially reducing gun violence among disadvantaged communities of color. Stricter gun laws and smaller supplies of legal firearms in the nation's urban centers result in minorities being more likely to purchase firearms through the secondary and underground gun markets than their White counterparts. Moreover, disproportionate minority participation in underground gun markets contributes to over-policing of young men of color in urban areas through practices like Stop, Question, and Frisk (SQF) (Fagan et al., 2010; Gelman et al., 2007) and the use of abusive "gang task force" practices in the name of reducing violent crime (Howell, 2015).

Over-policing in disadvantaged minority communities also manifests itself through police violence and the disproportionate officer-involved shootings of unarmed Black men. Police-involved shootings are concentrated in disadvantaged minority neighborhoods (Kane, 2002; Klinger et al., 2016). While roughly two-thirds of fatal officer-involved shootings entail the victim being armed, irrespective of the race of the victim, Black men are more than two times as likely than Whites to be shot while unarmed (Nix et al., 2017). It is worth noting that while scholars of officer-involved shootings often characterize police shootings as "extremely rare" (Nix et al., 2017, p. 327), police violence and harassment are often perceived as pervasive among residents of disadvantaged communities of color (Brunson, 2007; Brunson & Wade, 2019; Gau & Brunson, 2015; Rios, 2011). These perceptions of rampant police abuse and mistreatment of minority citizens contribute to the sentiment held by many residents that the police are at once a constant source of unwanted attention, yet absent when they are actually needed.

Recommendations for Equitable Gun Violence Reduction

It is clear that current firearm policy in the United States is entirely inadequate for limiting assaultive gun violence, especially in disadvantaged communities of color where violence is most prevalent. Firearm-specific policies have remained largely unchanged for decades due to political gridlock and the lobbying influences of grotesquely overreaching organizations like the National Rifle Association. When there is a public discourse on firearm policy, it most frequently focuses on legislation related to banning assault weapons and revising firearm licensing policies in legal markets, often in the immediate wake of a mass shooting. These policies are unlikely to contribute to a significant decrease in urban gun violence because they ignore illegal firearms markets and the broader sociohistorical context of violence and policing tactics in disadvantaged communities of color. It is apparent that this is a problem America will not solve simply by increased policing or incarceration. As such, we highlight three key areas of focus to more equitably address gun violence in the United States. We offer these recommendations in addition to factors like youth programming, root causes such as poverty and unemployment, environmental design, substance use reduction, and improved firearms data infrastructure outlined by other scholars (John Jay College Research Advisory Group, 2020; Roman, 2020).

Directly Address Firearm Access via Primary, Secondary, and Illicit Markets

Assault weapons and high-capacity magazine bans are unlikely to significantly reduce shootings that occur in urban communities of color because most shootings are committed with handguns and weapons with relatively limited ammunition capacity. Greater attention, instead, should be paid to expanding universal background checks to cover every transaction involving a firearm. Relatedly, red flag laws and waiting periods should be applied to all states to ensure that people with a prior history of violence and/or alcohol-related crimes cannot purchase a firearm. These are two evidence-backed risk factors that have been identified to predict future violence especially among gun owners (Resnick et al., 2004; Wintemute et al., 2018).

However, approaches to reduce firearm access through the primary legal market for high-risk individuals alone are unlikely to substantially reduce urban gun violence. Expanded universal background checks may somewhat limit the number of scofflaw dealers and straw purchasers that exploit secondary market loopholes and contribute to the flow of illegal guns. However, greater oversight at the federal level is required to reduce black market access to firearms through informal exchanges. Particular attention should be paid to networks of illicit firearm exchange that occur across state boundaries, typically from less regulated states into more heavily regulated states. The ATF lacks the capacity to properly oversee and enforce sanctions against illicit gun trades across state lines (Hureau & Braga, 2018; Webster & Vernick, 2013). Without adequate funding to properly track, document, and sanction the flow of illegal guns through secondary market sources, this agency will continue to fall short in limiting access to firearms through illegal means.

Relatedly, a law enforcement approach that emphasizes getting guns off the streets, rather than stopping the flow of illicit guns from its source, will always be akin to bailing water out of an imminently sinking ship. We concede that dismantling the black market for guns in the United States is no small task given the massive existing stock of firearms, but the fact that it is a foreboding problem does not make it an unsolvable one. An appropriate legislative response to reducing gun violence in the United States must consider policies that properly regulate the flow of guns through both primary and secondary markets across state lines. Realistically, however, this will remain challenging in an environment of patchwork, state-level gun laws that lack proper federal oversight and the urgency to reduce shootings across the country.

Invest in Community-Based, Anti-Violence Programs

Many policies to reduce gun violence target important neighborhood risk factors including community disadvantage, substance use, and gang membership. However, it is imperative to address violence directly through programs that place violence reduction at the forefront of their missions (Abt, 2019). Targeted programs that identify those at greatest risk for violence, those that intervene to offer alternatives and social services, and those that work to change community norms about violence like CureViolence and Operation Peacemaker Fellowship (OPF) have been shown to reduce violence in communities. These street outreach programs are designed to stop violence and prevent future altercations, rather than address the complex upstream risk factors related to root causes of violent crime like poverty and unemployment (Abt, 2019; Slutkin, 2017).

Street outreach programs have the benefit of operating effectively within disadvantaged communities of color because they employ culturally competent outreach workers well known by those in the communities in which they work. This provides legitimacy for the workers so that they can connect with those at greatest risk for violence involvement. Oftentimes, outreach workers share similar backgrounds and can relate to the criminal justice involvement, trauma, and victimization of the people they are looking to help. These programs have been shown to be effective across many cities in the United States and around the world (Butts et al., 2015). Although not all violence intervention programs effectively reduce violence, their success relies on ongoing, uniform, and properly compensated support for both outreach workers and the communities in which they are working.

Relatedly, hospital-based violence intervention programs (HVIP) can provide supplementary assistance to areas that implement street-based outreach programs. These programs deploy outreach workers to the bedsides of those who have been injured in a violent dispute to prevent retaliation and provide assistance and support to help move forward. These crisis intervention programs can be particularly effective because they work with violence-involved individuals during a time where they are most vulnerable yet open to change (Juillard et al., 2016; Rich, 2009). Proper support through trauma-informed services and diversionary programs to improve financial opportunities and social controls can steer people at high risk for repeat violence to a point where they are willing to consider a different path because they have experienced the pain and trauma of violence first-hand.

Despite their proven efficacy as gun violence reduction tools, many outreach programs are grossly underfunded. Research by The Trace analyzing the wages and labor conditions of street outreach workers across the country found that most of them make less than a living wage (Mascia, 2021). Additionally, many of these programs rely on favorable evaluations for continued funding. Yet the metrics used to evaluate these programs are often comparable to the evaluative measures of crime reduction efforts made by law enforcement even as street outreach workers have considerably less authority and powers of social control compared to the police (Papachristos, 2011; Skogan, 2011). These programs offer significant promise but must have the proper long-term funding and effective administrative oversight to reach their full potential.

Improve Community–Police Relations: Focused Deterrence and Procedural Justice

A holistic approach to reducing gun violence in disadvantaged communities of color necessarily includes reform to develop equitable policing practices. One community approach, focused deterrence, has been consistently shown to effectively reduce violent crime (Braga & Kennedy, 2021). Focused deterrence integrates multiple stakeholders and contributions from law enforcement, community mobilization organizations, and social service providers to generate a blended "carrot and stick" violence reduction approach. Within this framework, the police act as partners with the community to reduce gun violence, rather than strict enforcers, while working with organizations to provide resources for victims and offenders. The approach relies on a balance of careful communication, outreach and support, and swift yet certain punishment if offenders do not desist from violent behavior. A growing body of rigorous research continues to demonstrate the effectiveness of focused deterrence strategies for reducing community gun violence (Braga et al., 2018).

However, a focused deterrence approach can only be successful if it is built on a foundation of a strong community capacity, structures for accountability and sustainability, and ongoing problem analysis (Braga & Kennedy, 2021). A central tenet of focused deterrence success is procedural justice, or the extent to which citizens perceive that the actions of the justice system (e.g., the police) are fair and legitimate. Given the significant legal cynicism and lack of trust in the police among many communities of color (Brunson & Wade, 2019), procedural justice must be at the forefront of any violence reduction strategy, including focused deterrence. Research demonstrates that procedurally just interventions that limit the consequences of bias and promote community relations effectively reduce violent crime (Lawrence et al., 2019). Furthermore, communities with better perceptions of the legitimacy of the justice system and police have been shown to be more successful in implementing violence reduction strategies (Wakeling et al., 2016).

CONCLUSION

Gun violence is a multifaceted, complex, and enduring problem in the United States. The heavy burden of assaultive gun violence disproportionately falls on disadvantaged communities of color, yet public policy discussions often fail to consider these communities when debating how to tackle gun violence issues. Any policy to equitably reduce gun violence must consider not only primary legal firearms markets but also the complex secondary and illicit markets that drive the influx of guns into many communities. Violence reduction strategies must account for broader sociohistorical processes that influence community–police relationships to ensure that they will succeed and avoid further collateral damage. Significant investment in dismantling illegal firearms markets, long-term community violence programs, and focused deterrence strategies with procedural justice at their forefront all provide substantial opportunities to reduce the pain and suffering felt every day in so many communities. However, these strategies will only be successful if they are accompanied by the support of those they are designed to help alongside the political will and courage of lawmakers to make the necessary investments.

REFERENCES

Abt, T. (2019). *Bleeding out: The devastating consequences of urban violence--and a bold new plan for peace in the streets.* New York: Basic Books.

Anestis, M. D., Selby, E. A., & Butterworth, S. E. (2017). Rising longitudinal trajectories in suicide rates: the role of firearm suicide rates and firearm legislation. *Preventive Medicine, 100*, 159–166.

Bates, J. (2021). 2020 will end as one of America's most violent years in decades. *Time Magazine.* Accessed March 8, 2021. Available at: https://time.com/5922082/2020-gun-violence-homicides-record-year/.

Bazelon, E. (2020). *Charged: The new movement to transform American prosecution and end mass incarceration*: Random House Trade Paperbacks.

Bell, M. C. (2016). Police reform and the dismantling of legal estrangement. *Yale Law Journal, 126*, 2054–2150.

Braga, A. A., & Hureau, D. M. (2015). Strong gun laws are not enough: the need for improved enforcement of secondhand gun transfer laws in Massachusetts. *Preventive Medicine, 79*, 37–42.

Braga, A. A., & Kennedy, D. M. (2021). *A framework for addressing violence and serious crime: Focused deterrence, legitimacy, and prevention.* Cambridge, UK: Cambridge University Press.

Braga, A. A., Brunson, R. K., Cook, P. J., Turchan, B., & Wade, B. (2020). Underground gun markets and the flow of illegal guns into the Bronx and Brooklyn: A mixed methods analysis. *Journal of Urban Health*, 1–13.

Braga, A. A., Cook, P. J., Kennedy, D. M., & Moore, M. H. (2002). The illegal supply of firearms. *Crime and Justice, 29*, 319–352.

Braga, A. A., Papachristos, A. V., & Hureau, D. M. (2010). The concentration and stability of gun violence at micro places in Boston, 1980–2008. *Journal of Quantitative Criminology, 26*(1), 33–53.

Braga, A. A., Weisburd, D., & Turchan, B. (2018). Focused deterrence strategies and crime control: An updated systematic review and meta-analysis of the empirical evidence. *Criminology & Public Policy, 17*(1), 205–250.

Braga, A. A., Wintemute, G. J., Pierce, G. L., Cook, P. J., & Ridgeway, G. (2012). Interpreting the empirical evidence on illegal gun market dynamics. *Journal of Urban Health, 89*(5), 779–793.

Reeves, R.V. & Holmes, S.E. (2015). "Guns and race: The different worlds of black and white Americans." The Brookings Institute; Social Mobility Memos. Accessed April 28, 2021. Available at: https://www.brookings.edu/blog/social-mobility-memos/2015/12/15/guns-and-race-the-different-worlds-of-black-and-white-americans/.

Brunson, R. K. (2007). "Police don't like black people": African-American young men's accumulated police experiences. *Criminology & Public Policy, 6*(1), 71–101.

Brunson, R. K., & Wade, B. A. (2019). "Oh hell no, we don't talk to police": Insights on the lack of cooperation in police investigations of urban gun violence. *Criminology & Public Policy, 18*(3), 623–648.

Chesnut, K. Y., Barragan, M., Gravel, J., Pifer, N. A., Reiter, K., Sherman, N., & Tita, G. E. (2017). Not an 'iron pipeline,' but many capillaries: regulating passive transactions in Los Angeles' secondary, illegal gun market. *Injury Prevention, 23*(4), 226–231.

Cook, P. J., Harris, R. J., Ludwig, J., & Pollack, H. A. (2014). Some sources of crime guns in Chicago: Dirty dealers, straw purchasers, and traffickers. *Journal of Criminal Law and Criminology, 104*, 717–760.

Cook, P. J., Ludwig, J., Venkatesh, S., & Braga, A. A. (2007). Underground gun markets. *The Economic Journal, 117*(524), F588–F618.

Crifasi, C. K., Buggs, S. A., Booty, M. D., Webster, D. W., & Sherman, S. G. (2020). Baltimore's underground gun market: availability of and access to guns. *Violence and Gender, 7*(2), 78–83.

Currie, E. (2020). *A peculiar indifference: The neglected toll of violence on black America*. New York: Metropolitan Books.

Elliot, K., & Gebelhoff, R. (2015). Gun policies by state. *Washington Post*. Accessed March 22, 2021. Available at: https://www.washingtonpost.com/graphics/national/state-gun-policies/.

Everytown for Gun Safety. (2020, November 21). Mass shootings in America. Accessed April 28, 2021. Available at: https://everytownresearch.org/maps/mass-shootings-in-america-2009-2019/.

Fagan, J., Geller, A., Davies, G., & West, V. (2010). Street stops and broken windows revisited: Race and order maintenance policing in a safe and changing city. In S.K. Rice & M.D. White (Eds.), *Exploring race, ethnicity, and policing: New and essential readings* (pp. 309–348). New York: New York University Press.

Fox, J. A., & DeLateur, M. J. (2014). Mass shootings in America: moving beyond Newtown. *Homicide Studies, 18*(1), 125–145.

Fox, J. A., & Fridel, E. E. (2016). The tenuous connections involving mass shootings, mental illness, and gun laws. *Violence and Gender, 3*(1), 14–19.

Gau, J. M., & Brunson, R. K. (2015). Procedural injustice, lost legitimacy, and self-help: Young males' adaptations to perceived unfairness in urban policing tactics. *Journal of Contemporary Criminal Justice, 31*(2), 132–150.

Gelman, A., Fagan, J., & Kiss, A. (2007). An analysis of the New York City police department's "stop-and-frisk" policy in the context of claims of racial bias. *Journal of the American Statistical Association, 102*(479), 813–823.

Giffords Law Center to Prevent Gun Violence. (2021). Gun deaths are on the rise nationally. Accessed March, 8, 2021. Available at: https://giffords.org/lawcenter/gun-violence-statistics/.

Gius, M. (2014). An examination of the effects of concealed weapons laws and assault weapons bans on state-level murder rates. *Applied Economics Letters, 21*(4), 265–267.

Gius, M. (2015). The impact of state and federal assault weapons bans on public mass shootings. *Applied Economics Letters, 22*(4), 281–284.

Gun Violence Archive. (2021). Archive 2020. Accessed March 8, 2021. Available at https://www.gunviolencearchive.org/past-tolls.

Howell, K. B. (2015). Gang policing: The post stop-and-frisk justification for profile-based policing. *University of Denver Criminal Law Review, 5*, 1–32.

Hureau, D. M., & Braga, A. A. (2018). The trade in tools: The market for illicit guns in high-risk networks. *Criminology, 56*(3), 510–545.

Jacobs, J. B. (2015). Why ban assault weapons. *Cardozo Law Review, 37*, 681–712.

John Jay College Research Advisory Group on Preventing and Reducing Community Violence (2020). *Reducing violence without police: A review of research evidence.* New York: Research and Evaluation Center.

Johnson, N. J. (2012). Firearms and the black community: An assessment of the modern orthodoxy. *Connecticut Law Review, 45*, 1491–1604.

Juillard, C., Cooperman, L., Allen, I., Pirracchio, R., Henderson, T., Marquez, R., & Dicker, R. A. (2016). A decade of hospital-based violence intervention: benefits and shortcomings. *Journal of Trauma and Acute Care Surgery, 81*(6), 1156–1161.

Kane, R. J. (2002). The social ecology of police misconduct. *Criminology, 40*(4), 867–896.

Karberg, J. C., Frandsen, R. J., Durso, J. M., Lee, A., & Buskirk, T. D. (2017). *Background checks for firearm transfers, 2015-statistical tables.* Washington, DC: Bureau of Justice Statistics, US Department of Justice.

Kaufman, E. J., Morrison, C. N., Olson, E. J., Humphreys, D. K., Wiebe, D. J., Martin, N. D.,... Reilly, P. M. (2020). Universal background checks for handgun purchases can reduce homicide rates of African Americans. *Journal of Trauma and Acute Care Surgery, 88*(6), 825–831.

Kivisto, A. J., & Phalen, P. L. (2018). Effects of risk-based firearm seizure laws in Connecticut and Indiana on suicide rates, 1981–2015. *Psychiatric Services, 69*(8), 855–862.

Klinger, D., Rosenfeld, R., Isom, D., & Deckard, M. (2016). Race, crime, and the micro-ecology of deadly force. *Criminology & Public Policy, 15*(1), 193–222.

Koper, C. S. (2014). Crime gun risk factors: buyer, seller, firearm, and transaction characteristics associated with gun trafficking and criminal gun use. *Journal of Quantitative Criminology, 30*(2), 285–315.

Koper, C. S., & Roth, J. A. (2002). The impact of the 1994 federal assault weapons ban on gun markets: An assessment of short-term primary and secondary market effects. *Journal of Quantitative Criminology, 18*(3), 239–266.

Koper, C. S., Woods, D. J., & Roth, J. A. (2004). *An updated assessment of the federal assault weapons ban: impacts on gun markets and gun violence, 1994–2003.* Washington, DC: National Institute of Justice, US Department of Justice.

Lawrence, D., La Vigne, N. G., Jannetta, J., Fontaine, J., & Center, J. P. (2019). *Impact of the National Initiative for Building Community Trust and Justice on police administrative outcomes.* Urban Institute Justice Policy Center.

Lee, J. (2012). Wounded: life after the shooting. *The ANNALS of the American Academy of Political and Social Science, 642*(1), 244–257.

Lee, L. K., Fleegler, E. W., Farrell, C., Avakame, E., Srinivasan, S., Hemenway, D., & Monuteaux, M. C. (2017). Firearm laws and firearm homicides: a systematic review. *JAMA Internal Medicine, 177*(1), 106–119.

Lewiecki, E. M., & Miller, S. A. (2013). Suicide, guns, and public policy. *American Journal of Public Health, 103*(1), 27–31.

Mascia, J. (2021). The push to pay violence interrupters a living wage. *The Trace.* Accessed March 25th, 2021. Available at: https://www.thetrace.org/2021/03/gun-violence-interruptor-pay-los-angeles-milwaukee-chicago/.

McGinty, E. E., Webster, D. W., & Barry, C. L. (2013). Effects of news media messages about mass shootings on attitudes toward persons with serious mental illness and public support for gun control policies. *American Journal of Psychiatry, 170*(5), 494–501.

Metzl, J. (2019). *Dying of whiteness: How the politics of racial resentment is killing America's heartland.* New York: Basic Books.

Mozaffarian, D., Hemenway, D. A., & Ludwig, D. S. (2013). Curbing gun violence: lessons from public health successes. *JAMA, 309*(6), 551–552.

Nix, J., Campbell, B. A., Byers, E. H., & Alpert, G. P. (2017). A bird's eye view of civilians killed by police in 2015: Further evidence of implicit bias. *Criminology & Public Policy, 16*(1), 309–340.

Pallin, R., Schleimer, J. P., Pear, V. A., & Wintemute, G. J. (2020). Assessment of extreme risk protection order use in California from 2016 to 2019. *JAMA Network Open, 3*(6), 1–10.

Papachristos, A. V. (2011). Too big to fail: The science and politics of violence prevention. *Criminology & Public Policy, 10*, 1053–1062.

Papachristos, A. V., Wildeman, C., & Roberto, E. (2015). Tragic, but not random: The social contagion of nonfatal gunshot injuries. *Social Science & Medicine, 125*, 139–150.

Pierce, G. L., Braga, A. A., Wintemute, G. J., & Dolliver, M. (2012). *New approaches to understanding and regulating primary and secondary illegal firearms.* Washington, DC: National Institute of Justice.

Pierce, G. L., Braga, A. A., Hayatt Jr, R. R., & Koper, C. S. (2004). Characteristics and dynamics of illegal firearms markets: implications for a supply-side enforcement strategy. *Justice Quarterly, 21*(2), 391–422.

Ralph, L. (2014). *Renegade dreams: Living through injury in gangland Chicago.* Chicago, IL: University of Chicago Press.

RAND Corporation. (2020). Effects of waiting periods on violent crime. Accessed April 28, 2021. Available at: https://www.rand.org/research/gun-policy/analysis/waiting-periods/violent-crime.html.

Resnick, M. D., Ireland, M., & Borowsky, I. (2004). Youth violence perpetration: what protects? What predicts? Findings from the National Longitudinal Study of Adolescent Health. *Journal of Adolescent Health, 35*(5), 424-e1.

Rich, J. A. (2009). *Wrong place, wrong time: Trauma and violence in the lives of young black men*. Baltimore, MD: Johns Hopkins University Press.

Rios, V. M. (2011). *Punished: Policing the lives of Black and Latino boys*. New York: NYU Press.

Roberts, D. W. (2009). Intimate partner homicide: relationships to alcohol and firearms. *Journal of Contemporary Criminal Justice, 25*(1), 67–88.

Roman, J. (2020). *A blueprint for a US firearms data infrastructure*. Bethesda, MD: NORC at the University of Chicago.

Sierra-Arévalo, M. (2016). Legal cynicism and protective gun ownership among active offenders in Chicago. *Cogent Social Sciences, 2*(1), 1–21.

Skogan, W. G. (2011). Community-based partnerships and crime prevention. *Criminology & Public Policy, 10*, 987–990.

Slutkin, G. (2017). Reducing violence as the next great public health achievement. *Nature Human Behaviour, 1*(1), 1.

Smart, R., Morral, A. R., Smucker, S., Cherney, S., Schell, T. L., Peterson, S., Gresenz, C. R. (2020). *The science of gun policy: A critical synthesis of research evidence on the effects of gun policies in the United States*: RAND Corporation.

Vernick, J. S., & Webster, D. W. (2013). Curtailing dangerous sales practices by licensed firearm dealers. In D.W. Webster & J.S. Vernick (Eds.), *Reducing gun violence in America: Informing policy with evidence and analysis* (pp. 130–140). Baltimore, MD: Johns Hopkins University Press.

Vittes, K. A., Vernick, J. S., & Webster, D. W. (2013). Legal status and source of offenders' firearms in states with the least stringent criteria for gun ownership. *Injury Prevention, 19*(1), 26–31.

Wakeling, S., Crandall, V., & Gilbert, D. (2016). *Notes from the field: Strengthening police-community relationships goes hand in hand with reducing violence: An update on Oakland Ceasefire*. Oakland, CA: California Partnership for Safe Communities.

Walker, H., Collingwood, L., & Bunyasi, T. L. (2020). White response to black death: A racialized theory of white attitudes towards gun control. *Du Bois Review*, 1–24.

Webster, D. W., Vernick, J. S., & Bulzacchelli, M. T. (2009). Effects of state-level firearm seller accountability policies on firearm trafficking. *Journal of Urban Health, 86*(4), 525–537.

Wintemute, G. J., Pear, V. A., Schleimer, J. P., Pallin, R., Sohl, S., Kravitz-Wirtz, N., & Tomsich, E. A. (2019). Extreme risk protection orders intended to prevent mass shootings: A case series. *Annals of Internal Medicine, 171*(9), 655–658.

Wintemute, G. J., Teret, S. P., Kraus, J., & Wright, M. (1988). The choice of weapons in firearm suicides. *American Journal of Public Health, 78*(7), 824–826.

Wintemute, G. J., Wright, M. A., Castillo-Carniglia, A., Shev, A., & Cerdá, M. (2018). Firearms, alcohol and crime: convictions for driving under the influence (DUI) and other alcohol-related crimes and risk for future criminal activity among authorised purchasers of handguns. *Injury Prevention, 24*(1), 68–72.

Chapter 2

Policing Is Punishment

Defunding the Police as Sentencing Reform

Jalila Jefferson-Bullock and Jelani Jefferson Exum

The summer of 2020 birthed what some considered a revived Civil Rights Movement (Strauss, 2020).[1] The police killings of George Floyd, Breonna Taylor, and others displayed a reality of which Black people in the United States have always been keenly aware: systemic racism, in the form of police brutality, is alive and well. The American policing model has been to "target discriminatorily, surveil persistently, prosecute fervently, and punish vigorously" (Jefferson-Bullock & Jefferson Exum, 2021, p. 3). This includes using deadly force against individuals through a variety of means, but most frequently by shooting Black people (Sinyangwe et al., 2020; Swaine et al., 2015). Police officers kill Black people at more than twice the rate of White people (Connelly et al., 2020; Johnson et al., 2019; Swaine et al., 2015; Gabrielson et al., 2014). These racially disparate outcomes are no surprise given the racist roots of policing in the United States. While various reform-seeking legislative measures have been taken across the nation over the past years, this particular moment sparks demands for different, systemic changes. One emerging demand for a systemic response is the call to defund the police.

Two models of police defunding have emerged most prominently among activists and scholars. Under one, jurisdictions completely disband entire police departments—offering leaders the opportunity to begin afresh and draft community-led public safety prototypes that do not include police (Searcy, 2008; Andrew, 2006). Under the other, police coffers are divested, to varying degrees, with funds reallocated to various social services to reduce— but not wholly eliminate— police contact with the community (Searcy, 2008; Andrew, 2006). While different, these models seek to shift the sole responsibility for public safety away from the traditional "surveillance and punishment" model that typifies police practice to more appropriate entities that seek to foster more equitable, healthier, and safer communities (Lowrey,

2020; Andrew, 2006). Under each, police funding, often the greatest line item of large city budgets, is diverted to various community services, strengthening crisis care capacity, and hiring and training social service workers, with the hope of decreasing negative interactions with police and bettering community relations and aid (Collins, 2020; Baranauckas & Sullivan, 2020). In essence, the modern alarm to defund the police is actually both an appeal and an opportunity to improve the administration of justice. It is "a call to reinvent our criminal justice system to better honor our national pledge of equal justice under the law" (Gammage & Hostetler, 2020, p. 27.). Even more, it is a pronouncement that our legal order is a systemically racist enterprise that can only be sufficiently remedied by a total reimagining.

While there has been increased recognition of systemic racism throughout the country and broad support for police reform, the particular call to defund the police has created considerable controversy, and has not reached widespread consensus (Goodkind, 2020). The long-held belief in police "superpowers" is crumbling, but the majority of Americans advocate specific reforms instead of wholesale defunding ("Poll: Voters Oppose 'Defund the Police,'" 2020; Butler, 2016). Despite considerable evidence that the system is inherently flawed, only 25 percent of Americans endorse decreased spending on police forces (Pew Research Center, 2020). In many ways, however, polling reveals a prominent public misunderstanding of what defunding the police means. Polls indicate that people balk at the term "defund the police" but appear more open if asked if they support shifting money allocated to police toward specific social services (Russonello, 2020). This pushback against defunding the police may be rooted in a misunderstanding of the true nature of policing in the United States. Many fall prey to status quo bias and consider policing, in its current form, as absolutely necessary for crime control and protection against violence. However, understanding policing as a form of punishment clarifies how reforming policing, including defunding the police, fits within the broader, more widely accepted sentencing reforms that have enjoyed bipartisan support in recent years. Further, defunding the police is likely the only avenue to uproot the racism embedded in modern policing.

Criminal sentencing's crushing retributive structure and reliance on racial bias is not atypical in American institutions and is central to police-initiated punishment as well. The dangerous myth of Black criminality, which guides both police use of force and sentencing determinations, bespeaks centuries of ingrained, institutionally sanctioned discrimination and oppression. Through various proposals, modern-day sentencing reformers seek to overhaul the entire system by eliminating bias, reintroducing the concept of rehabilitation, and prohibiting unreasonable lengthy criminal sentences (Jefferson-Bullock, 2016). The history of police use of force is no different. Modern-day sentencing reformers request that judgeswho are constrained by objective, purpose-informed sentencing goals—make more individualized and informed sentencing decisions. Likewise, police reformers petition that the courts determine guilt and punishment instead of empowering police to do so on the streets. When policing is recognized as punishment that is operating improperly, defunding is merely a means of moving the resources used to punish to their proper place, the courts, and adjusting responses to community crises away from the police and toward professionals who are equipped to offer a non-punitive response to the situation.

This chapter reframes the call to defund the police by positioning it within the larger, more familiar discourse regarding sentencing reform. The authors contend that police use of force, most notably lethal force, is government-sanctioned punishment. Thus, similar to more traditionally recognized modes of punishment (imprisonment, fines), police use of force must also comport with legitimate theories, purposes, and precepts of punishment, which it often cannot accomplish (Jefferson-Bullock & Jefferson Exum, 2021). Further, the police should not be empowered to punish in situations that call for a non-punitive response. This chapter posits that protecting people from illegitimate police-based punishment can only be accomplished through the type of complete, systemic overhaul that police defunding offers. To understand the need for such a systemic overhaul, we must first acknowledge the racist underbelly of American policing.

POLICING, RACISM, AND TRAUMA

American policing is systemically racist. In petitioning for systemic overhaul, the police defunding movement relies, in part, on policing's ties to slavery—specifically brutal slave patrols—and argues that the entrenched racism that anchors the foundations of policing must be unearthed and wholly dismantled (Hasbrouck, 2020; Carter, 2004). Scholars note that "racial profiling is a modern manifestation of the historical presumption, still lingering from slavery, that African Americans are congenital criminals rightfully subject to constant suspicion because of their skin color" (Carter, 2004, p. 56). In short, "[p]olice have long been the face of oppression to Black people" (Hasbrouck, 2020, p. 210).

Like the genesis of policing itself, the justification for excessive spending on police budgets is also steeped in racism. Scholars note that the rise in federal aid to police departments was directly informed by racial threat theory. Racial threat theory suggests that White perceptions of communities of colors' encroachment on their economic resources led to the creation of initiatives aimed at preserving the White status quo and White dominance, even in the form of increased police spending (Hasbrouck, 2020). Ironically, increased police spending does not create safer streets. Despite increased spending, rates of solved crimes have remained roughly identical for decades (Hasbrouck, 2020). Quite simply, governments have accepted racial threat theory's fiction, thereby wasting tremendous resources. The cost of compounded, racially motivated spending over time is unsustainable fiscal pressure on state and local governments. Studies demonstrate that in 35 of the 50 most populous US cities, police department appropriations generally account for the largest budget allotment. Likewise, local annual police budgets can range from $100 million to over $5 billion, often outpacing social services spending (Baranauckas & Sullivan, 2020). The effects of exorbitant spending on police budgets justified by the mirage of racial threat theory range far beyond the obvious. A brief consideration of cultural trauma proves instructive.

American policing—with its focus on bloated police budgets, racial profiling, and racially biased enforcement strategies—regularly inflicts trauma on Black people, which must be viewed as a punishment (Charney, 2019; *Floyd v. City of New York*, 2013; Carter 2004). "Cultural trauma" is the socially sanctioned traumatic stress and mental and psychological outcomes that Black people suffer due to the lasting impacts of systemic oppression, discrimination, and racism (Carter et al., 2017; Bryant-Davis, 2007). It "occurs when groups endure horrific events that forever change their consciousness and identity" (Onuwuachi-Willig, 2016, p. 335). Due to the United States' overwhelmingly tragic history of discrimination against minority groups, communities of color often experience shared trauma, transmitted collectively and intergenerationally over time (Tuchinda, 2020). This is especially true for Black people in the United States, for whom systemic racism is an everyday ordeal (Tuchinda, 2020). Cultural trauma ignites from a collective, disruptive memory that, in turn, forms the group's identity. For Black people, that shared, disruptive memory is slavery, whose legacy endures through continued discrimination, degradation, humiliation, and oppression. Studies conclude that constant exposure to such trauma can affect DNA structure, "adding a potential biological factor to the mix," such that cultural trauma "come[s] to reside in the flesh [of Black people] as forms of memory reactivated and articulated at moments of collective spectatorship" (Sanders, 2018, p.71; Onuwachi-Willig, 2016, p. 336).

Unlike other recognized traumas, cultural trauma often presents as two separate experiences. Its more latent form is coined *background cultural trauma*, and acts as the backdrop to everyday life for Black people (Carter et al., 2017; Bryant-Davis, 2007). In its more active form, cultural trauma disrupts ever-present background trauma, adding to the daily trauma narrative that Black people must navigate. Background cultural trauma manifests as a "pattern of racist events . . . across the life domains of minority citizens

... that requires ongoing coping and expenditures of psychic energy" and "provides a more precise description of the psychological consequences of interpersonal or institutional traumas motivated by the devaluing of one's race," even in the absence of physical contact (Bryant-Davis, 2007; Bryant-Davis & Ocampo, 2005, p. 137). Though it originates from slavery, background cultural trauma resides in all facets of "familiar and habitual society," including racial profiling and police brutality (Jefferson-Bullock & Jefferson Exum 2021, p. 6).

The second type of cultural trauma, *cultural trauma from the routine*, posits that background trauma may be augmented by unexpected traumatic occurrences. In previous works, we note that when three specific factors converge,

> The ongoing, background cultural trauma narrative widens and works to publicly retraumatize the group in question, such that they are reminded, by the exposed shame of highlighting their subordinated status, that they have not yet won society's respect nor any of its attendant rights and privileges. (Onuwachi-Willig, 2016, p. 336; Jefferson-Bullock & Jefferson Exum 2021, p. 5)

As a result, the "subordinated group's consciousness of its second-class citizenship [is reignited] and punctuates its already existing distress and suffering, thereby causing such tensions and pains to boil over and lay a foundation for the development of a cultural trauma narrative" (Onuwachi-Willig, 2016, p. 337). Those three specific factors are the following:

(1) An established history or accumulation of the routine harm for the trauma group;
(2) Widespread media attention, usually based on preceding events, that brings regional, national, or international attention to the occurrence of the routine harm; and
(3) Public discourse ... about the meaning of the routine harm, which consists of public or official affirmation of the subordinated group's marginal status (Onuwachi-Willig, 2016, p. 346).

Every publicized instance of police brutality, especially the use of deadly force, disrupts the daily background cultural trauma that Black Americans face and thrusts discrimination against Black people back into the spotlight in a welcoming, yet highly, retraumatizing way. The cultural trauma that Black people must suffer from the routine experience of police brutality is more than debilitating—it is, quite simply, exhausting. Cultural trauma, however, is a cognizable pain that, through targeted and deliberate efforts, can be successfully interrupted. It must be noted that the change sought is not only for an end to police brutality. Instead, it is an appeal for the abolishment of institutionalized racism. That can begin with defunding the police as a part of reforming punishment as a whole. The integrity of the entire criminal justice system demands such change.

A BRIEF LOOK AT RECENT DEFUNDING EFFORTS AND WHY THEY PROVE INSUFFICIENT

Since the summer of 2020, some reforms in police funding have emerged. In 2020, the New York City Council approved $88.19 billion executive fiscal budget, which included $1 billion shift in funding from the New York City Police Department to various civilian agencies in an effort to transfer responsibilities to offices best suited to handle them ("Agreement of FY 2021 Budget," 2021; Booker, 2020). An extensive accompanying reallocation plan included funding transfers to the Departments of Education, Health and Mental Hygiene, and Homeless Services, among others, in an effort to strengthen summer youth programs, education, family, and social services; another aim was to provide for capital investments in parks, community centers, and technology services for low-income and minority families (Speaker Corey Johnson, 2021; Booker, 2020). The new spending plan also reduced two incoming police classes (Speaker Corey Johnson, 2021; Booker, 2020). Likewise, in the summer of 2020, the Baltimore City Council voted to cut $22 million in police spending for the 2021 executive fiscal year (Summary of the Adopted Budget, 2021; Richman and Wenger, 2020). The budget cuts were designed to revive community services, including opening recreation centers on Sundays, increasing trauma services, and offering Black-owned businesses forgivable loans (Summary of the Adopted Budget, 2021; Wenger & Richman, 2020). In like manner, in the summer of 2020, the Austin City Council unanimously voted to cut its police department budget by $150 million and shift that funding to homeless services, mental health services, and family violence prevention initiatives, among other social programs (Venkataraman, 2020). While these steps are welcome, they represent meager strides in the movement to create a more equal and just system.

Though there are successes, the backlash has been swift. On June 1, 2021, Texas Governor Greg Abbott signed legislation prohibiting municipalities with a population of over 250,000 from reducing law enforcement budgets. Separate legislation would require counties with a population over one million to hold elections before reducing or reallocating law enforcement budgets. Per this legislation, non-compliant counties' property tax revenues will be frozen. Though far less egregious, New York City has increased police spending yet again, with the assistance of federal stimulus funds. The 2022 executive fiscal budget allows New York to expand alternatives to policing without reducing spending. Today, it is unclear whether New York City will take further steps to defund the police since it is able to maintain alternatives to policing without further instituting budget cuts to the police department. Still, other states and municipalities simply refuse to entertain any police defunding conversation. Like many issues involving race, increasing protections for minorities, and preserving Black lives, these reactions and reversals indicate both a prominent misunderstanding of the purposes and effects of police defunding and the influence of petty, partisan politics. States and municipalities that have passed defunding measures recognize that they have over-relied on, and thus overfunded, law enforcement. These defunding approaches would go further toward systemic change, however, if they were rooted in an understanding that when police use force—especially deadly force—they are inflicting punishment on communities. By shifting particular funds and responsibilities from the police to community and social services, jurisdictions are beginning to reframe the criminal justice narrative to acknowledge that policing has operated in a manner that is highly inappropriate, incredibly traumatizing, and wholly unnecessary. By adding to this understanding that policing has acted as unjust punishment, the defunding approach can go even further. It can work to remove police from most everyday interactions with individuals by funding the creation of appropriate, non-punitive responses that do not include the police.

We must completely retool our thinking concerning the criminal justice system. Viewing policing as punishment, as an avenue to true reform, is possible with the assistance of abolitionist democracy theory. Whether through the imposition of particular purpose sentencing or the inclusion of experimentalist theory in determining how much punishment is enough, modern-day reforms must pursue a total dismantling of our unjust system (Jefferson Exum, 2015; Jefferson-Bullock, 2016).

Abolitionist democracy is central to the concept of police defunding. Traditional reform efforts attempt to operate within the existing system. Proponents of abolitionist theory properly identify and acknowledge the backdrop of racial oppression that is attached to every level of every institution in the United States and assert that reform of any systemically racist system requires disruption of racist narratives (McLeod, 2019). Abolitionist democracy theory "calls for a constellation of democratic institutions and practices to displace policing and imprisonment while working to realize more equitable and fair conditions of collective life" (McLeod, 2019, p. 1618). The overarching goal of abolitionist democracy theory is to overhaul unjust resource allocations, and to "build local democratic power to reinvest public resources in projects that actually provide meaningful security, while simultaneously reducing the violent theft perpetrated daily by mainstream economic practices and institutions" (McLeod, 2019, p.1613). It can be used as a lens through which to critically consider, respond to, and fight against the inequities inherent in our legal system.

With candor, abolitionist democracy theory challenges status quo reforms. Abolitionists claim that even convictions for officers engaged in police brutality would ultimately fail to produce equitable outcomes because they would neglect to change the "institutional and cultural dynamics responsible for the pervasive violence of policing" (McLeod, 2019, p. 1639). Per abolitionists, the problem is not that deserving "isolated bad apples" were not appropriately punished (McLeod, 2019, p. 1639). Instead, it is that policing methods, systems, and processes that permit brutality as a regular occurrence remain intact. They continue to operate against "the backdrop of a status quo" that is steeped in racism and inequality (McLeod, 2019, p. 1640). In the case of policing, abolitionist democracy theorists urge a complete reimagining of police functioning and practice. This model is critical in attempting to view punishment differently, such that genuine rebuilding can be realized. As a first step, abolitionist democracy theory can be used to assist in reconceptualizing the Supreme Court's position regarding the reasonableness of police action.

THE UNREASONABLENESS OF A REASONABLENESS APPROACH TO POLICE USE OF FORCE

Due in large part to policing's characterization in the courts, there remains a prevalent misconception that policing and punishment are different issues. For decades, the Supreme Court has ignored the authentic nature of the consequences of police use of force, especially deadly force, by analyzing excessive police force claims under the Fourth Amendment's protection against unreasonable seizures—instead of viewing them as more akin to punishment (*Graham v. Connor*, 490 U.S. 386, 386 (1989)). Arguably, a person is seized when police use force against them; yet confining police force cases to such traditional Fourth Amendment analyses egregiously limits appropriate methods of challenging police conduct in the courts (*United States v. Brignoni-Ponce*, 422 U.S. 873, 878 (1975)). A closer look at the reasonableness standard applied to cases claiming unconstitutional policing reveals its extraordinary shortcomings.

In the 1985 case, *Tennessee v. Garner*, the Supreme Court considered the constitutionality of the use of deadly force by police and held that deadly force "may not be used unless it is necessary to prevent the escape and the officer has probable cause to believe that the suspect poses a significant threat of death or serious physical injury to the officer or others" (*Tennessee v. Garner*, 471 U.S. 1, 3 (1985)). The Court explained:

> [N]otwithstanding probable cause to seize a suspect, an officer may not always do so by killing him. The intrusiveness of a seizure by means of deadly force is unmatched. The suspect's fundamental interest in his own life need not be elaborated upon. The use of deadly force also frustrates the interest of the individual, and of society, in judicial determination of guilt and punishment. (*Tennessee v. Garner*, 471 U.S. 1, 3 (1985))

Though the Court's words suggest that the use of deadly force by officers would only be allowed in limited circumstances, just five years later, the Court invoked a reasonableness approach that would make it extremely difficult to challenge an officer's use of force. In 1989 the Court decided *Graham v. Connor* and held that "all claims that law enforcement officers have used excessive force, deadly or not, in the course of an arrest, investigatory stop, or other 'seizure' of a free citizen should be analyzed under the Fourth Amendment and its 'reasonableness' standard" (*Graham v. Connor*, 490 U.S. 386, 386 (1989)). According to the Court, this standard is judged "from the perspective of a reasonable officer on the scene, rather than with the 20/20 vision of hindsight" (*Graham v. Connor*, 490 U.S. 386, 386 (1989)). The Court further explained that this reasonableness inquiry "is an objective one," asking "whether the officers' actions are 'objectively reasonable' in light of the facts and circumstances confronting them, without regard to their underlying intent or motivation" (*Scott v. United States*, 437 U.S. 128, 137–39 (1978); *Terry v. Ohio*, 392 U.S. 1 (1968)).

Though the Court posed the review as an objective one, in reality, the reasonableness assessment is subjective. It relies on the subjective impressions of prosecutors in deciding whether to charge an officer for excessive force or the subjective impressions of jurors in deciding whether to hold an officer accountable for force used against an individual. A punishment approach to policing would allow for the Eighth Amendment's legal standards of non-arbitrariness, proportionality, and respect for human dignity to have a more uniform application to police encounters where force is used (Jefferson Exum, 2015). By applying a traditional Fourth Amendment reasonableness analysis to excessive force claims, the Court has not effectively protected the individual's "fundamental interest" in their own lives (*Tennessee v. Garner*, 471 U.S. 1, 9 (1985)). Instead, the Court has diminished the police-individual encounter to one that depends upon the inconsistent views of prosecutors or jurors about what is appropriate in a given situation. It only takes a survey of recent reports of killings by police officers for that failed protection to become apparent.

The death penalty on the streets—when police officers kill individuals as punishment for that person's objectionable behavior—operates outside of the criminal justice system's procedural safeguards (Jefferson Exum, 2015). Between 2005 and 2015, police officers fatally shot over 1,000 people each year, but only 44 officers were criminally charged (Kindy, 2015). Judging police use of force by its reasonableness, which is informed by police officers' discretionary judgment, has contributed to an unjust system. This is especially true for those who have lost their lives in police encounters when the use of nonfatal police tactics could have safely avoided that loss of life. The tragedies of Breonna Taylor, Michael Brown, and other unarmed individuals who have been killed by police officers who went unpunished for their actions demonstrate the incompleteness of the reasonableness standard (Jefferson Exum, 2015; Jefferson-Bullock & Jefferson Exum, 2021). That standard fails to capture the full harm inflicted on individuals, families, and communities when police use extreme levels of force against individuals. This is especially true given the racist roots of policing, the racial trauma it inflicts, and the view of Black criminality that it perpetuates.

The true consequences of the police force—that individuals are physically penalized or executed for their perceived objectionable response to a police encounter—demonstrate that it is more akin to punishment than a seizure. Rather than an unsatisfactory reasonableness analysis, the Supreme Court's Eighth Amendment death penalty analysis should govern. In interpreting the Eighth Amendment cruel and unusual punishment clause, the Supreme Court has expressed the importance of human dignity and that "the fundamental premise of the [cruel and unusual punishment] Clause [is] that even the vilest criminal remains a human being possessed of common human dignity" (*Furman v. Georgia*, 408 U.S. 238, 270 (1972)). The same respect for human life that fuels the protections and guarantees given in the death penalty context can be incorporated into the reasonableness standard that now governs excessive force claims.

The Court's treatment of the death penalty provides a strong example of how the Supreme Court centers its Eighth Amendment jurisprudence on human dignity in a manner that could be adopted in the police force context. In keeping with this concern, the Supreme Court has developed several limits on when the death penalty can be imposed through the Court system. For instance, the death penalty must be proportionate to the crime of conviction, and death cannot be a mandatory punishment (*Gregg v. Georgia*, 428 U.S. 153, 154 (1976); *Woodson v. North Carolina*, 428 U.S. 280, 280–81 (1976)).

Proportionality between the crime committed and the punishment imposed is one bedrock protection that the Supreme Court has read into the cruel and unusual punishment clause (*Gregg v. Georgia*, 428 U.S. 153, 154 (1976)). The Court deems punishment unconstitutionally excessive if it is "grossly out of proportion to the severity of the crime" and has described the death penalty as "unique in its severity and irrevocability" (*Coker v. Georgia*, 433 U.S. 584, 592 (1977)). Due to this severity, the Court has limited the death penalty for "those offenders who commit 'a narrow category of the most serious crimes' and whose extreme culpability makes them 'the most deserving of execution'" (*Kennedy v. Louisiana*, 554 U.S. 407, 420 (2008)). For this reason, the Supreme Court repeatedly declined to uphold the death penalty in situations where the defendant did not intentionally cause the death of another human (*Kennedy v. Louisiana*, 554 U.S. 407 (2008); *Coker v. Georgia*, 433 U.S. 584, 592 (1977)).

The Supreme Court has also shown respect for human dignity in the death penalty context by invalidating statutes that make death a mandatory penalty. In the 1976 case, *Woodson v. North Carolina*, the Supreme Court explored the country's history of moving away from the mandatory imposition of such a final and severe sentence (*Woodson v. North Carolina*, 428 U.S. 280, 298–299 (1976)). The Court quoted Chief Justice Burger's dissent in *Furman v. Georgia* in which he said that the change from mandatory death sentences "was greeted by the Court as a humanizing development" (*Woodson v. North Carolina*, 428 U.S. 280, 298–299 (1976)). As the Court elegantly stated:

> Process that accords no significance to relevant facets of the character and record of the individual offender or the circumstances of the particular offense excludes from consideration in fixing the ultimate punishment of death the possibility of compassionate or mitigating factors stemming from the diverse frailties of humankind. It treats all persons convicted of a designated offense not as uniquely individual human beings, but as members of a faceless, undifferentiated mass to be subjected to the blind infliction of the penalty of death. (*Woodson v. North Carolina*, 428 U.S. 305 (1976))

The Supreme Court has acknowledged that just punishment sees people as individuals with value beyond their punishable actions. By allowing each defendant to be seen as a unique individual, possibly worthy of compassion, death penalty jurisprudence incorporates respect for human dignity into even the most severe and final sentence. The traditional Fourth Amendment reasonableness standard misses what the Eighth Amendment captures—a concern for the human who is subject to police violence. Unfortunately, by limiting the Eighth Amendment to post-conviction punishment, the Supreme Court has foreclosed a victim of police violence from the human dignity protection that the Eighth Amendment could provide.

The force law enforcement officials use to carry out criminal law's investigatory power is a form of punishment. Criminal punishment is imposed upon a person as a response to that person's objectionable behavior—the violation of a particular jurisdiction's criminal statutes. Punishment is inflicted to deter criminal behavior, rehabilitate the criminal offender, incapacitate dangerous individuals, or express society's desire for retribution against the lawbreaker (Campbell, 1991). When law enforcement officials seize individuals, it is because of some perceived criminal violation committed by that individual (which may or may not be a pretextual reason). Rather than depending on a flimsy assessment of reasonableness, courts and the public should instead view certain aspects of policing as a form of control and punishment—especially over Black bodies. When this more fitting punishment lens is used to assess the excessiveness of policing, it becomes clearer that the police repeatedly use force as punishment in situations in which the punishment imposed is an arbitrary and disproportionate response. The appropriate punishment reform, then, is to move away from punitive police interactions by defunding the police, and instead, funding non-punishment approaches to dealing with community crises.

CONCLUSION: ANTIRACIST SENTENCING REFORM INCLUDES DEFUNDING THE POLICE

This unique moment, when there is increased public interest in being antiracist—"a radical choice in the face of history, requiring a radical reorientation of our consciousness"—presents an opportunity for reform (Kendi, 2019, p. 23). The face of American history is fraught with using police force to control, oppress, and traumatize Black Americans (Williams & Murphy, 1990). Still today, police force is imposed in racially discriminatory ways that display the incidences and badges of policing's roots in slavery; the police funding model supports and institutionalizes this racism (Hasbrouck, 2020).

Defunding the police answers the antiracist call to radically reorient the public consciousness and faith in the entire criminal justice system, which has been undermined by the routine use of force against Black Americans. Legal standards for challenging the excessiveness of police force based on reasonableness reap unreasonable outcomes that reflect biased views of Black criminality. Reconceptualizing these aspects of policing as punishment situates the defund movement within the widely accepted sentencing reform movement and reorients policing as punishment outside of the protections of the criminal process. This reorientation recognizes that police-initiated punishment fails to fulfill the legitimate purposes of criminal punishment and is, therefore, in need of an entire overhaul.

True systemic change can only happen in conjunction with eradicating racism. The movement to defund the police is "a call to reinvent our criminal justice system to better honor our national pledge of equal justice under the law" (Gammage & Hostetler, 2020, p. 27). We can do this by calling policing what it is—punishment—and no longer standing for a racist system of sentencing, whether on the streets or in the courts, to stand.

NOTE

1. This article was initially published in Volume 48, Book 3, of the *Fordham Urban Law Journal* and is republished with permission. Jefferson-Bullock, J and Jefferson Exum, J. (2021). That is enough punishment: Situating defund the police within antiracist sentencing reform. *The Fordham Urban Law Journal, 48*(3), 625.

REFERENCES

Andrew, S. (2020, June 17). There's a Growing Call to Defund the Police. Here's What It Means. *CNN*. https://www.cnn.com/2020/06/06/us/what-is-defund-police-trnd/index.html.

Baranauckas, C and Sullivan, C. (2020, June 26). How Much Money Goes to Police Departments in Largest Cities Across the U.S. *USA Today*. https://www.usatoday.com/ story/money/2020/06/26/how-much-money-goes-to-police-departments-in-americas-largest-cities/112004904/.

Booker, B. (2020, July 1). De Blasio on Shifting $1 Billion from NYPD: 'We Think It's the Right Thing to Do': Updates: The Fight Against Racial Injustice. *NPR*. https://www.npr. org/sections/live-updates-protests-for-racial-justice/2020/07/01/886000386/de-blasio-on-shifting-1-billion-from-nypd-we-think-it-s-the-right-thing-to-do.

Bryant-Davis, T. (2007). Healing Requires Recognition: The Case for Race-based Traumatic Stress. *The Counseling Psychologist, 35*(1), 135–143.

Bryant-Davis, T. and Ocampo, C. (2005). Racist Incident-based Trauma. *The Counseling Psychologist, 33*(4), 479–500. doi: 10.1177%2F0011000005276465.

Burkel, N. Cesario, J. Johnson, D. Taylor, C. Tress, T. (2019). Officer Characteristics and Racial Disparities in Fatal Officer-involved Shootings. *Proceedings of the National Academy of Sciences - PNAS, 116*(32), 15877–15882. doi: 10.1073/pnas.1903856116.

Buter, P. (2016). The System Is Working the Way It Is Supposed to: The Limits of Criminal Justice Reform. *The Georgetown Law Journal, 104*(6), 1419.

Carter, R. (2019). Relationships Between Trauma Symptoms and Race-based Traumatic Stress. *American Psychology Association 26*, 11–16. PowerPoint Presentation (ctacny.org).

Carter, R. Roberson, K. Johnson, V. (2020). Race Based Traumatic Stress, Racial Identity Statuses, and Psychological Functioning: An Exploratory Investigation. *Journal of Multicultural Counselling and Development, 48*(2), 95–107. doi: 10.1002/jmcd.12168.

Carter, W. (2004). A Thirteenth Amendment Framework for Combatting Racial Profiling. *Harvard Civil Rights-Civil Liberties Law Review, 17*(39), 56–57.

Charney, D (2019, December 16). Stop and Frisk Report: NYPD Racial Bias Persists. *Center for Constitutional Rights.* https://ccrjustice.org/home/press-center/press-releases/ stop-and-frisk-report-nypd-racial-bias-persists.

Collins, S. (2020, September 23). The Financial Case for Defunding the Police. *Vox.* https://www.vox.com/the-highlight/21430892/defund-the-police-funding-abolish-george-floyd- breonna-taylor-daniel-prude.

Floyd v. City of New York, 959 F. Supp. 2d 540 (S.D.N.Y. 2013).

Gabrielson, R. Sagara, E, Grochowski Jones, R. (2014, October 4). Deadly Force, in Black and White: A ProPublica Analysis of Killings by Police Shows Outsize Risk for Young Black Males. *ProPublica.* https://www.propublica.org/article/deadly-force-in-black-and-white.

Gammage, A and Hostetler, S. (2020). Ok Boomers, What's Going On? *Res Gestae, 19*, 27.

Goodkind, N. The Vast Majority of Americans Don't Want to Defund the Police. (2020, July 9). *Fortune.* https://fortune.com/2020/07/09/defund-the-police-poll-most-americans-oppose -defunding-police-departments/.

Hasbrouck, B. (2020). Abolishing Racist Policing with the Thirteenth Amendment. *UCLA Law Review, 67*(5), 200.

Jefferson-Bullock, J. (2016). How Much Punishment is Enough?: Embracing Uncertainty in Modern Sentencing Reform. *Journal of Law and Policy, 24*(2). Available at: https://brooklynworks.brooklaw.edu/jlp/vol24/iss2/2.

Jefferson-Bullock, J and Jefferson Exum, J. (2021). That is Enough Punishment: Situating Defund the Police Within Antiracist Sentencing Reform. *The Fordham Urban Law Journal, 48*(3), 625.

Jefferson Exum, J. (2015). The Death Penalty on the Streets: What the Eighth Amendment Can Teach About Regulating Police Use of Force. *Missouri Law Review, 80*(4), 987.

Kendi, I. (2019). *How to be an Antiracist.* OneWorld.

Kindy, K. et al., (2015, April 11). Thousands Dead, Few Prosecuted. *Washington Post.* http://www.washingtonpost.com/sf/investigative/2015/04/11/thousands-dead-few-prosecuted/.

Law Enforcement and Violence: The Divide Between Black and White Americans. (2021). Associated Press and NORC. Accessed October 21, 2020. Available at: https://apnorc.org/projects/law-enforcement-and-violence-the-divide-between-black-and-white-americans/.

Lowrey, A. (2020, June 5). Defund the Police. *The Atlantic.* https://www.theatlantic.com/ideas/archive/2020/06/defund-police/612682/.

McLeod, A. (2019). Envisioning Abolition Democracy, *Harvard Law Review, 132*(6), 1613.

Onwuachi-Willig, Angela. (2016). The Trauma of the Routine: Lessons on Cultural Trauma from the Emmett Till Verdict. *Sociological Theory, 34*(4), 335–357.

Pew Research Center (2020, July 9). *Majority of Public Favors Giving Civilians the Power to Sue Police Officers for Misconduct.* https://www.pewresearch.org/politics/2020/07/09/ majority-of-public-favors-giving-civilians-the-power-to-sue-police-officers-for-misconduct/.

Poll: Voters Oppose 'Defund the Police' But Back Major Reforms (2020). Politico. Accessed July 9, 2021. Available at: https://www.politico.com/news/2020/06/17/poll-voters-defund-police-reforms-324774.

Russonello, G. (2020, July 3). Americans Warmed to Calls to 'Defund the Police'? *New York Times.* https://www.nytimes.com/2020/07/03/us/politics/polling-defund-the-police.html.

Sanders, Kindaka J. (2018). Defending the Spirit: The Right to Self-Defense Against Psychological Assault. *Nevada Law Journal 19*(1), 227.

Searcey, D. (2020, June 8). What Would Efforts to Defund or Disband Police Departments Really Mean? *New York Times.* https://www.nytimes.com/2020/06/08/us/what- does-defund-police-mean.html.

Sinyangwe, S., McKession, D. & Elzie, J. (2020). Mapping Police Violence. Accessed October 22, 2020. Available at: Mapping Police Violence.

Speaker Corey Johnson, Finance Committee Chair Daniel Dromm, and Capital Budget Subcommittee Chair Vanessa Gibson Announce Agreement on FY 2021 Budget – Press. (2021, June). New York City Council.

Strauss, V. (2020, June 6). This is my generation's civil rights movement. *The Washington Post.* https://www.washingtonpost.com/education/2020/06/06/this-is-my-generations-civil-rights-movement.

Summary of the Adopted Budget Fiscal 2021 Preliminary Budget. (2021, July). The City of Baltimore Department of Finance. Fiscal 2021 Preliminary Budget (baltimorecity.gov).

Swaine, J., Laughland, O., Lartey, J. & McCarthy, M. (2015, June 1). The Counted: People Killed by Police in the US. *The Guardian.* https://www.theguardian.com/us-news/ng-interactive/2015/jun/01/the-counted-police-killings-us-database.

Tuchinda, N. (2020). The Imperative for Trauma-Responsive Special Education. *New York University Law Review (1950), 95*(3), 766–836.

Venkataramanan, M. (2020, August 14). Austin City Council Votes to Cut Police Department Budget by One-Third. *The Texas Tribune.* Austin City Council votes to cut police department budget by one-third | The Texas Tribune.

Wenger, Y and Richman, T. (2020, June 17). The Baltimore City Council Eliminated $22 Million from the Police Budget. What Does that Look Like? *Baltimore Sun.* https://www.baltimoresun .com/politics/bs-md-pol-police-budget-explainer-20 200617-4yjweepbkreknjlef4f45jiblm-story.html.

Williams, H. & Murphy, P. (1990). *The Evolving Strategy of Police: A Minority View.* U.S. Dept. of Justice, Office of Justice Programs, National Institute of Justice.

Chapter 3

Four Racial Justice Principles for Policy Response to Carceral Technology

Emily Tucker

In February 2019, police in the city of Woodbridge, New Jersey, arrested Nijeer Parks, a thirty-three-year-old Black man, when facial recognition software matched Parks's picture with the photograph of a man accused of stealing candy from a hotel gift shop (Hill, 2020). Parks was denied pretrial release because his "risk score," computed by an algorithm, was too high. Though Parks was eventually able to prove that he was 30 miles away at the time of the incident, he spent ten days in jail, and thousands of dollars in legal fees, before the case against him was dismissed for lack of evidence due to his indisputable alibi. Parks is one of three people, all of them Black men, publicly known to have suffered wrongful arrest as a result of police reliance on facial recognition software. Given that police have been using facial recognition for over twenty years and given that there are no rules requiring disclosure to a defendant when police use the technology, it seems reasonable to assume that the actual number of people who have been arrested and incarcerated based on a bad facial recognition match is much higher. In spite of research demonstrating that facial recognition software is less accurate on images of people of color and on women (Buolamwini & Gebru, 2018), police departments all over the country continue to use it in their investigations. Risk assessment algorithms also remain ubiquitous in the face of mounting criticism that the data used to train those algorithms are tainted by racial bias (Mayson, 2019). Unfortunately, these are only two examples of the many digital technologies that now suffuse our systems of policing and punishment.

Will the next evolution of the carceral state be digital? In the wake of the most recent wave of police violence against Black people in the United

States, which has forced open a window of receptivity to large-scale system change, this is a question keeping many racial justice activists and allies up at night. While the US government has always used surveillance as one means of controlling and coercing communities of color (Browne, 2015), never before in our history has the state had the technological capability to look so closely, so continuously, or so secretly into the lives of so many people. At the same time, policymakers and government officials are pointing to those very technological capabilities as offering alternatives to, or cures for, everything from mass incarceration to discriminatory policing, and to racially disparate sentencing practices. How should people engage in the struggle for transformative change around technology-centric "solutions" in policy conversations about racial equity and social justice? This chapter offers a framework of four principles for thinking about that question. These four principles share the central idea that policymaking focused on the technology itself (as opposed to policymaking about the people affected by technology) will always serve the purpose of system preservation.

HISTORICAL CONTEXT

To understand the system-preserving potential of carceral technologies, it is important to put their new popularity into historical context. Since the end of slavery, the American criminal legal system has been the primary resource of the power structure that thrives on the exploitation of Black lives. Over the last two decades, a corpus of scholarship has emerged to explain the contemporary tragedy of mass incarceration as the result of a perpetual refusal—since the Civil War—to enter into a new social covenant co-imagined with formerly enslaved people and their descendants (Alexander, 2020; Benjamin, 2019b; Blackmon, 2009; Murakawa, 2014; Simon, 2007). In *Abolition Democracy*, Angela Davis builds on W.E.B. Du Bois's account of the failures of Reconstruction to give historical context to the current constellation of political and social systems of which policing and prisons are part:

> [I]n order to fully abolish the oppressive conditions produced by slavery, new democratic institutions would have to be created. Because this did not occur; black people encountered new forms of slavery—from debt peonage and the convict lease system to segregated and second-class education. The prison system continues to carry out this terrible legacy. It has become a receptacle for all of those human beings who bear the inheritance of the failure to create abolition democracy in the aftermath of slavery. (Davis, 2005, pp. 73–74)

While there is a long history of White elites using the legal category of "criminal" to circumvent laws that limit exploitation based explicitly on race (Blackmon, 2009; Gilmore, 2007), the concept of "criminality" expanded throughout the 1970s to become the primary means by which the state coerces and constrains Black people (Alexander, 2020; Simon, 2007). Since the dawn of the era of mass incarceration, the most iconic criminal legal system reforms have consisted primarily in the judicial allowance of certain rights that individuals may invoke for their personal defense. Cases like *Miranda* (*Miranda v. Arizona*, 1966)—which requires police officers to notify persons under investigation of their Fifth Amendment rights—and *Gideon* (*Gideon v. Wainwright*, 1963)—which established the right to appointed counsel for defendants in criminal cases—still enjoy a popular reputation as progressive touchstones. Those cases certainly made it more possible for particular defendants to fight for their freedom within the legal system. But one consequence of that new set of possibilities was to focus attention on questions of procedural fairness for individuals and away from questions of substantive justice within the political community. The post *Gideon-Miranda* criminal legal regime created the illusion of a fair shake for poor people and people of color at least in the arena of the courtroom; this helped to legitimate the broader criminal legal system, even as law and policy mutated to subject more and more of the population to harsher and harsher punishment (Butler, 2013; Murakawa, 2014; Seidman, 1992).

That fairness illusion—after decades of resistance by abolitionist thinkers, writers, and organizers—is finally crumbling. The Movement for Black Lives has articulated a set of demands (*Policy Platform*, n.d.) which, if adopted, could make possible the new social and political covenant that Du Bois saw as the lost hope of Reconstruction (Du Bois, 1935). Municipal policymakers are voting to significantly reduce funding for law enforcement (McEvoy, 2020), and legislative proposals to reduce incarceration and mitigate direct and indirect harms of the criminal legal system at the state level are becoming more common (Nichanian, n.d.). The new cultural currency of abolitionist ideas and the collective sense that American Democracy is at an inflection point, if not a precipice, suggest that those who benefit from our current structures of political authority may once again be considering what they can sacrifice in order to preserve their power (Pew Research Center, 2020).

Applying these lessons from history, we should anticipate system reforms that change the cosmetics of oppression while keeping certain fundamental assumptions (such as the threat of "crime" rightly justifying state violence) firmly in place (Simon, 2007). In the era of big data and exploding digital infrastructure, mass surveillance is easier, more scalable, and more cost-effective than mass incarceration. If the next wave of reforms proposes to eliminate millions of prison cells in exchange for our consent to the creation of billions of virtual ones, that may be very hard to resist (Jefferson, 2020; Zuboff, 2019).

Unlike prison walls, digital infrastructure can be built invisibly, without the awareness of the communities it touches. Unfortunately, the landscape for digital systems of social control has been made ready, over the last decade, through the suffusion of new technologies throughout every part of our criminal legal system. Police, prosecutors, and judges have adopted a wide range of powerful tools to surveil communities and automate adjudicative processes. For example, hundreds of local law enforcement agencies already rely on "crime prediction" software that uses historical arrest data to generate recommendations for which individuals and neighborhoods law enforcement should target (Ferguson, 2017). Facial recognition technology, aerial drones, street cameras, cell-site simulators, and automated license plate readers gather, integrate, and process enormous amounts of data that police can then use to track and identify almost anyone (Electronic Frontier Foundation, n.d.). In the courts, prosecutors use algorithms to estimate the likelihood that a person will engage in future criminal activity and then use those predictions in their charging decisions, sentencing and bail recommendations, and in case resolution (Ferguson, 2016). Judges use algorithmic risk assessment tools in sentencing, bail, and other pretrial decisions, and corrections officials use them for case management inside prisons and for parole determinations.

Not only is the technological scaffolding already in place to support a shift from incarceration to surveillance, but policymakers, prison corporation executives, and academics have been talking explicitly about such a shift for over a decade. Most of that conversation has centered around devices like GPS-enabled electronic ankle monitors, which would—in theory—allow corrections officials to engage in continuous remote surveillance of individuals who would otherwise remain incarcerated (Bagaric et al., 2018; Kilgore, 2013). Although there is no evidence of any surveillance technology actually reducing incarceration rates (as opposed to expanding the overall custody net), its advocates argue that it will reduce costs and suffering. These are the same arguments that we can expect to encounter in the policy debates that will ensue in response to new calls for a criminal legal system overhaul.

It might seem clear from this overview that mass surveillance is already a reality in the United States, and that it helps to fuel, rather than to displace, mass incarceration. This is certainly true to a large degree, but it would be a mistake to think that the potential of carceral technology is anywhere close to fully manifested. Consider, for example, the mass collection of personal information that occurs *not* primarily through law enforcement, but through digital record keeping by state and local government agencies and—even more crucially—by corporations. As a harbinger of one potential future, consider the example of the company known as Clearview AI, which developed a face recognition app that allows users to upload a photograph of a person, compare it with Clearview's database of over five billion images, and view a list of matching images along with links to the website where the image occurs. Clearview built its database by scraping images from websites like Facebook, Instagram, Twitter, and LinkedIn, often in violation of the terms of service. According to the company's CEO, more than 2,400 law enforcement agencies are using their database (Lopatto, 2020).

The possible applications for databases like Clearview's, especially when combined with the increasingly sophisticated surveillance hardware and software that is becoming more common in policing, are vaster than we can currently imagine (Hill, 2021b). Corporations that build algorithms to exploit the massive digital datasets we now generate through our online lives, and the law enforcement agencies that buy those algorithms, have argued that they are in fact tools for reducing human bias (Miller, 2018). The notion that racism within our criminal legal system can be removed through a filter of machine calculation, though now thoroughly debunked (Mayson, 2019; Richardson et al., 2019; Schwartzapfel, 2019), has helped to justify the insertion of powerful digital policing and surveillance technologies throughout our legal system. This notion has also enriched tech company executives who operate on principles of profit maximization, without any public interest commitments and with little oversight or regulation (Garvie et al., 2016; Joh, 2017).

One of the most common temptations in considering how law and policy should respond to the ways that technology redistributes power is to frame the question in terms of the technology, rather than power distribution. What follows is a set of four principles to guide political deliberation about, and to prevent political diversion by, questions of technology within carceral systems. It is important to note that these are policy principles rather than political principles, and as such they are incomplete as a normative account of what democracy requires in decision making about the operation of disciplinary structures within society. The question of whether a policy is just can never be solely a question of the words on the page, or even of the effect of those words in the world; it must always also be a question of how the policy came to be, whose experiences it values, and whose power it expresses. The purpose of articulating these four principles is, therefore, not to offer a rubric by which policies on carceral technology can be evaluated as finally good or bad, but a heuristic by which those engaged in the longer-term fight for racial justice can orient themselves in live policy debates about technology in carceral systems.

FOUR PRINCIPLES

First Principle: Refuse Any New Expansion of Carceral Technology Absolutely

A primary goal of any effort to reduce the harms of carceral technology should be to stop its spread within policing and punishment. The digital infrastructure upon which mass surveillance and algorithmic policing depend is not only already very advanced but taken for granted as part of the law enforcement landscape. A posture of absolute refusal toward new proposals to expand this infrastructure is necessary if there is any hope of challenging the technologies upon which actors in the criminal legal system already rely.

In other contexts, it might make sense to think of tensions about policy responses to technology within movements for social change in terms of a continuum of beliefs about the political feasibility of a given idea for reform. For example, reasonable individuals, all committed to protecting the power of workers to organize, might disagree about whether to push for a federal bill that places limitations on the *collection* of worker data, or whether a bill that limits the ways that employers may *use* worker data is the best that can be hoped for in a given legislative session (Ajunwa et al., 2017). In this hypothetical scenario, both of the policy options on the table have the potential to restore some power to workers not only within their individual relationship with their employer but also within the corporate ecosystem. There is no analogy to be made in the context of the criminal legal system because, to the extent that the system takes account of the rights of those subject to policing and punishment, such rights are all individual, all defensive, and do not involve any power over or participation in system design.

The effect of digital overlay in the criminal legal system will therefore always be to amplify the power of the state and to shrink the space available for those who experience the most violent manifestations of state power to resist. As Jefferson (2020, p. 192) argues:

> If opposition to digitized modes of criminalization is to gain momentum, it cannot be only defensive; it must be abolitionist. This is to say that it must question the very society that incentivizes the production of technologies for racialized social management.

Insisting on an abolitionist approach rather than an approach of compromise when it comes to technology in the criminal legal system encourages a political discourse that is about the problems with policing, prosecution, adjudication, and punishment instead of a discourse about the problems with the tools of policing, prosecution, adjudication, and punishment.

A further, more practical reason for using a refusal framework to respond to proposals to expand carceral technology is that it is very difficult for political communities to make accurate judgments about the implications of any particular extension of technology within the system. This is both because of how quickly technologies themselves now evolve, and because of how they build upon one another over time. Consider New York City's "Domain Awareness System" (DAS), which is currently the world's largest, most sophisticated digital surveillance system. DAS integrates data from thousands of CCTV cameras, license plate readers, aerial drones, cell-site simulators, gunshot detectors, and other surveillance hardware throughout the city. Officers using DAS can run searches on millions of policing records (arrest records, complaints, warrant information, police reports, etc.) through an interface equipped with facial recognition, crime "prediction" software, and other algorithmic surveillance tools (Levine et al., 2017). While DAS itself was launched in 2012, the components that make it the powerful system it is today were developed and put in place piecemeal over the course of a decade—mostly through procurement processes that received little public scrutiny. And even if the city had engaged in a robust political process to debate each of the system components that would one day comprise DAS, those debates would not have taken place in full comprehension of the very near future in which all of those tools would work together in amplifying synchronicity.

Second Principle: Reject Cures for Carceral Technology That Build Carceral Bureaucracy

Because of the opaque, corporate-driven processes by which policymakers introduce digital technologies into the criminal legal system, there are rarely opportunities for grassroots resistance to those technologies before their implementation. Instead, communities discover after the fact—through specific experiences with police, prisons, and courts—that technology played a significant, often harm-increasing, role in those experiences. Most organizing and advocacy against carceral technology is therefore reactive rather than preemptive, and most policy response occurs in a context of deep system investment—contracts already signed, software already purchased, databases already linked, cameras already mounted, and employees already trained to view all of these technologies as necessary to their basic job functions. The risk of policymaking in contexts where digital infrastructure is already constitutive of the carceral systems in question is that policy intended to mitigate the harms of the technology will actually have the effect of embedding them further. In order to avoid this pitfall, policy about existing carceral technology should resist creating new political mechanisms that will build up bureaucracy around the technology. Examples of policy provisions that typically have this effect are: transparency and oversight procedures, allocation of funds to government entities or individuals to mediate on questions of carceral technology, the articulation of judicial standards or other rules or sets of conditions to authorize the use of carceral technology, and the creation of new procedural rights for those subjected to carceral technologies.

While it may be that robust regulation of a given technology within the criminal legal system will have the potential to reduce some harms, complex governance structures also work to legitimize carceral technologies, and can therefore end up hindering community-led movements for transformative change. Legal scholars in the "critique of rights" tradition have described the way that judicial annunciation of rights for individuals that belong to a class of people suffering from systemic exclusion, persecution, or exploitation can actually work against progressive causes (Kennedy, 2002; Tushnet, 1993; West, 2011). In applying this critique to *Gideon*, Paul Butler observes:

> Gideon makes it more work—and thus more difficult—to make economic and racial critiques of criminal justice. This is not to say people cannot and do not make those claims, but rather that Gideon makes their arguments less persuasive. It creates a formal equality between the rich and the poor because now they both have lawyers. (Butler, 2013, p. 2197)

While most of this literature focuses on judge-made law, its insights are equally relevant in the context of legislation and policymaking. And given how little case law exists at this point on the constitutional questions raised by carceral technologies, the primary norm-setting activity in this context is happening through political processes—some at the federal level, but most at the state and local levels. Much of the policy being proposed and enacted takes for granted that digital surveillance will remain part of the criminal legal system and responds by imposing a purportedly "rights protecting" scaffolding to structure and shape its use. For example, the American Civil Liberties Union (ACLU), which is the largest and one of the most influential civil rights organizations in the country, has—for several years—been promoting model legislation to establish public disclosure and reporting requirements for police departments that use surveillance technologies. The bill, titled Community Control Over Police Surveillance (CCOPS) has so far been adopted in 21 jurisdictions. CCOPS requires governments to hold public hearings and regular reporting on police departments' use of surveillance technology. It also calls for the establishment of a community advisory board that is charged with investigating and reporting on the impact of the technology on local communities.

On the surface, these provisions might look like mechanisms for accountability. But when it comes to carceral systems, the necessary question about any proposed reform is: how does the proposal vest power and how does it vest resources? In the case of CCOPS, the answer is that it vests power and resources in the police. The police are the ones with control over the initial disclosures about the technologies, and those disclosures then frame the public hearings, which are planned and run by city officials. Similarly, the police write their own annual reports and are in charge of the public engagement process that the CCOPS bill prescribes as follow up to the annual reports. The police departments receive funding to undertake these processes and police officers are of course paid for their participation; the community members are not. The community advisory board has no enforcement powers, and neither the police nor any other part of the government is required to follow any of the recommendations the advisory board may make.

In criticizing CCOPS style policies, Hamid Khan, the founder of the Stop LAPD Spying Coalition, a grassroots group that fights against police surveillance in Los Angeles, points out that when LAPD solicited public comment on its proposed facial recognition program, 98 percent of responses opposed the program. And that did not stop the city from moving forward with the program. Community engagement is neither equivalent to community empowerment nor is transparency equivalent to truth-seeking. In discussing a similar reform effort in New York City, Khan (2021) remarked:

> The CCOPS approach to surveillance creates structures that we will later regret. For example, last summer politicians in New York City responded to the George Floyd rebellion by passing a law that requires the New York City Police Department to publish self-audits and set self-governance policies. Last month, the NYPD published those reports, which of course announce that all their surveillance is harmless and valuable.

The problem with bureaucracy-building reforms is that they create an illusion of a democratic process, which may diffuse public pressure and scrutiny. Transparency, oversight, and public engagement can be powerful democratic mechanisms when communities already have some measure of power within the systems where those mechanisms are being imposed. However, these mechanisms cannot by themselves bring democratic integrity to the parts of a political system where it is lacking. The American system of policing and punishment is predicated on a conception of those targeted by law enforcement as non-participants in decisions about either law or enforcement of the law (Tucker, 2022). For those who acknowledge and seek to redress the corruption, violence, and brutality that this conception of policing and punishment entails, transparency and oversight and public engagement are a political show which blocks that deeper conversation.

Another bureaucracy-building approach that is common when it comes to policymaking about carceral tech is the articulation of rules for the technology's use and standards the technology must achieve in order to qualify for that use. For example, alongside a growing movement to completely ban police use of facial recognition technology (mostly at the municipal level) is a concurrent push for the adoption of regulations (mostly at the state and federal levels). These regulatory proposals often include lists of permitted and prohibited uses, use authorization processes like judicial warrant requirements, testing requirements to ensure that the technology is accurate and unbiased, and training for law enforcement. The Center on Privacy & Technology at Georgetown Law proposed model legislation along these lines in a 2016 report (Garvie et al., 2016), and the states of Washington (Tracy, 2020) and Massachusetts (Hill, 2021a) have recently passed bills with several similar provisions.

The implementation of these policies will entail: (a) significant public expenditure to test facial recognition software and train police to use it, (b) the creation of incentives for corporations to continue to develop increasingly powerful surveillance systems, (c) the integration of facial recognition into routine policing, and (d) the establishment of case law enshrining facial recognition as a legitimate law enforcement tool. Nothing in these regulations restores any power to the communities against whom the police are using facial recognition, and to the extent that the passage of regulations represents at least a temporary political conclusion, it may become harder for communities to build organizing momentum to push for stronger policy. This preemptive effect is in many ways the most serious harm of bureaucracy building when it comes to carceral technologies because it replaces an important discourse about the dangers of mass surveillance in a democracy with a trivial discourse about the correct way to operate the surveillance gadgets. A common misconception about regulation is that it represents a form of opposition by the state to a given practice. In fact, regulation is a disciplinary force that creates a space within the state for that practice to fit. That is, regulation is not a cage, but a home.

It may be that, in certain political contexts, the communities most affected by policing and surveillance will make the judgment that advocating for bureaucracy-building regulations like those described above is strategic for any number of reasons, such as to reduce immediate suffering of community members or as part of a longer-term project of building their own political power. The point here is not to critique the trade-offs that any particular community has made, or might make in the future, but to say—with rigor and clarity—what those trade-offs actually are when it comes to carceral technologies.

Third Principle: Reduce Digital Record Keeping and Digital Record Sharing

The problem with regulatory frameworks for carceral technology is not that regulation falls short of immediate abolition. Given the indisputable political infeasibility of banning all digital surveillance at any time in the near future, policy change in this area will necessarily be incremental. But the question is what kinds of incremental policy demand organized communities can make without undercutting longer-term work to overhaul systems of policing and punishment in this country. Somewhat counterintuitively, the policies that will do the most to restore community power to resist carceral technology do not actually center on systems of policing and punishment, but on much broader systems of data collection and sharing (Brayne, 2018, 2021).

While each type of carceral technology comes with its own set of concerns, the Orwellian potential arises neither from hardware nor from software, but from their integration with the massive sets of digital data containing detailed, personal information about almost everyone. Increasingly, this data does not originate with law enforcement agencies, but with other government agencies, or with corporations. Data gets from its initial point of collection to law enforcement through any one of a number of complicated networks and information sharing systems, including through data brokers who compile data from multiple sources to package and sell to a range of public and private sector clients (Miller, 2017; O'Neil, 2017).

When state and local bureaucracies first began making the shift to digital record keeping in the 1990s, the motivation was convenience and administrative efficiency. Neither the officials who authorized the change nor their constituents could have contemplated that within three decades all of their electronic information would be linked with electronic information from thousands of other governmental and nongovernmental sources to form the basis for a digital panopticon. At the federal level however, there is considerable evidence that the government saw the opportunity for large scale surveillance that the move to digital record keeping represented. In 2010, through Freedom of Information Act (FOIA) litigation about the immigration enforcement program "Secure Communities," the Center for Constitutional Rights obtained a trove of documents in which federal officials described Secure Communities as one aspect of a massive biometrics database (known as Next Generation Information or NGI) (Center for Constitutional Rights & NDLON, 2011). A 2009 memo included in the government's FOIA response outlines the concept of "record linking," which, the memo explains, will enable interoperability between NGI and other government databases (CJIS, 2009). Another document, prepared to help Department of Homeland Security officials persuade local law enforcement agencies to participate in Secure Communities, explicitly characterizes Secure Communities as a kind of pilot program which DHS hopes will help local agencies become comfortable with a much larger scale information sharing project they have planned. Secure Communities, the memo explains, "is simply the first of a number of biometric interoperability initiatives being brought online" by NGI. "Signing on to Secure Communities now is an opportunity for Local Law Enforcement Agencies to see the future and become comfortable with it" (FBI/CJIS, n.d.).

Just as Secure Communities was only the tip of the NGI iceberg, NGI (while massive) is today only one small part of the complex information gathering and sharing landscape that local, state, and federal law enforcement entities inhabit, and which feeds and is fed by digital surveillance technologies. Because there is so little transparency about these systems and practices, communities are forced to piece together an understanding of how they work based on the ways that they show up in the lives of those targeted by law enforcement. But increasingly—lurking behind each new story about arrests, incarceration, or deportation—there is another story about databases, networks, and algorithms.

Consider a recent case study from Maryland. In 2013, the Maryland legislature passed the Highway Safety Act (Highway Safety Act, 2014), which extended eligibility for driver's licenses to Maryland residents regardless of immigration status. Many undocumented people took advantage of the new law, applied for and received Maryland licenses, and began driving with those licenses. Maryland's Motor Vehicle Administration stores all of its driver photos in a database known as the Maryland Image Repository System (MIRS) which also includes millions of mugshots uploaded by law enforcement. MIRS is part of Maryland's "Criminal Justice Dashboard," the main digital interface for police in Maryland, which includes searchable records on millions of people. The Dashboard is equipped with facial recognition software, and anyone with access to Dashboard can upload a probe photo to search for a match in MIRS. Dashboard, in turn, is linked to a sprawling network of law enforcement databases called the International Safety and Justice Network, but popularly known as "Nlets" (*Nlets—The International Justice And Public Safety Network*, n.d.). Virtually all law enforcement agencies in the country (as well as several international ones) participate in Nlets, which allows its members to query one another's databases for a wide range of information such as a name and address, warrant information and court records, employment information, and driver information.

In February of 2020, Immigration and Customs Enforcement (ICE) knocked on the door of the home where José Santos Quintero Hernandez was living with his wife and five children. One of the children opened the door, and ICE arrested Mr. Hernandez and incarcerated him in an ICE detention center. The ICE agents informed Mr. Hernandez that they located him through information on his driver's license (Bedoya et al., 2021). As it turns out, ICE has automatic access to Maryland's driver information database through Nlets, and ICE officers can even run facial recognition searches on driver photos without the approval or awareness of any Maryland official. Policymakers were unaware, when they passed the 2013 bill with the intention of improving the lives of immigrants living in Maryland, that there was a digital back door that would allow ICE to exploit driving records to carry out deportations. We only know this part of Mr. Hernandez's story because of a slip of the tongue by an ICE agent, and it would be irrational to believe that he is the only person who has ended up in deportation proceedings as a result of information sharing between government agencies. This is unfortunately the nature of carceral technology: its harms are hidden within other harms we are already used to, invisibly accelerating the rate of injury.

The impossibility of full knowledge about the scope and function of digital surveillance means that policies targeting the uses of carceral technology will always be to some extent unseeing and ill-fitting. But however the technologies themselves develop, we do know that their power is dependent on ease of access to ever metastasizing pools of digital data. Policy to curtail the creation, storage, sharing, and sale of personal data gets at the *function* rather than the *use* of carceral technologies. The principle of data minimization is central to the General Data Protection Regulation in Europe (General Data Protection Regulation, 2016), but so far has very little legislative traction in the United States. Organizations that advocate for new federal privacy laws focus on the need to improve economic sector protections, for the most part ignoring the relationship between big data and the criminal legal system. Organizers and advocates looking for ways to address carceral technology as part of the larger movement for racial justice in the United States should consider adopting a set of policy demands that would: (a) limit digital record keeping by state and local governments, (b) cut off avenues of access to digital records by law enforcement agencies especially when it comes to data generated by non-law enforcement sources, (c) remove the profit incentive for data brokers and developers of carceral hardware and software, (d) and curtail database interoperability even among law enforcement agencies. Minor changes in these areas, even if only enacted at the local level, would have the potential to return some power and autonomy to the communities most impacted by policing and punishment.

Fourth Principle: Resist in Terms of Root Causes

Technology cannot solve problems that are not technological in nature (Morozov, 2013). Yet, even in the midst of the most sustained public uprising against policing and incarceration in American history, the temptation to understand our criminal legal system in terms that would make it fixable using existing digital gadgets remains quite strong. Policymakers and pundits hailed algorithmic risk assessment tools as a race-blind cure for human subjectivities in sentencing and, after an enormous body of sociological research, demonstrated that risk assessment tools do not lead to less biased judging (Eckhouse et al., 2019; Green, 2020;

The Use of Pretrial "Risk Assessment" Instruments: A Shared Statement of Civil Rights Concerns, 2018). Government officials and corporations have continued, undeterred, in their conversations about how the algorithms can be "fixed." The recent surge of public attention to facial recognition has produced a mountain of commentary weighing the various problems with the technology (its inaccuracies and biases and inherent privacy infringement) against its power as a law enforcement tool (Hill, 2021b). Very few critiques have pointed out that the power of facial recognition as a law enforcement tool, at a moment of intense political reckoning with the fundamental injustices of law enforcement in the United States, should *itself* be a grave cause for concern.

Policymaking is only ever partly about the substance of the policy; equally important is the discourse that a given policy proposal makes possible within a given political community. When it comes to carceral technology, communities will need to work to redirect policy conversations about technologies toward conversations about the deeper questions of what it will take to achieve racial and economic equity in our world. What is rhetorically possible, for the communities against whom police use facial recognition, in a policy debate about the software's "error rates"? Arguments about the harms of being wrongfully arrested are possible, arguments about the harms of being racially profiled are possible, but arguments about the problems with underlying conceptions of policing are not possible.

Resisting in terms of root causes, in policy conversations around carceral technology, may mean focusing on the underlying problems with our systems of policing and punishment, but it also means expanding that focus to include other social and political systems that have failed communities of color for generations. Instead of debating whether and how surveillance might displace mass incarceration, we have the opportunity to ask: what are the activities of the political community that surveillance has already displaced? The Movement for Black Lives has put forth a Policy Platform which, while very much motivated by experiences of state-sponsored violence in Black communities, emphasizes economic and political reforms over reforms to law enforcement:

> We demand repair for the harms that have been done to Black communities, in the form of reparations and targeted long-term investments. We demand economic justice. We demand defunding and dismantling of the systems and institutions that criminalize, control, and cage us. . . . . We demand political power and community control over the institutions which govern our lives. (*Policy Platform*, n.d.)

Ultimately no policy can cure the problems with carceral technology and no technology can cure the problems with policing and punishment.

Conclusion

Resisting mass surveillance as the next mutation of mass incarceration will mean thinking about the policymaking spaces that are now opening up around the criminal legal system as a chance to insist on a discourse that is about liberation rather than efficiency, about justice rather than accuracy (Benjamin, 2019a). To do so will require enormous discipline on the part of those leading the movement because we all suffer somewhat from imaginative capture by digital culture. But the practice of searching together for the right question, and of rejecting answers that offer to delay that searching, is the practice of revolution.

REFERENCES

Ajunwa, I., Crawford, K., & Schultz, J. (2017). Limitless Worker Surveillance. *California Law Review, 105*, 735–776. doi: 10.15779/Z38BR8MF94.

Alexander, M. (2020). *The New Jim Crow* (10th ed.). The New Press.

Bagaric, M., Hunter, D., & Wolf, G. (2018). Technological Incarceration and the End of the Prison Crisis. *The Journal of Criminal Law & Criminology, 108*(1), 73–135.

Beckett, K. (1999). *Making Crime Pay: Law and Order in Contemporary American Politics.* Oxford University Press.

Bedoya, A. M., Lam, C., & Stein, D. (2021, February 16). Maryland bill would restrict ICE access to MVA data | COMMENTARY - Baltimore Sun. *Baltimore Sun.* https://www.baltimoresun.com/opinion/op-ed/bs-ed-op-0217-ice-mva-20210216-jpcuulqlgvcuxe5iamfi3n6qoy-story.html.

Benjamin, R. (Ed.). (2019a). *Captivating Technology: Race, Carceral Technoscience, and Libertory Imagination in Everyday Life.* Duke University Press.

Benjamin, R. (2019b). *Race After Technology: Abolitionist Tools for the New Jim Code.* Polity Press.

Blackmon, D. (2009). *Slavery by Another Name.* Anchor.

Brayne, S. (2018). The Criminal Law and Law Enforcement Implications of Big Data. *Annual Review of Law and Social Science, 14*, 293.

Brayne, S. (2021). *Predict and Surveil.* Oxford University Press.

Browne, S. (2015). *Dark Matters: On the Surveillance of Blackness.* Duke University Press.

Buolamwini, J., & Gebru, T. (2018). Gender Shades: Intersectional Accuracy Disparities in Commercial Gender Classification. *Proceedings of Machine Learning Research, 81*, 1–15.

Butler, P. (2013). Poor People Lose: Gideon and the Critique of Rights. *Yale Law Journal, 122*(8), 2176–2204.

Center for Constitutional Rights, & NDLON. (2011, July 6). *SECURE COMMUNITIES AND NEXT GENERATION IDENTIFICATION: The FBI's "Big Brother"*

Surveillance Agenda. Uncover the Truth. https://uncoverthetruth.org/wp-content/uploads/2011/07/7-6-11-Scomm-NGI-Fact-Sheet.pdf.

CJIS. (2009). *CJIS Advisory Board Staff Paper*. http://uncoverthetruth.org/wp-content/uploads/2011/07/FBI-SC-1333-1336.pdf.

Community Control Over Police Surveillance (CCOPS) Model Bill. (2020, October). American Civil Liberties Union. https://www.aclu.org/legal-document/community-control-over-police-surveillance-ccops-model-bill.

Davis, A. Y. (2005). *Abolition Democracy: Beyond Prison, Torture and Empire*. Seven Stories Press.

DuBois, W. E. B. (1935). *Black Reconstruction in America: An Essay Toward a History of the Part Which Black Folk Played in the Attempt to Reconstruct Democracy in America, 1860–1880*.

Eckhouse, L., Lum, K., Conti-Cook, C., & Ciccolini, J. (2019). Layers of Bias: A Unified Approach for Understanding Problems with Risk Assessment. *Criminal Justice and Behavior, 46*(2), 185–209. doi: 10.1177/0093854818811379.

Electronic Frontier Foundation. (n.d.). *Atlas of Surveillance*. Electronic Frontier Foundation. Retrieved April 3, 2021, from https://atlasofsurveillance.org/.

FBI/CJIS. (n.d.). *Deployment Outreach Deep Dive*. http://uncoverthetruth.org/wp-content/uploads/2011/07/FBI-SC-2246-2261.pdf.

Ferguson, Andrew G. (2016). Predictive Prosecution. *Wake Forest Law Review, 51*, 705–744.

Ferguson, Andrew G. (2017). Policing Predictive Policing. *Washington University Law Review, 94*, 82.

Garvie, C., Bedoya, A. M., & Frankle, J. (2016). *Perpetual Line-up: Unregulated Police Face Recognition in America*. Center on Privacy & Technology at Georgetown Law. https://www.perpetuallineup.org/.

General Data Protection Regulation, 2016/679 (2016).

Gideon v. Wainwright, 372 U.S. 335 (U.S. Supreme Court 1963).

Gilmore, R. W. (2007). *Golden Gulag: Prisons, Surplus, Crisis, and Opposition in Globalizing California*. University of California Press.

Green, B. (2020). The False Promise of Risk Assessments: Epistemic Reform and the Limits of Fairness. *Proceedings of the ACM Conference on Fairness, Accountability, and Transparency*. https://scholar.harvard.edu/files/bgreen/files/20-fat-risk.pdf.

Haskins, C. (2020). The Los Angeles Police Department Says It Is Dumping a Controversial Predictive Policing Tool. *BuzzFeed*. https://www.buzzfeednews.com/article/carolinehaskins1/los-angeles-police-department-dumping-predpol-predictive.

Highway Safety Act, Maryland Code Annotated § §16-122 (2014).

Browne, S. (2015). *Dark Matters: On the Surveillance of Blackness*. Duke University Press.

Buolamwini, J., & Gebru, T. (2018). Gender Shades: Intersectional Accuracy Disparities in Commercial Gender Classification. *Proceedings of Machine Learning Research, 81*, 1–15.

Hill, K. (2020, December 29). Another Arrest, and Jail Time, Due to a Bad Facial Recognition Match. *The New York Times.* https://www.nytimes.com/2020/12/29/technology/facial-recognition-misidentify-jail.html.

Hill, K. (2021a, February 27). How One State Managed to Actually Write Rules on Facial Recognition. *The New York Times.* https://www.nytimes.com/2021/02/27/technology/Massachusetts-facial-recognition-rules.html.

Hill, K. (2021b, March 18). What Happens When Our Faces Are Tracked Everywhere We Go? *The New York Times.* https://www.nytimes.com/interactive/2021/03/18/magazine/facial-recognition-clearview-ai.html.

Jefferson, B. (2020). *Digitize and Punish: Racial Criminalization in the Digital Age.* University of Minnesota Press.

Joh, E. E. (2017). The Undue Influence of Surveillance Technology Companies on Policing. *New York University Law Review Online, 91,* 101. doi: 10.2139/ssrn.2924620.

Kennedy, D. (2002). The Critique of Rights in Critical Legal Studies. In W. Brown & J. Halley (Eds.), *Left Legalism/Left Critique.* Duke University Press.

Khan, H. (2021, March 10). Police Surveillance Can't Be Reformed. It Must Be Abolished. *Vice.* https://www.vice.com/en/article/xgzj7n/police-surveillance-cant-be-reformed-it-must-be-abolished.

Kilgore, J. (2013). Progress or More of the Same? Electronic Monitoring and Parole in the Age of Mass Incarceration. *Critical Criminology, 21*(1), 123–139.

Levine, E. S., Tisch, J., Tasso, A., & Joy, Mi. (2017). The New York City Police Department's Domain Awareness System. *Interfaces, 47*(1), 70–84.

Lopatto, E. (2020, August 26). *Clearview AI CEO Says 'Over 2,400 Police Agencies' Are Using Its Facial Recognition Software.* The Verge. https://www.theverge.com/2020/8/26/21402978/clearview-ai-ceo-interview-2400-police-agencies-facial-recognition.

López, I. F. H. (2010). Post-Racial Racism: Racial Stratification and Mass Incarceration in the Age of Obama. *California Law Review, 98,* 1023.

Mayson, S. (2019). Bias In, Bias Out. *Yale Law Journal, 128,* 2218.

McEvoy, J. (2020, August 12). *At Least 13 Cities Are Defunding Their Police Departments.* Forbes. https://www.forbes.com/sites/jemimamcevoy/2020/08/13/at-least-13-cities-are-defunding-their-police-departments/?sh=41d657ff29e3.

Miller, A. P. (2018, July 26). Want Less-Biased Decisions? Use Algorithms. *Harvard Business Review.* https://hbr.org/2018/07/want-less-biased-decisions-use-algorithms.

Miller, C. R. (2017, June 6). I Paid to Find Out Everything a Data Broker Knows About Me. *The Atlantic.* https://www.theatlantic.com/technology/archive/2017/06/online-data-brokers/529281/.

Miranda v. Arizona, 384 U.S. 436 (U.S. Supreme Court 1966).

Morozov, E. (2013). *To Save Everything Click Here.* Penguin.

Murakawa, N. (2005). *Electing to Punish: Congress, Race, and the American Criminal Justice State.* Yale University Press.

Murakawa, N. (2014). *The First Civil Right: How Liberals Built Prison America.* Oxford University Press.

Nichanian, D. (n.d.). *Criminal Justice Reform in the States: Spotlight on Legislatures.* The Appeal Political Report. Retrieved March 28, 2021, from political-report

Nlets—*The International Justice And Public Safety Network.* (n.d.). Retrieved April 18, 2021, from https://www.nlets.org/.

O'Neil, C. (2017). *Weapons of Math Destruction.* Crown.

Pew Research Center. (2020). *In Views of U.S. Democracy, Widening Partisan Divides Over Freedom to Peacefully Protest.* https://www.pewresearch.org/politics/2020/09/02/in-views-of-u-s-democracy-widening-partisan-divides-over-freedom-to-peacefully-protest/.

Policy Platform. (n.d.). *Movement for Black Lives.* Retrieved February 14, 2021, from https://m4bl.org/policy-platforms/.

Richardson, R., Schultz, J. M., & Crawford, K. (2019). Dirty Data, Bad Predictions: How Civil Rights Violations Impact Police Data, Predictive Policing Systems, and Justice. *New York University Law Review, 94,* 192.

Schwartzapfel, B. (2019, July 1). Can Racist Algorithms Be Fixed? *The Marshall Project.* https://www.themarshallproject.org/2019/07/01/can-racist-algorithms-be-fixed.

Seidman, L. M. (1992). Brown and Miranda. *California Law Review, 80,* 763.

Simon, J. (2007). *Governing Through Crime: How the War on Crime Transformed American Democracy and Created a Culture of Fear.* Oxford University Press.

Stop LAPD Spying Coalition. (2018). *Before the Bullet Hits the Body: Dismantling Predictive Policing in Los Angeles.* https://stoplapdspying.org/wp-content/uploads/2018/05/Before-the-Bullet-Hits-the-Body-May-8-2018.pdf.

The Use of Pretrial "Risk Assessment" Instruments: A Shared Statement of Civil Rights Concerns. (2018). http://civilrightsdocs.info/pdf/criminal-justice/Pretrial-Risk-Assessment-Full.pdf.

Tracy, R. (2020, March 31). Washington State OKs Facial Recognition Law Seen as National Model—WSJ. *Wall Street Journal.* https://www.wsj.com/articles/washington-state-oks-facial-recognition-law-seen-as-national-model-11585686897.

Tucker, E. (2022). Deliberate Disorder: How Policing Algorithms Making Thinking About Policing Harder. *NYU Review of Law and Social Change, 46.*

Tushnet, M. (1993). The Critique of Rights. *SMU Law Review, 47,* 23–34.

West, R. (2011). Tragic Rights: The Rights Critique in the Age of Obama. *William and Mary Law Review, 53,* 713–746.

Zuboff, S. (2019). *The Age of Surveillance Capitalism: The Fight for a Human Future at the New Frontier of Power.* PublicAffairs.

Chapter 4

Marijuana Legalization

Angela S. Murolo

America's relationship with marijuana—also referred to as cannabis—is complex and rooted in racist rhetoric, policies, and laws. Recreational use in the United States was first documented in the early 1900s (Griffin III et al., 2013). Shortly thereafter, efforts to control marijuana began (Courtwright, 2001). Racist media reports linked marijuana use to violence and immigrants, which created a moral panic (Bonnie & Whitebread, 1999). A moral panic occurs when an initial fear or problem is amplified by media reports to create an adverse societal reaction (Cohen, 1972). Based on this reaction, lawmakers and other agents of social control (e.g., police officers) responded with new policies and enforcement strategies to calm the public (Cohen, 1972). Unfortunately, this response tended to label marijuana users as "criminals."

Henry Anslinger, the first director of the Federal Bureau of Dangerous Drugs (later renamed the Drug Enforcement Agency), was primarily responsible for the initial moral panic and subsequent prohibition of marijuana through racist rhetoric and strategic use of the media. This led to the Marihuana Tax Act of 1937 (Griffin III et al., 2013). His article, "Marihuana: Assassin of Youth," claimed that those who used marijuana—especially young people—became unpredictable, violent, insane murderers. He also linked marijuana use to jazz musicians, African American people, and immigrants, including those who originated from Mexico, Greece, and Latin-American countries (Anslinger & Cooper, 1937; Griffin III et al., 2013). After the passage of the Marihuana Tax Act of 1937, there was little change in marijuana's legal status until the 1960s, when marijuana use became fashionable again among White American youths (Moran, 2011). During this period, President Nixon found new ways to disparage the use of marijuana and create a moral panic. He labeled the substance as a sign of the counterculture and a destructive force against American values (Moran, 2011). Vietnam war protestors, hippies, liberals, and Black nationalists were arrested for marijuana possession during this period (ACLU, 2020). Nixon's domestic policy adviser, John Ehrlichman, was interviewed by Dan Baum in 1994 and was very candid in stating their intentions:

> The Nixon campaign in 1968, and the Nixon White House after that, had two enemies: the antiwar left and black people. You understand what I'm saying? We knew we couldn't make it illegal to be either against the war or black, but by getting the public to associate the hippies with marijuana and blacks with heroin, and then criminalizing both heavily, we could disrupt those communities. We could arrest their leaders, raid their homes, break up their meetings, and vilify them night after night on the evening news. Did we know we were lying about the drugs? Of course we did. (Baum, 2016)

After relative acceptance during the Carter era (1977–1981), the political pendulum swung toward prohibition, the war on drugs, and—in effect—the war on minorities. During the Reagan and Bush administrations, low-level offenses were targeted for arrest, ultimately leading to mass incarceration (Mitchell, 2011). Ronald Reagan officially announced the war on drugs in October 1982. However, less than 2 percent of the population viewed drugs as a pressing issue (Alexander, 2012). Much like Anslinger and Nixon, Reagan exploited racial hostility and resentment for political gain by using "colorblind" rhetoric that centered personal responsibility or irresponsibility as the cause of drug use. This campaign ultimately led to the disproportionate arrest and incarceration of African American people. Specifically, despite similar drug use patterns, African American people were arrested and charged at approximately four times the rate of White Americans (Bunting et al., 2013). Recognizing the link between racialized rhetoric, drug arrests, and mass incarceration, the legalization of marijuana has been framed as one way to "right the wrongs" of the war on drugs and the disproportionate impact of flawed policies on the African American community. Moreover, marijuana's rising popularity coupled with increased favorability has prompted many states to legalize or decriminalize marijuana for adult recreational use (Brenan, 2020). Decriminalization removes the criminal punishment associated with marijuana use or possession; however, the substance remains illegal—unlike legalization, which eliminates criminal punishments with exceptions (Svrakic et al., 2012).

This chapter aims to discuss the costs and benefits of marijuana legalization through a critical lens. First, we will begin with a focus on the financial benefits touted by lawmakers to fill budget gaps and the unknowns that come with projecting future marijuana consumption. Following this, the conversation will focus on business and job creation through the legal marijuana market and how laws create exclusions for those with a criminal history or lack of capital.

Next, the discussion will shift to the promise of legalization and the expectation that people will no longer be arrested or incarcerated for marijuana-based offenses. Unfortunately, the reality has not lived up to its promise. However, some communities have taken progressive measures in the form of reparations, economic empowerment, and restorative justice policy. Finally, the conclusion will include recommendations that create opportunities to enter the marijuana industry and establish a more equitable system.

FINANCIAL CURE-ALL?

Tax and Budgets

Lawmakers looking to legalize recreational marijuana often cite tax revenue and padding state budgets as a reason to pass legislation, but results are mixed. States that have legalized marijuana have found that it is not a predictable revenue stream. For instance, to estimate how much tax revenue can be generated, lawmakers need some indication of how many people use marijuana and their frequency of use. The state of Alaska conducted a poll of citizens that asked about their marijuana usage before legalization to gauge consumption habits. Not surprisingly, people were less than forthcoming, which made potential tax revenue challenging to predict (Chapman et al., 2019). Additionally, revenue projections are contingent on the history of a product's sales. Still, the prior illegality of marijuana makes accurate predictions difficult (Chapman et al., 2019). For example, proponents of marijuana legalization in California estimated $1 billion would be generated in tax revenue per year, but the first full year of marijuana legalization generated $345 million, less than one-third of the projected revenue (Becker, 2019). Opponents of legalization, such as Smart Approaches to Marijuana, have also stressed that tax revenue from legal marijuana sales is less than 1 percent of state tax revenues—a drop in the proverbial bucket (Smart Approaches to Marijuana, n.d.-b).

Predicting future consumption patterns is another factor that influences state tax revenue. Will more people use marijuana if it is legal, and for how long? This complicated issue is shaped by many factors, including (a) the price compared to the illegal underground market, (b) taxation levels in the state, (c) competition from neighboring states, (d) any changes at the federal level related to legalization or decriminalization, and (e) lag times from legalization to the beginning of sales (Pew Charitable Trusts, 2019). For example, California's legal marijuana is more expensive than the black-market cost of marijuana, which has negatively impacted legal sales (Chapman et al., 2019). Marijuana advocates argue that the taxes are too high, which is infringing on legal sales. However, policymakers would argue that tax revenue is the reason for legalization in the first place (Becker, 2019). Ultimately, retail sale prices will significantly impact legal sales (Kilmer, 2016). Another challenge to a robust marijuana economy is competition from neighboring states. If neighboring states have legal marijuana markets, they are competing for sales and revenue. Therefore, if taxes are lower and marijuana is cheaper, it is possible that one state may siphon off sales from another (Kilmer, 2016). Other unexpected financial challenges that come with legalization include lengthy lag times from legalization to retail sales. States looking to legalize marijuana fail to understand just how long it can take to get tax infrastructure and retail markets up and running. This includes time to set up regulations, establish licensing guidelines, and process applications, and the length of time it takes to grow and process marijuana, which can be as long as a year (Biolchini, 2019; Cazentre, 2021; Chapman et al., 2019).

Despite the unpredictability of marijuana-generated tax revenue, the taxes collected from marijuana sales are used to fund state programs that benefit the public. Illinois is one state that is using tax revenue from adult marijuana sales to support programs that serve communities disproportionately impacted by the war on drugs. The Restore, Reinvest, Renew (R3) program, which was part of the Cannabis Regulation and Tax Act of 2019, earmarks 25 percent of all marijuana ta revenue for grants and funds to communities (Illinois Criminal Justice Information Authority, 2021). Tax revenue totaling $31.5 million has been used for restorative justice grants, mental health and substance abuse treatment, and economic development (Jaeger, 2021). Similarly, Colorado used tax revenue from the 2017–2018 fiscal year to fund public schools. Additional revenue was set aside for future funding. Washington state used tax revenue to fund Medicaid for low-income residents (Perez et al., 2019).

Businesses and Jobs

While policymakers argued that legalization would be a windfall for state budgets, business entrepreneurs contend that legalization will generate income and create new businesses and jobs. The marijuana industry is a multibillion-dollar business, with sales of legal marijuana totaling nearly $10 billion in 2018 (32 Incredible Cannabis, n.d.). The industry is projected to generate $30 billion per year by 2025 (Uzialko, 2020). However, financial projections are based on federal laws that continue to criminalize marijuana (NORML, n.d.).

The growth of the marijuana industry also signals job growth. In 2018, the marijuana industry added 64,389 jobs (Cox, 2019). This number is expected to increase as states continue to legalize marijuana. There are two types of marijuana-related businesses—plant-touching and ancillary businesses—which provide various employment opportunities (Uzialko, 2020). Salaries for plant-touching-related employment vary greatly. For example, a "budtender" or a staff member who works at a dispensary can earn between $12 and $16 an hour. In contrast, those involved with cultivation and extraction and sales representatives can make upward of six figures (Cox, 2019). The median pay in the legal marijuana industry is 11 percent higher than the average median salary among US workers (Cox, 2019).

It is clear that legalization is trending, with over 60 percent of the American public and 18 states supporting legalization for adult use (Brenan, 2020; NORML, n.d.). Although unpredictable, tax revenues have provided increased cash flow to states to provide social programs and add cushion to strapped state budgets (Jaeger, 2021). These social programs aim to serve and repair the communities that have been disproportionately impacted by the war on drugs (Illinois Criminal Justice Information Authority, 2021). Business owners and investors are generating wealth and creating jobs (Uzialko, 2020). But who benefits from business opportunities, wealth, and marijuana industry-based jobs?

Who Is Benefited?

While marijuana legalization has benefitted several African American people—including some high-profile celebrities—legalization has profited the wealthy and well-connected. Most of the beneficiaries are White investors or the White business class. Famous basketball players like Al Harrington and John Salley own large-scale growing, cultivation, manufacturing, and distribution facilities (Johnson, 2020). Rapper and entrepreneur Snoop Dogg has a stake in several marijuana-based businesses, including Casa Verde Capital—a venture capital firm investing "in scalable, capital efficient businesses . . . addressing long-term market needs" (Casa Verde Capital, n.d.). Moreover, several Black-owned marijuana businesses were founded by less well-known entrepreneurs (see table 4.1 for a partial list of Black-owned marijuana-based companies); however, most marijuana businesses are owned and operated by White investors, who have a vast stake in legalization. Only 4 percent of marijuana-based businesses are Black-owned (McVey, 2017).

It is important to note that the elite's embrace of legalization is not without controversy. Legalization is framed as a social justice issue that can bring relief from criminalization and provide opportunities for Black entrepreneurs. Unfortunately, access to opportunities within the marijuana industry is often blocked. For example, 24 investors in Ohio (only one African American) intended to get marijuana legalization on the ballot. Still, the provision limited growing operations to 10 parcels of land controlled by the same investors who lobbied for the law's passage, effectively setting up a monopoly and blocking access for others to benefit from the bill (Ross, 2018). Although

Table 4.1 Black-Owned Cannabis Companies (Partially or Fully Owned)

Company Name	Owner(s)
American Cannabinoid Clinics	Dr. Jessica Knox, Dr. Janice Knox, and Dr. Rachel Knox, a family of doctors
Ardent Cannabis	Shanel Lindsay, lawyer, entrepreneur
Blunts and Moore	Alphonso "Tuck" Blunt Jr. and Brittany "Bri" Moore
Canopy Growth	Snoop Dogg, rapper, entrepreneur
Casa Verde Capital	Snoop Dogg, rapper, entrepreneur
Deuces 22	John Salley, former NBA player
Green Thumb Industries	Eugene Monroe, former NFL player
Kush and Cute	Iyana Edouard
Mary & Main	Dr. Octavia Wiseman, Dr. Larry Bryant, and Hope Wiseman
Pure Oasis	Kobie Evans and Kevin Hart
Simply Pure	Wanda James and Scott Durrah, military veterans
The Farmacy	Sue Taylor
Tyson Ranch	Mike Tyson, boxer
Viola	Al Harrington, former NBA player
Whoopi & Maya	Whoopi Goldberg, actress
99th Floor	Doug Cohen and Miguel Trinidad

this bill did not pass, it highlights the obstacles ordinary people could face if they were interested in starting a legal marijuana business. Many marijuana businesses are multistate, multi-million-dollar, and multi-billion-dollar corporations that are publicly traded and generally run by White Boards of Directors members. Marijuana is a big business that provides limited access to opportunities for the underprivileged (Ross, 2018).

Who Is Not Benefited?

One of the primary obstacles to entering the marijuana business is a lack of access to capital. Many states have costly licensing fees and startup costs that would be unaffordable for most. For example, medical marijuana licensing for growers and processors in Pennsylvania requires $2 million in capital in addition to a $10,000 initial nonrefundable fee and a $200,000 permit fee (Pennsylvania Department of Health, 2020). Pennsylvania is not unique in requiring excessive startup costs. Some states require as much as $3 to $5 million dollars to apply for a marijuana license (Bender, 2016). African American people were drastically impacted by the Great Recession of 2007–2010, and median wealth continued to decline in 2010–2013 (Kochnar & Cilluffo, 2017). More recently, African American households have experienced negative consequences from the COVID-19 pandemic; African American women disproportionately suffer from unemployment and loss of liquid assets (Moss et al., 2020). The average White person has a net worth

10 times that of African Americans and holds 84 percent of total household wealth in the United States (Kochnar & Cilluffo, 2017). Therefore, one can infer that legalization favors those who have the wealth to invest, which prevents African Americans and other non-White minority citizens from gaining access to the market.

Finding financial investors may be difficult as well. For instance, Shanel Lindsay—the founder of Ardent Cannabis, a biotech and medical marijuana company that develops devices that can improve the processing of medical marijuana (Sumner, 2020)—spoke about the obstacles that people of color face in obtaining capital. In an interview with Green Entrepreneur, Lindsay noted that "it was very difficult as a woman of color who was bringing in a new technology . . . to raise money" (as cited by Sumner, 2020). Lindsay noted her ability to go to family and friends for financial support, without which she would not have launched her business (Sumner, 2020).

Access to bank loans may be problematic. Bankers may not be willing to lend money to marijuana entrepreneurs due to concerns over federal trafficking crimes (Mitchell, 2019). Of the 5,276 banks in America, less than 190 serve the marijuana industry (Heras, 2021). While Congress agreed not to pursue violations of federal marijuana laws in the 2015 Omnibus spending bill, it did not agree to allow banks to provide financial services to marijuana businesses, further complicating efforts to enter the industry (Bender, 2016).

Challenges with entering the marijuana market extend beyond finances. There is little to no chance to secure a license or retail employment if one has a criminal record. Many states have what is known as a "good moral character" clause (Thompson, 2017) that bans anyone with a prior criminal conviction or felony from obtaining a license (Clarke, 2019). If someone has good moral character, legally, this implies that the individual does not have a criminal history and fulfills their legal obligations (USCIS Policy Manual Part F, 2020). Criminal history denies access to employment where "good moral character" is considered necessary. Although some states, like Oregon, grant license exceptions to those who have gone 5 years without a conviction, have only one marijuana-based conviction, or whose history shows only non-drug-related misdemeanors (Measure 91, 2014, Section 29), other states, like Colorado, are especially stringent with financial restrictions. Colorado excludes individuals with outstanding child support obligations, delinquent student loans, and tax debt (Wyatt, 2015).

Although the legal language is race-neutral, the message is clear. Travis (2005) would posit that the exclusion of formerly incarcerated people, particularly African American people, from this burgeoning market is another form of invisible punishment. These sanctions eliminate opportunities and relegate formerly incarcerated persons to second-class citizen status. Alexander

(2012) would argue this is part of the new Jim Crow, where White privilege and racialized social control remain the status quo. Many African Americans are removed from the legal drug market because they are almost four times more likely to be arrested for marijuana possession than their White counterparts (Bunting et al., 2013). This disparity is evident because 99 percent of license holders for the "growing" sector of the marijuana industry are White (Clarke, 2019). Because marijuana is not legal on the federal level, there are no guidelines for racial equity in employment (Charles, 2020).

LEGALIZATION WILL REDUCE ARRESTS AND MASS INCARCERATION, RIGHT?

Marijuana legalization has not been a financial cure-all. However, supporters of legalization have argued that we can reduce prison populations through pardons, expungements, and resentencing. We might also expect a reduction in arrests and racial disparities in the criminal justice system through legalization. Unfortunately, the reality is a bit more complicated.

Arrests in Post-Legalization States

States that legalized marijuana still arrest people for possession and personal use. Arrests in marijuana-legal states disproportionately impact both adult and juvenile African Americans (Resing, 2019). Bans on public consumption, marijuana possession in "plain view," and the inability to use marijuana indoors perpetuate policies that disproportionately criminalize African American people and the poor. African American juveniles are more likely to be arrested on school property for simple possession (Way, 2018). However, overall arrests and racial disparities in arrests have dropped in states that have legalized or decriminalized marijuana (Todd, 2018). Conversely, states that continue to criminalize marijuana use, such as South Dakota and Utah, have increased marijuana-related arrests (ACLU, 2020).

Washington approved the use of both medical (1998) and recreational marijuana (2012) but has a history of arresting people for marijuana at alarmingly high rates (ACLU, 2020). After medical marijuana was legalized, arrest rates for marijuana grew between 1998 and 2010, including individuals with proof of medical marijuana authorization from their doctors (Levine et al., 2012). Medical marijuana laws do not immunize people from arrest or prosecution (Levine et al., 2012). Before the passage of the recreational use law, African American people were arrested at 2.9 times the rate of White people (Levine et al., 2012). Post legalization, Washington continues to arrest

Table 4.2 States Ranked by Racial Disparity in Marijuana Arrests

Times More Likely Black People Arrested in 2018	State	Year Legalized
6.1×	Vermont	2018
4×	Massachusetts	2016
4×	Maine	2016
3.6×	Michigan	2018
3×	Nevada	2016
2.1×	Washington	2012
1.8×	Oregon	2014
1.8×	California	2016
1.6×	Alaska	2014
1.5×	Colorado	2012

African American adults at a disproportionate rate. African Americans were arrested 2.1 times the rate of White adults (Levine et al., 2012). This is just one example of how changes do not materialize into broad reform; instead, they perpetuate the status quo.

In Colorado, marijuana arrests for possession and cultivation dropped by 80 percent between 2010 and 2014 (just before and after legalization), excluding the city of Denver (Gettman, n.d.). However, racial disparities persisted, with African American people still being arrested at rates 2.4 times higher than White Coloradans 2 years after marijuana was legalized (Gettman, n.d.). By 2018, African American people were arrested 1.5 times more than White people (ACLU, 2020) (see table 4.2 below). This disparity can be explained by a shift in law enforcement priorities to arrest those using marijuana in public (Gettman, n.d.). Reasons for public marijuana use vary. People who are homeless are likely to smoke marijuana outdoors. Other people may smoke outdoors due to fear of public housing policies that mandate eviction for drug possession or arrest due to "one strike and you're out" laws (as cited in Travis, 2005). Public use arrests are primarily concentrated in impoverished African American communities and are often used as gateways to investigate other crimes (Schwartzman & Harden, 2020).

Resentencing, Expungement, and Pardons

Many people remain incarcerated for drug crimes that are no longer illegal. As states vote to legalize marijuana, the response to those already incarcerated for marijuana offenses varies; some states are more willing to assist incarcerated persons in revisiting their sentences than others. For example, the state of Oregon allows eligible persons to apply to have a sentence reduction, their criminal records sealed, or their "charges set aside" through expungement (Drug Policy Alliance, 2015). To be eligible for a sentence change, one must go through a lengthy legal application process. The process includes applying for a change in status, serving the prosecutor's office with a notice, and hiring a lawyer to represent one's case, which will be presented in front of a judge. This process begins after the appropriate time has been served to be eligible (Thompson, 2017). This law (ORS 137.225) assumes people in prison have time, money, and access to appropriate legal representation to reduce or eliminate the charges against them. The Colorado law that considers marijuana convictions (*Colorado v. Brandi Jessica Russel*, 2004) only considers cases that were pending during the legalization process and does not apply retroactively to cases before legalization (RT Staff, 2014). This ruling benefitted very few people; those who were in possession of small amounts of marijuana were already subject to decriminalization, and incarceration for possession was unlikely (Peralta, 2014).

Before legalization, some cities, including San Francisco, automatically expunged and sealed thousands of marijuana convictions without requiring a petition. This directly helped people who may have been victims of the war on drugs (Aiello, 2018). This runs contrary to California's overall strategy of having people previously convicted of a marijuana offense file a petition, pay a fee, and retain an attorney. Overall, this process makes participation by minorities and the poor unlikely (Aiello, 2018).

Alaska's legalization statute does not address those who were incarcerated before the legalization change at all. Instead, those who want a sentence reduction must rely on a pardon from the governor, which is another tool to reverse criminal convictions (Woodham, 2015). Some states like Pennsylvania use an expedited pardon process to address past criminal convictions (Hughes, 2019). Previously, the pardon process would take up to 2.5 years to be processed, but the current goal is to process low-level marijuana offenses in less than a year (Hughes, 2019). Additionally, in 2019, Pennsylvania waived the application fee, making it more accessible to people with financial obstacles.

Some states are more proactive in their approach to reduce the harm of past drug policies. Pennsylvania and New York are automatically removing obstacles to clearing criminal history records (New York Marihuana Tax and Regulation Act, 2021). Other states like Oregon require people to initiate action to clear their records (Drug Policy Alliance, 2015). This action can be costly, lengthy, and out of reach for those without the time or money to clear their names and records. Nonetheless, this change in philosophy on marijuana use has many activists and stakeholders positing that legalization can also reduce mass incarceration.

Reducing Mass Incarceration?

Marijuana legalization has been promoted as a racial justice issue that would decrease mass incarceration. Places like Washington, DC ran legalization campaigns arguing that "legalization ends discrimination" (Smart Approaches to Marijuana, n.d.-a). But only a handful of states have successfully decreased prison populations, albeit indirectly. Rhode Island and Alaska are two states that have seen declines in prison populations but for very different reasons.

Rhode Island decreased incarceration rates by decriminalizing marijuana and using civil penalties or summonses instead of arrest and incarceration (Schrantz et al., 2018). This, in turn, decreased court admissions and reduced incarceration rates (Schrantz et al., 2018). The change in incarceration strategy, coupled with decriminalization of marijuana, has de facto reduced the prison population and the likelihood of being incarcerated for a marijuana offense (Schrantz et al., 2018).

Alaska also decreased prison populations, but that drop was not related to marijuana legalization specifically. With the passage of Senate Bill (S.B.) 91 in 2005, Alaska readdressed incarceration as a punishment for various offenses, including drug possession, to reserve imprisonment for the most heinous crimes (Kelly et al., 2017). This daring change of strategy led to a decrease in the prison population and the elimination of people who could be incarcerated for marijuana-related offenses (Smart Approaches to Marijuana, n.d.-a). Alaska and Rhode Island have readdressed how they look at marijuana legalization and incarceration, which has led to decreases in the prison population.

There have been varied responses to marijuana usage ranging from arrest and decarceration to expungement and pardons for those who have been incarcerated (Resing, 2019). While the nation moves toward more favorable attitudes about marijuana and relaxation of punishment, some states still opt to be "tough" on drugs (Levine et al., 2012). Other states are shifting to repair the harms done by the war on drugs (New York Marihuana Tax and Regulation Act, 2021). In the next section, solutions to this complicated issue will be addressed.

SOLUTIONS

Malcolm X once claimed "Racism is like a Cadillac; they bring out a new model every year" (Lipsitz, 1998). One could argue that legalization is the new Cadillac. It could explain the disproportionate incarceration of African Americans for the use and distribution of marijuana, followed by its legalization, which has systematically locked African Americans out of opportunities that primarily benefit the wealthy, White investor class. Moving forward, the goal should be to provide solutions to address racial disparities and make legalization fair. Laws and policies should address the impact of a marijuana arrest on long-term prosperity and aid those looking to enter one of the fastest-growing employment and business industries (Cox, 2019). Below, solutions are presented as a path forward.

Invest in Impacted Communities

State tax revenue from marijuana sales should be used to invest in communities impacted by disproportionate drug arrests. Having a criminal record decreases the likelihood of obtaining employment, a fair wage, and suitable housing; moreover, it negatively impacts long-term earning outcomes (Pager, 2002). Arrests and incarceration remove workers, family members, and breadwinners from their communities. If people are separated from their families, they cannot support their children or contribute to the tax base. Employment and other taxes provide funding for educational programming and other public services (Perez et al., 2019). Therefore, using tax revenue to give back to communities that have been disproportionately impacted is a way to begin to repair the harms done by the war on drugs and mass incarceration.

How do we do this? One way to improve employment opportunities in impacted communities is to expand or initiate the Ban the Box program. This program restricts employer's access to the applicant's criminal history until after the initial application process (Avery & Lu, 2020). This is a small step to open opportunities that can begin the process of offering employment opportunities. Another way to invest in communities is to create public sector jobs in neighborhoods with high concentrations of drug arrests (Perez et al., 2019). This would provide opportunities to people who may be excluded from good-paying public jobs. At the federal level, the Marijuana Justice Act (2019), sponsored by Senator Cory Booker of New Jersey, aims to provide grants to impacted communities for programming, job training, reentry services, and expungement for convictions.

This is a step forward, but does it go far enough? Grandpre (2020) argues that Booker's Marijuana Justice Act does not go far enough and focuses on reinvestment rather than reparations. Grandpre (2020) suggests a framework like the People's Assembly in Jackson, Mississippi, where an independent body decides where funds should be allocated to provide the greatest impact to their community. Decisions are presented to the local government, which sets spending priorities—underscoring the impact of collective efficacy on community outcomes (Grandpre, 2020). New York legalized recreational marijuana use on March 31, 2021 (New York Marihuana Tax and Regulation Act, 2021). Before passage, African American lawmakers publicly stated that they would not vote for legalization unless some profits were redirected to communities of color (Charles, 2020). This insistence by African American lawmakers was successful. The legislation requires 40 percent of the tax revenue from adult-use sales be allocated to communities impacted by the war on drugs (New York Marihuana Tax and Regulation Act, 2021). Evanston, Illinois is an example of how tax revenue from marijuana sales can repair community harm. Evanston's ground-breaking program allocates a percentage of its marijuana tax revenue (3 percent) to provide reparations to African American citizens impacted by discriminatory housing practices (Adams, 2021). Housing subsidies of $25,000 will go to residents for mortgage assistance or property repairs. Still, some argue direct cash payments are a more effective use of funds (Adams, 2021).

Job and Business Opportunities

For those looking for an entryway into the marijuana-based market, there are many ways opportunities should be increased at the federal and state levels. The Marijuana Opportunity Reinvestment and Expungement Act (MORE) Act would effectively "cancel low-level federal convictions and marijuana arrests," which would increase the possibility of employment (Walsh, 2020). Tax on marijuana sales would be directed to communities impacted by the war on drugs as well. Marijuana legalization on the federal level would also create jobs in the marijuana industry and ancillary services, such as banking (to provide loans), marketing, and packaging. For those who cannot gain access to plant-touching positions because of their criminal records, ancillary functions may be obtainable and lucrative (Charles, 2020). Estimates suggest that federal legalization would generate $105.6 billion in tax proceeds and one million jobs by 2025 (Song, 2018).

At the state level, laws should ensure equitable access to business and job opportunities. Equitable access allows all citizens to obtain a license by removing the "good morals" clauses from states that have already legalized marijuana. States that have not legalized marijuana yet should not include provisions that address prior behaviors. If they must include such language, there should be a time limit attached to consideration of one's criminal history. After a period of "noncriminal behavior," one's history should be wiped clean, a notion which is currently gaining momentum in New York State (Clean Slate NY, n.d.). New Jersey's citizens voted on a ballot measure to approve recreational marijuana use in November 2020. One clause required that 30 percent of the licenses be set aside for minorities, women, and disabled veterans (Smith, 2021). Some may argue that this does not go far enough. States that have legalized marijuana have learned that it is not enough to talk about ending discriminatory practices. Legislators must provide access to opportunity, particularly to those impacted by punitive drug policies. Last, to create job and business opportunities, there must be increased access to capital through, for example, microloans. With federal legalization, bank loans will give business opportunities to those traditionally locked out. According to Charles (2020), greater access to capital will increase minority ownership.

Criminal Justice-Based Solutions

In the future, criminal justice-based solutions must be more rigorous and retroactive in their scope to undo the harm done by punitive punishments for marijuana-based offenses. States that have legalized marijuana must engage in decriminalization and decarceration for marijuana offenses. On the ground level, this means not arresting people for marijuana use in public places. There are many ways of addressing this, including giving "warnings" instead of citations, prescribing community service in place of citations for those who cannot afford to pay, and providing private and public spaces where consumption is permitted (Thompson, 2017). States that have legalized marijuana have seen a drop in racial disparities in arrests; however, this is not enough (Woodham, 2015). For legal marijuana to live up to its racial justice potential, policing marijuana use should not be a law enforcement priority.

Beyond policing, prosecutors can choose not to prosecute marijuana-based arrests. For instance, Manhattan District Attorney Cyrus Vance declined to prosecute marijuana possession and use cases beginning in 2018, three years before legalization in New York (Manhattan, 2018). This policy change was expected to reduce prosecutions for marijuana up to 96 percent, or down to 200 prosecutions per year in Manhattan alone (Manhattan, 2018). There have also been efforts by New Jersey to avoid arresting minors for marijuana possession. Instead, officers must notify parents if they are caught with marijuana or alcohol (Davis, 2021). Police officers were ultimately barred from notifying parents of marijuana possession when marijuana legalization was passed (Davis, 2021). However, parental notification as an initial response is preferable to arresting juveniles for marijuana possession, introducing criminalization at a young age (Way, 2018).

There should also be automatic reviews of marijuana convictions to address retroactive harms, and people in prison should be resentenced based on current laws. This is costly and time-consuming, but it should be a priority with increased tax revenue from legalization. When people return to the community from prison, opportunities for reentry assistance should be available. Job training, education, and housing are the primary concerns of those returning from prison (Travis, 2005). Assisting those returning from prison should be considered a form of community reinvestment that tax revenue from legal marijuana sales should fund. States like Arizona and New Jersey have taken note of states that legalized early and strived to provide a more racially and socially just law with their version of legalization.

CONCLUSION

Marijuana's history has been fraught with racist and classist undertones. From moral panics to cultural and social shifts, recreational marijuana use has become popular and socially accepted. These changes have led many states to pass medical and recreational marijuana use laws. Many people thought legalization would end discriminatory arrest policies and bring an end to mass incarceration. Unfortunately, the results of this grand experiment have not been far-reaching. While some states like Colorado and Alaska have reduced racial disparities in marijuana arrests, other states like South Dakota and Utah have increased arrests. Additionally, African Americans have been disproportionately impacted by mass incarceration and the war on drugs, which has effectively locked them out of the windfall of legal marijuana sales.

Knowing this, we must advocate for decarceration, decriminalization, and opportunities for entrance into the legal market. Like Alaska, states should reconsider "crimes" that require incarceration with an eye toward maintaining public safety. No one should be criminalized for using a legal drug. Providing alternatives to incarceration—such as summons for public use or community service for those who cannot afford to pay—could keep people out of prison. States and communities should also consider that some people simply cannot use marijuana in their homes for fear of repercussions. We have bars and restaurants to drink alcohol; there should be public or semipublic places where people can use marijuana without fear of arrest. Addressing marijuana rationally instead of using a punitive approach will lessen the harm caused by criminalization.

REFERENCES

ACLU. (2020). *A tale of two countries: Racially targeted arrests in the era of marijuana reform.* American Civil Liberties Union. https://www.aclu.org/report/tale-two-countries-racially-targeted-arrests-era-marijuana-reform.

Adams, C. (2021, March 26). *Evanston is the first U.S. city to issue slavery reparations. Experts say it's a noble start.* NBC News. https://www.nbcnews.com/news/nbcblk/evanston-s-reparations-plan-noble-start-complicated-process-experts-say-n1262096.

Aiello, C. (2018, January 31). *The San Francisco DA will dismiss thousands of marijuana-related convictions in an unprecedented move.* CNBC. https://www.cnbc.com/2018/01/31/the-san-francisco-da-will-dismiss-thousands-of-marijuana-related-convictions.html.

Alexander, M. (2012). *The new Jim Crow: Mass incarceration in the age of colorblindness.* The New Press.

Anslinger, H. J., & Cooper, C. R. (1937). *Marijuana: Assassin of youth.* Crowell Publishing Company.

Avery, B. & Lu, H. (2020, September 20). *Ban the box: U.S. cities, counties and states adopt fair hiring policies.* National Employment Law Project. https://www.nelp.org/publication/ban-the-box-fair-chance-hiring-state-and-local-guide/.

Baum, D. (2016, March 25). *Legalize it all: How to win the war on drugs.* Harpers Magazine. Retrieved from: https://harpers.org/archive/2016/04/legalize-it-all/.

Becker, B. (2019). *Cannabis was supposed to be a tax windfall for states. The reality has been different.* Politico. https://www.politico.com/agenda/story/2019/10/14/marijuana-tax-revenue-001062/.

Bender, S. (2016). The colors of cannabis. Race and marijuana: *UC Davis Law Review*, 50, 689.

Biolchini, A. (2019, August 4). After marijuana legalization, the wait for retail sales is the national norm. *MI Live*. https://www.mlive.com/news/2019/08/after-marijuana-legalization-the-wait-for-retail-sales-is-the-national-norm.html.

Bonnie, R. J., & Whitebread, C. H. (1999). *The marihuana conviction: A history of marihuana prohibition in the United States* (2nd ed.). The Lindesmith Center.

Brenan, M. (2020). *Support for legal marijuana inches up to new high of 68%.* Gallup Poll. https://news.gallup.com/poll/323582/support-legal-marijuana-inches-new-high.aspx.

Bunting, W. C., Garcia, L., & Edwards, E. (2013). *The war on marijuana in black and white.* American Civil Liberties Union. https://www.aclu.org/report/tale-two-countries-racially-targeted-arrests-era-marijuana-reform.

Casa Verde Capital. (n.d.). About us. Casa Verde. https://www.casaverdecapital.com/.

Cazentre, D. (2021, April 6). New York is about to legalize marijuana. But it will take a year or more before you can buy it. New York Upstate. https://www.newyorkupstate.com/news/2021/03/new-york-is-about-to-legalize-marijuana-but-it-will-take-a-year-or-more-before-you-can-buy-it.html.

Chapman, J., Levin, A., Murphy, M., & Zhang, A. (2019, August). *Forecast hazy for state marijuana revenue.* Pew Charitable Trusts. https://www.pewtrusts.org/-/media/assets/2019/08/marijuana-brief_v2.pdf.

Chapman, J., Levin, A., & Zhang, A. (2020, December 8). *Can revenue from legalized recreational marijuana help states close budget gaps?* Pew Charitable Trusts. https://www.pewtrusts.org/en/research-and-analysis/articles/2020/12/08/can-revenue-from-legalized-recreational-marijuana-help-states-close-budget-gaps.

Charles, N. (2020, February 11). *Black entrepreneurs struggle to join legal weed industry.* NBC News. https://www.nbcnews.com/news/nbcblk/black-entrepreneurs-struggle-join-legal-weed-industry-n1132351.

Clarke, K. (2019). *Cannabis industry shouldn't expand until we fix marijuana's racial inequities, injustices*. USA Today. https://www.usatoday.com/story/opinion/2019/02/22/marijuana-legalization-exposes-cannabis-industry-racial-injustice-incarceration-minorities-column/2836449002/.

Clean Slate NY. (n.d.). Clean Slate New York. https://www.cleanslateny.org/.

Cohen, S. (1972). *Folk devils and moral panics*. Routledge.

Courtwright, D. T. (2001). *Forces of habit: Drugs and the making of the modern world*. Harvard University Press.

Cox, J. (2019). *The marijuana industry looks like the fastest-growing job market in the country*. CNBC. https://www.cnbc.com/2019/03/14/the-marijuana-industry-looks-like-the-fastest-growing-job-market-in-the-country.html.

Davis, M. (2021, March 25). *NJ legal weed changes coming? Parental notification for underage marijuana, alcohol use OK'd*. Asbury Park Press. https://www.app.com/story/news/local/new-jersey/marijuana/2021/03/25/nj-marijuana-legalization-legal-weed-parent-notification/6996705002/.

Drug Policy Alliance. (2015, March 25). *New report provides comprehensive data on marijuana arrests and charges in Colorado after legal regulation for adult use*. Drug Policy Alliance. https://drugpolicy.org/news/2015/03/new-report-provides-comprehensive-data-marijuana-arrests-and-charges-colorado-after-leg.

Gettman, J. (n.d.). *Marijuana arrests in Colorado after the passage of Amendment 64*. Drug Police Alliance. https://drugpolicy.org/sites/default/files/Colorado_Marijuana_Arrests_After_Amendment_64.pdf.

Grandpre, L. (2020, June 17). *A path to reparations for the war on drugs*. The Forge. https://forgeorganizing.org/article/path-reparations-war-drugs.

Griffin III, O. H., Fritsch, A. L., Woodward, V. H., & Mohn, R. S. (2013). Sifting through the hyperbole: One hundred years of marijuana coverage in The New York Times. *Deviant Behavior, 34*(10), 767–781.

Heras, R. (2021). *FINCANN launches the cannabis industry's first and only federally-insured banks counter*. Ganjapreneur. https://www.ganjapreneur.com/fincann-launches-the-cannabis-industrys-first-and-only-federally-insured-banks-counter/.

Hughes, S. A. (2019, October 29). *Pennsylvanians with minor cannabis convictions can apply for expedited pardon*. The Philadelphia Tribune. https://www.penncapital-star.com/blog/pennsylvanians-with-minor-cannabis-convictions-can-apply-for-an-expedited-pardon/.

Illinois Criminal Justice Information Authority. (2021, January 21). *Delivering on key equity goal, Pritzker Administration Awards $31.5 million in first ever restore, reinvest, and renew program grants to organizations across the state*. Illinois Criminal Justice Information Authority. https://r3.illinois.gov/downloads/01.21.21_ICJIA_R3_Grants_Release_Final.pdf.

Jaeger, K. (2021, January 4). *Illinois sold more than $1 billion worth of legal marijuana in 2020, new state data shows*. Marijuana Moment. https://www.marijuanamoment.net/illinois-sold-more-than-1-billion-worth-of-legal-marijuana-in-2020-new-state-data-shows/.

Johnson, C. (2020). *9 black-owned cannabis companies you should know.* Revolt. https://www.revolt.tv/2020/4/20/21224491/9-black-owned-marijuana-companies.

Kelly, D., Boots, M.H., & Herz, N. (2017, October 23). How SB 91 has changed Alaska's criminal justice system. *Anchorage Daily News.* https://www.adn.com/alaska-news/crime-courts/2017/10/21/how-sb-91-has-changed-alaskas-criminal-justice-system/.

Kilmer, B. (2016, January). *Marijuana legalization, government revenues, and public budgets: Ten factors to consider.* RAND Office of External Affairs. https://www.rand.org/pubs/testimonies/CT449.html.

Kochnar, R. & Cilluffo, A. (2017, November 1). *How wealth inequality has changed in the U.S. since the Great Recession, by race, ethnicity and income.* Pew Research Center. https://www.pewresearch.org/fact-tank/2017/11/01/how-wealth-inequality-has-changed-in-the-u-s-since-the-great-recession-by-race-ethnicity-and-income/.

Levine, H. G., Gettman, J. B., & Siegel, L. (2012). *240,000 Marijuana arrests: Costs, consequences and racial disparities of possession arrests in Washington, 1985-2010.* Marijuana Arrest Project. https://drugpolicy.org/sites/default/files/240.000-Marijuana-Arrests-In-Washington.pdf.

Lipsitz, G. (1998). *The possessive investment in whiteness: How whites benefit from identity politics.* Temple University Press.

Manhattan D.A. (2018, July 31). *Tomorrow: D.A. Vance ends prosecution of marijuana possession and smoking cases.* Manhattan District Attorney's Office. https://www.manhattanda.org/tomorrow-d-a-vance-ends-prosecution-of-marijuana-possession-and-smoking-cases/.

Marijuana Justice Act of 2019, 597 U.S.S. https://www.congress.gov/bill/116th-congress/senate-bill/597/text.

McVey, E. (2017, September 11). *Chart: Percentage of cannabis business owners and founders by race.* MJ Biz Daily. https://mjbizdaily.com/chart-19-cannabis-businesses-owned-founded-racial-minorities/.

Measure 91. (2014). *Control, regulation, and taxation of marijuana and industrial hemp act.* Oregon State. https://www.oregon.gov/olcc/marijuana/Documents/Measure91.pdf.

Mitchell, O. (2011). Drug and other specialty courts. *In M. Tonry (Ed.), The Oxford handbook of crime and criminal justice* (pp.843–871). Oxford University Press.

Mitchell, T. (2019, September 25). *House passes landmark marijuana banking bill.* West Word. https://www.westword.com/content/printView/11492056.

Moran, T. J. (2010). Just a little bit of history repeating: the California model of marijuana legalization and how it might affect racial and ethnic minorities. *Washington. & Lee Journal of Civil Rights & Social Justice,* 17, 557.

Moss, E., McIntosh, K., Edelburg, W., & Broady, K. (2020, December 8). *The Black-white gap left Black households more vulnerable.* The Brookings Institute. https://www.brookings.edu/blog/up-front/2020/12/08/the-black-white-wealth-gap-left-black-households-more-vulnerable/.

New York Marihuana Tax and Regulation Act, N.Y. Stat. §854A (2021). https://legislation.nysenate.gov/pdf/bills/2021/s854a.

NORML. (n.d.). Decriminalization. NORML. https://norml.org/laws/decriminalization/.

Pager, D. (2002). *The mark of a criminal record*. Paper presented at the annual meeting of the American Sociological Association, Chicago, August 16–19.

Pennsylvania Department of Health. (2020). *Official Report. This two-year report of the Pennsylvania Department of Health's Office of Medical Marijuana is to comply with 35 P.S. § 10231.1105*. Pennsylvania Department of Health. https://www.health.pa.gov/topics/Documents/Programs/Medical%20Marijuana/DOH%20MM%20Official%20Two%20Year%20Report%20-%20May%2015%202020.pdf.

Peralta, E. (2014, March 13). *Colorado court rules some marijuana convictions can be overturned*. NPR. https://www.npr.org/sections/thetwo-way/2014/03/13/289961369/colo-court-rules-some-marijuana-convictions-can-be-overturned.

Perez, M., Ajilore, O., & Chung, E. (2019). *Using marijuana revenue to create jobs*. Center for American Progress. https://cdn.americanprogress.org/content/uploads/2019/05/16135643/Marijuana-Jobs-Guarantee.pdf.

Resing, C. (2019). *Marijuana legalization is a racial justice issue*. American Civil Liberties Union. https://www.aclu.org/blog/criminal-law-reform/drug-law-reform/marijuana-legalization-racial-justice-issue.

Ross, J. (2018, December 31). *Legal marijuana made big promises on racial equity- and fell short*. NBC News. https://www.nbcnews.com/news/nbcblk/legal-marijuana-made-big-promises-racial-equity-fell-short-n952376.

RT Staff. (2014, March 24). *Colorado approves retroactive reversal of marijuana convictions*. RT. https://www.rt.com/usa/colorado-marijuana-reverse-convictions-929/.

Schrantz, D., DeBor, S. T., Mauer, M. (2018). *Decarceration strategies: How 5 states achieved substantial prison population reductions*. The Sentencing Project. https://www.sentencingproject.org/publications/decarceration-strategies-5-states-achieved-substantial-prison-population-reductions/.

Schwartzman, P. & Harden, J. D. (2020, September 15). *D.C. legalized marijuana, but one thing didn't change: Almost everyone arrested on pot charges is Black*. The Washington Post. https://www.washingtonpost.com/local/legal-issues/dc-marijuana-arrest-legal/2020/09/15/65c20348-d01b-11ea-9038-af089b63ac21_story.html.

Smart Approaches to Marijuana. (n.d.a.). *Prison population in AK, CO, DC, OR, and WA since legalization*. SAM. https://learnaboutsam.org/state-prison-populations/

Smart Approaches to Marijuana. (n.d.b.). *Revenues vs reality*. SAM. https://learnaboutsam.org/wp-content/uploads/2020/05/Revenues-vs-Reality-0520-4.pdf.

Smith, J. (2021, February 22). *New Jersey recreational marijuana implementation law signed, setting stage for $1 billion market*. Marijuana Business Daily. https://mjbizdaily.com/new-jersey-governor-signs-recreational-marijuana-law/.

Song, B. (2018, March 13). *Cannabis taxes could generate $106 billion, create 1 million jobs by 2025*. New Frontier Data. https://newfrontierdata.com/cannabis-insights/cannabis-taxes-generate-106-billion-create-1-million-jobs-2025/.

Sumner, W. (2018, July 26). *Why are only 4 percent of cannabis businesses owned by African Americans?* Green Entrepreneur. https://www.greenentrepreneur.com/article/315528.

Svrakic, D. M., Lustman, P. J., Mallya, A., Lynn, T. A., Finney, R., & Svrakic, N. M. (2012). Legalization, decriminalization & medicinal use of cannabis: a scientific and public health perspective. *Missouri Medicine*, 109(2), 90–98.

32 Incredible Cannabis Industry Statistics 2020. (n.d.). Marijuana SEO. https://www.marijuanaseo.com/cannabis-industry-statistics/.

Thompson, B. Y. (2017). "Good moral characters": how drug felons are impacted under state marijuana legalization laws. *Contemporary Justice Review*, 20(2), 211–226.

Todd, T. (2018). The benefits of marijuana legalization and regulation. *Berkeley Journal of Criminal Law*, 23, 99.

Travis, J. (2005). *But they all come back: Facing the challenges of prisoner reentry.* The Urban Institute Press.

U.S. Citizenship and Immigration Services. (2021, May 28). Policy Manual Part F. Good Moral Character. U.S. Citizenship and Immigration Services https://www.uscis.gov/policy-manual/volume-12-part-f-chapter-1.

Uzialko, A. (2020, September 16). *Cannabis industry growth potential for 2021.* Business News Daily. https://www.businessnewsdaily.com/15812-cannabis-industry-business-growth.html.

Walsh, D. (2020, December 4). *House approves decriminalizing marijuana; Bill to stall in Senate.* NPR. https://www.npr.org/2020/12/04/942949288/house-approves-decriminalizing-marijuana-bill-to-stall-in-senate.

Way, A. (2018, February 8). *Two most talked about marijuana legalization issues in Colorado: The hype and the reality.* Drug Policy Alliance. https://drugpolicy.org/blog/two-most-talked-about-marijuana-legalization-issues-colorado-hype-and-reality.

Woodham, S. (2015, September 17). *Can people convicted of pot crimes get their records cleared after Alaska's vote to legalize?* ADN. https://www.adn.com/highly-informed/article/can-people-convicted-pot-crimes-get-their-records-cleared-after-alaska-vote.

Wyatt, K. (2015, May 5). Dispute over felons in pot industry flares at Statehouse. CBS Denver. https://denver.cbslocal.com/2015/05/05/dispute-over-felons-in-pot-industry-flares-at-statehouse/.

Chapter 5

American Dream into Nightmare

Immigration, Systemic Structural Racism, and Health Inequity in the United States

Jay Pearson

INTRODUCTION

Racialized health disadvantage in the United States is long-standing, well-established, and reliably patterned. This patterning reflects the US history of structurally rooted racism playing out through racial construction, racial hierarchy, and racial bias. Efforts to improve entrenched US racialized health disadvantage remain largely unsuccessful. Failure to recognize or meaningfully address racism undergirds this failure. Such shortcomings are evident when contrasted against findings documenting a pattern of racialized health advantage for recently arrived diverse immigrant populations compared to their US-born co-racial counterparts.

This chapter introduces, conceptualizes, and integrates components from these phenomena to construct an explanatory framework implicating Systemic Structural Racism (SSR) as the fundamental causal driver of US racialized health disadvantage. The framework is then utilized to inform and develop equitable policy suggestions to reduce this health inequity.

Racialized Health Disadvantage and Immigrant Health Phenomena

A few notable exceptions notwithstanding, considerable research dating back to W.E.B Du Bois (1899) documents that, when compared to White Americans, US-Black and Indigenous as well as other populations of color (BIPOC) are at a distinct social well-being and health disadvantage. Persistent and pernicious racialized health disadvantages manifest across mental health, heart disease, high blood pressure, and diabetes among others (James, 1994; Williams, 1999; Geronimus, 1994; Jackson, 1998; Hudson, 2013). Racialized differences in birth outcomes provide the best example.

Compared to White American mothers, Black and native American mothers and infants have much higher rates of preterm birth, low birthweight, and infant mortality (Geronimus, 1992; MacDorman, 2011). Money does not explain these findings as richer households and neighborhoods improve birth outcomes for Whites and do not improve or even worsen outcomes for Blacks (Collins & Rankins, 2011; Braveman et al., 2014). Education also fails to explain these findings. Among mothers over 20, White women without a high school diploma have better birth outcomes than Black women with at least an undergraduate degree (Hunh & Parker et al., 2005; Jackson & Williams, 2006). US maternal mortality is particularly telling with Blacks 3.2 times and natives 2.3 times more likely to die from complications associated with childbirth than Whites (Tucker & Berg et al., 2007; Creenga & Syverson et al., 2017). Finally, among mothers with college degrees, Blacks are 5.2 times more likely than Whites to die from complications associated with giving birth (Petersen et al., 2019).

Early on, public health and medical care professionals proposed that racialized health disadvantages, as well as policy suggestions to address them, combined biological inferiority, culture of poverty, irresponsible behavior, reduced medical coverage and services utilization, or socioeconomic disadvantage as the causes of these differences (Lewis, 1966; Moynihan, 1967; Kaplan, 2001).

A parallel course of more recent research shows diverse US-immigrant populations doing better on multiple health measures, including birth outcomes, compared to US-born groups of the same race (Abriado-Lanza, 1998). Strongest for recently arrived immigrants, this health advantage is lost over time for the first generation and disappears entirely for their children and grandchildren (Kaestner et al., 2007; Collins, 2001). The magnitude and rate of immigrant health degradation vary by race. Darker-skinned immigrants' health gets worse faster than those with lighter skin (Langellier et al., 2020; Hamilton, 2011).

Early explanations for immigrant health advantages suggested one or some combination of younger healthier immigrants arriving at the United States, maintenance of traditional sociocultural orientations that support healthy relationships and behaviors, and older sicker immigrants returning home to die (Marks, 1990; Thomas, 1995; Abriado-Lanza, 1999). Early explanations for immigrant health loss suggested loss of health-promoting traditional sociocultural practices, adoption of less healthy US practices, and acculturative distress (Kaplan & Marks, 1990; Finch, 2001; Antecol Bedard, 2006).

Spanning this range of phenomena is the history of biased immigration policy intertwined with US race making (Takaki, 1998; Frisbie et al., 2001). Indeed, contemporary immigration policy and subsequent immigrant racialization provide a natural experiment to investigate the historical and current impacts of racism. Research on BIPOC social well-being, life chances, and lived experience demonstrates how historical and current racial inequality drives BIPOC health disadvantage and insight into how BIPOCS respond to secure social well-being and improve health (Viruell-Fuentes et al., 2012; Pearson, 2008; Ford & Harawa, 2010). Consequently, public policies to improve racialized health disadvantage must first acknowledge dehumanizing US racist history and recent, racist, immigration practices before proposing other interventions.

Getting under the Dark Skin: Social Vulnerability, Distress, and Health

A growing body of conceptual and theoretical work—as well as accompanying empirical evidence—challenges and refutes the aforementioned early explanations for US racialized health disadvantage and both immigrant health phenomena (Dressler, 2005; Kaestner et al., 2009; Geronimus et al., 2016). This research instead argues that Structural Inequalities (SI) generally and US-based SSR specifically are the fundamental causal social determinants influencing these processes (Viruell-Fuentes et al., 2012; Gee et al., 2006, 2009; Kaestner et al., 2009; Geronimus, 2000). Research on these phenomena shows that stress from struggling within a racist society changes how human bodies function to worsen health for US and non-US-born BIPOCs (Kaestner et al., 2009; James, 1993; Williams & Collins, 2000; Hamilton & Hummer, 2011; Krieger, 2021; Gee & Ford, 2011).

Per this perspective, BIPOC health disadvantage comes from many factors other than simple differences in behaviors, education, or income and even insurance and medical coverage which most people describe as health disparities (Dressler & Ots, 2005; Braveman & Gruskin, 2011). The enduring nature of US racialized health disadvantage reflects lifetimes of racism causing disconfirming social experiences translating into more disease and earlier death. Defined as differences in population health and death rates as well as the underlying social determinants of them that are preventable, avoidable, and consequently unnecessary, but additionally unfair and unjust, Health Inequity best describes this phenomenon (Whitehead, 1992; Braveman, 2011). This definition highlights two important points: first, racialized health disadvantages persist despite better behaviors, more money, health insurance, and medical service (Geronimus & Pearson, 2016; Kaestner et al., 2009; Pearson & Geronimus, 2011; Braveman et al., 2014); second, this persistence also reflects resistance to develop or implement promising health equity initiatives designed to benefit BIPOCS (Braveman et al., 2011; Krieger, 2021; Petteway, 2021). In simple language, doing the same "right" thing in the same wrong system does not improve health for BIPOCS the same as for Whites. Additionally, public as well as population health scientists and practitioners have considerable insight into how these phenomena operate and develop programs to prevent or reduce BIPOC health inequity. So far, these programs have not been widely used because the sociopolitical and policymaking support to make them happen does not yet exist (Krieger, 2021; Braveman et al., 2011; Geronimus & Thompson, 2004).

Structural Inequality and Systemic Structural Racism

SI are sets of social processes and mechanisms that (a) reliably establish and maintain stratified hierarchies of differential human valuation and (b) support dominating relationships of unequal status across diverse population groups (Dani & Haan, 2008; Rahman, 2019). Structural refers to basic beliefs informing public policy decision making. Inequality refers to how ideas about natural group-level differences justify socially sorting people into different categories and positions. These practices define relationships within and across groups that influence opportunities for human development in ways that build social systems advantaging majority groups at the cost of disadvantaging minority groups (Sorenson, 1996).

The majority/minority status distinction is not who is more than 50% of the population, instead, it is about social asymmetries in power, status, and standing favorable to majority populations and, at the same time, unfavorable to minority populations (Anderson, 2016). Power implies the direction of influence whereby majorities construct and define experiences of minorities while minorities cannot do the same to majorities. The status reflects majorities having direct, easy access to values and socially desirable things like positions, titles, material resources, and other possessions. Standing establishes that majorities construct narratives describing historical and contemporary events for themselves *and* for all minority groups. Consequently, majority groups, in ways that exclude minorities, build societies reflecting positively upon themselves and negatively upon minority populations. At the crux, structural inequality is about majority groups humanizing themselves while simultaneously dehumanizing minorities. Racism in the United States is the most well-researched example of structural inequality.

SYSTEMIC STRUCTURAL RACISM

Structural racism holds that macro-level social processes associated with racial construction, racial hierarchy, as well as racial bias are central organizing features of the United States and that informed public policy decision making (Bonilla-Silva, 1997; Feagin, 2006). Frederick Douglas, in his classic oration "The Meaning of July 4th for the Negro," argues that oppressive racism is central to US national identity and consequently structural. Manifesting as government-sanctioned dehumanization of African slaves and native Americans running parallel to an ethos of human equality, Structural racism was established before the United States was formally founded and remained salient to the national social order until Douglas's time. These parallel but opposing narratives continue unabated until the present.

In contemporary times, structural racism entails multifaceted, interconnected, and co-occurring racial construction, racial stratification, and racial bias processes inextricably linked to US national identity. These processes operate within and across virtually every major institution comprising US society (Feagin, 2006). This pervasive institutionalization of structural racism makes it systemic. SSR negatively impacts BIPOCS to the benefit of White Americans far beyond individual acts of interpersonal racial discrimination, internalized racism, and even institutional racism (Ford & Gee, 2011). In fact, these other forms of racism exist because SSR informs them and is the platform upon which they are built.

Dr. Camara Phyllis Jones (2000) utilizes the analogy of planter boxes holding different colored flowers to illustrate the multilevel nature of SSR. Contingent upon their color, Dr. Jones argues that gardeners (representing policy decision makers) plant flowers in soils of varying nutritional value (representing institutional forces differentially influencing power and material conditions). Flowers planted in the more nutritional soil sprout and grow more rapidly and stronger than those planted in poor soil. The gardener then judges the weaker slower-growing flowers as less appealing and plucks them. Judgment without consideration to differences in the soil is prejudice and the plucking is biased action. When combined, these represent interpersonal discrimination. Finally, the weaker slower-growing flowers, after being subjected to the gardener's differential soil distribution and plucking, consider themselves inferior to the more privileged flowers, admire and aspire to be like them. This represents internalized racism.

Gee and Ford (2011) integrate these perspectives to define structural racism as macro-level systems of thought, ideology, and philosophy which inform social forces, institutions, and processes interacting with one another to generate and reinforce inequalities and inequities among racial and ethnic groups. The authors highlight racism as interactive multilevel phenomena operating from the structural down through the individual. They analogize an iceberg to illustrate this point. The tip of the iceberg extended out of the water represents easily seen and recognized interpersonal racism (racial slurs, for example), while the much larger portion of the iceberg, below the water, represents the more challenging not often seen and acknowledged, structural racism (belief in genetic differences influencing racially biased medical policy).

Suggestions for how best to define SSR have recently increased (Pearson, 2020; Hicken et al., 2020). Nevertheless, other than residential segregation, not a lot of research measures and causally links SSR to racialized health inequity. Despite this, policymakers can justify interventions given that legislative and other policymaking processes most often reflect social values being later supported by scientific evidence (Brighouse et al., 2018).

Establishing these contexts of race making is essential to integrating the full range of findings associated with social well-being and health at the intersection of race, ethnicity, and immigration. Moreover, policies proposing to improve racialized health inequity must first explicate SSR as the foundation upon which multiple manifestations of racialized experiences, positive and negative, are rooted and influence health.

Race and Ethnicity

The terms race and ethnicity are often used interchangeably and uncritically in US social scientific and public health research. While integrally related, understanding the distinction between these identity constructs has implications for addressing racialized health inequity. Imposed racial minority status compromises social well-being and health. Alternatively, self-constructed ethnic identity, people deciding who they are, provides a path toward improved social well-being and better health (Airhihenbuwa & Liburd, 2006).

Race

Northwestern European immigrants to the emerging United States designed and imposed a system of socialized racial categorization (race) to dehumanize the social other. This served to justify the material exploitation of native Americans through the appropriation of their historical lands and economic exploitation of Black Africans through chattel slavery (Pounder et al., 2003). Race suggested that differences in sets of desirable and undesirable traits like intelligence, work ethic, rascality, and deceptiveness were inherently and differentially associated with one or some combination of what people looked like (phenotype), where they came from (geographic origin), or who their forebears were (ancestry) (Cornell & Hartman, 2007). This typology of inferior racialization was then adapted and applied to BIPOCS subsequently immigrating to the United States.

Members of the White race argued that differences in these characteristics implied a natural hierarchy of humanity with themselves having more desirable traits and worthy of majority status (American Anthropological Association, 1999). The White racial majority then suggested that all BIPOCS and some Europeans diverse on national origin, ethnicity, and religion had more undesirable characteristics, and naturally occupied lower positions. The belief that this was true led to race "science" that, over time, validated ideas of natural racial differences.

National policy decision making then baked this idea into major institutions like courts, work, government, schools, and medicine. These policy practices effectively established and maintained a rigid stratified racial hierarchy of differential human valuation that uses one or some combination of phenotype, geographic origin, and ancestry as *social markers* for where people are placed and how they are treated (American Sociological Association, 2003). Today, inequalities between so-called racial groups are not about biological differences, but the results of historical and contemporary social, economic, educational, and political circumstances reflecting how diverse human populations were and are differentially identified, socially ordered, and subsequently treated.

This history establishes that race is an externally constructed and imposed minoritizing process reflecting how Whites viewed and humanized themselves, then viewed, oppressed, and dehumanized BIPOCs. This dehumanization compromises the social well-being, and by extension health, of BIPOCs in a range of ways. These same (de)humanization processes influence US ethnic identity construction.

Ethnicity

Ethnicity reflects how different population groups conceive, develop, and implement self-perceived identity construction as well as sociocultural orientations representing these self-perceptions (Smaje, 1996). Because group identity construction occurs in relationship with other groups, how much ethnicity can be actually self-determined is influenced by whether its development happens inside or outside of imposed race. To this point, ethnic identity construction entails context-specific social processes of attribution and relationship (Ford & Harawa, 2011). The attributional dimension of ethnicity addresses independent sociocultural characteristics reflecting how groups view themselves and practices/behaviors to represent these self-perceptions. The relational dimension of ethnicity represents a group's relative position, majority or minority, within stratified social hierarchies, and reflects how groups in different positions interact with each other. Healthy, humanizing interactions (for racial majorities) promote self-determined identity construction while dehumanizing ones (for racial minorities) constrain it. Consequently, ethnicity outside the United States addresses self-perceived identity construction while ethnicity in the United States additionally and simultaneously addresses relationship to the structure of racial stratification (Nazroo, 1988; Geronimus, 2000; Pearson, 2008). These differences have implications for health.

In the United States, BIPOC ethnic identity builds resistant sociocultural orientations and resources designed to resist negative stereotypes often associated with minority racial status (Pearson, 2008). Conversely, BIPOCS born or raised outside the United States are not subjected to pervasive daily reminders of minority status and benefit from more liberated, self-determined traditional sociocultural orientations and resources brought with them upon immigration (James, 1993; Geronimus, 2000; Pearson, 2008). In both cases, unique sets of sociocultural resources are used to mitigate, resist, or undo the effects of minority racial status.

To summarize, White Americans imagined themselves to be superior and occupied majority of the positions, then constructed and imposed systems of dehumanizing racial classification relegating BIPOCS to minority positions. This majority/minority racial distinction informs unjust distributions of resources and risks supporting and compromising health respectively. Ethnicity provides an alternative identity option related to, but distinct from, race. US constructed ethnicity resists race while non-US ethnicity avoids it. Where race constrains, ethnicity aspires to liberate by offering alternative more positive and health enhancing ways of being.

Racial Bias

Over the long course of US history, racial bias has selectively determined how opportunity structures that regulate distributions of resources and risks were constructed and subsequently employed. Positive racial bias supports access to resources and protection from risks for White Americans, while negative racial bias restricts access to resources and increases exposure to risks for BIPOCs. Historicizing racial bias is essential to policymakers competently integrating and synthesizing the full range of findings on race, ethnicity, social well-being, and health. In broad strokes, historical review establishes that a society constructed to enforce the notion that Whites were inherently superior reflects Systemic White Racial Supremacy (SWRS) and directly informs BIPOC oppression (Feagin, 2013).

Deeply rooted SWRS conferring White racial hegemony is the foundation upon which subsequent racial bias was constructed and is enforced (Leonardo, 2004). Supremacy refers to the normalization and institutionalization of belief that a preferred category of people is inherently superior to other categories (Guess, 2006). SWRS is secured when this belief is reified and reinforced through the construction of political, economic, and cultural systems granting Whites exclusive control of decision making processes, virtually exclusive access to social and material resources, protection from social and material risks as well as narrative setting (Ansley, 1989; Petteway, 2021).

SWRS effectively allows White racial actors, or those perceived as such, to construct and impose oppressive social orders that reliably relegate populations of color into inferior subaltern positions. These oppressive social orders ensure that majority group members secure a disproportionate share of the good things in life (powerful roles, good housing, good health) and minority group members receive a disproportionate share of the bad things (inferior roles, bad housing, poor health) (Young, 1990). Finally, domination entails the social dialogue between racial actors assigned different positions within these hierarchies (Pratto et al., 1994; Ansley, 1989). This dynamic plays out as normalization of roles, actions, and expectations assuring the likelihood of conventional success for majority populations and increasing the likelihood of marginal survival for minority populations (Sidanius & Pratto, 1999; Steele, 2011). In short, all populations, Whites and BIPOCs, work to maximize the sets of resources and risks apportioned them. These dynamics detail the historical processes informing contemporary structurally rooted and institutionally (re)enforced sets of privileges conferring unearned advantages benefitting Whites and discrimination imposing sets of un-incurred disadvantages burdening BIPOCS.

Per this perspective, racial bias uses racial identifiers to determine different distributions of the resources and risks constituting opportunity structures. Racial bias also influences the types and quality of lived experiences that diverse racial actors have as they engage the institutions regulating access to these sets of resources or exposure to risks.

Research on social mobility and bias indicates that conventional resource acquisition confirms notions of egalitarian justice and status congruence for US Whites but reflects disconfirming inequality, injustice, and status incongruence for racial minorities (Braveman et al., 2014; Gee & Ro, 2012; Duleep & Sanders, 1992). Similarly, individual-level risk behaviors appear more damaging for racial minorities than for racial majorities (Kandel, 1995). These opposing mechanisms operate beyond the influence of conventional predictors of health like income and residence (Pearson, 2008). Individual efforts to do the right thing per dominant narratives suggesting that health improves with greater resources and worsens with increased risks may actually cause more racialized health inequity if the regulating institutions reflect a positive bias for Whites and negative bias against BIPOCS. Consequently, racialized health inequities represent the physiological manifestation of this diverse range of underlying differences in life chances *and* lived experiences. These mechanisms operate through broad sets of confirming and disconfirming social interactions that may or may not line up neatly with simple resource and risk distribution counts. Efforts proposing to investigate or reduce racialized health disadvantages, but that fail to address socially biased lived experience, are fundamentally misaligned. Such efforts will be ineffective at best and may worsen racialized health inequities.

The order in which researchers, legislators, and policymakers consider how the range of racial biases influence life chances and lived experience as well as their impact on racialized health inequity has implications for how best to theorize relationships between these constructs and propose interventions to reduce their negative health effects (Dressler & Ots, 2005; Peck, 2019). Focusing first, exclusively or disproportionately on interpersonal discrimination leaves unacknowledged and unaddressed the more fundamentally rooted phenomena of supremacy, oppression, and domination. A more promising approach engages the process of conceptualizing, measuring and linking these more fundamental social biases to racialized health inequity.

Social Determinants of Health and the Theory of Fundamental Cause

The US Department of Health and Human Services (2011) defines social determinants of health as "conditions in the environments in which people are born, live, learn, work, play, worship and age that affect a wide range of health functioning and quality of life outcomes and risks." Also known as social and physical determinants of health, these factors impact a wide range of functioning and quality of life outcomes (Healthy People, 2020). Any policy influencing social determinants is indeed health policy.

Per these perspectives, the social determinants of health entail variable distributions and exposures associated with resource and risk allocations as opportunity structures or life chances, and the lived experience of engaging biased institutions regulating access to them. The sum of these processes become physically embodied (getting under the skin through disconfirming or affirming social cues and interactions) and biologically embedded (affecting body systems even down to the cellular level) to determine interpopulation level differences in social well-being and health. The degree to which health promotion efforts only address conventional proximal health predictors like economic resources, individual behaviors, health insurance, and medical care or additionally aspire to incorporate a social determinants perspective has implications for how health equity is conceived and proposed (James, 2008; Diez-Roux, 2016).

The Theory of Fundamental Cause proposes that majority/minority asymmetries in underlying social conditions are fundamental drivers of pernicious health disadvantage across multiple outcomes (Link & Phelan,

1995). These conditions ensure that health disadvantage persists even when proximal risk factors for singular conditions are identified and positively altered (Geronimus, 2000). Per this perspective, significant differences in mechanisms like socioeconomic resources, residential segregation, and influential social relationships help to prevent disease-causing exposures in the first place and increase coping capacity in the event of exposure. These differences manifest as the reliable reproduction of health vulnerability for social minority populations relative to majority populations across multiple outcomes.

To summarize, variable distributions of life chances and lived experiences associated are the inevitable manifestations of stratified racial hierarchies resulting from SSR. SWRS is the central guiding principle upon which SSR is constructed and is implicated as the fundamental causal social determinant of racialized health inequity (Link & Phelan, 1995; Geronimus, 2000; Krieger, 2021). The social condition of minority racial status fundamentally structures different resource and risk distributions and institutional mechanisms regulating them that drive disconfirming social experiences—producing chronic distress that increases disease susceptibility thereby increasing rates of racialized health inequity.

Systemic Structural Racism and Racialized Health Inequity: The Way Forward

Research examining how racial bias and interpersonal discrimination constrain social well-being and compromise BIPOC health is well-established (Williams; 1999; Krieger & Sidney, 1996). Conversely, to date, there remains sparse research investigating the ways that positive social bias grants privilege to supporting the social well-being and health of Whites. Virtually no research investigates SWRS as the primary driver of SSR and health inequity.

To this last point, if SWRS is the foundation of both positive and negative racial bias linked to health inequity, then SWRS should also be the foundation upon which racialized health promotion is rooted. Put another way, populations of color have not minoritized themselves. Proposing and expecting BIPOCS to engage unjustly biased systems with resilient efforts to overcome racial minority status is simply another form of dehumanizing oppression.

To illustrate this point, Larry Davis (2014) proposes the analogy of children being hit in the head with a baseball bat. Resiliency researchers then examine those atypical positive deviants hard-headed or lucky enough to avoid the expected outcomes of death or a large bump on their heads. Interventionists then propose to learn and teach victims what allows some to survive the natural effects of the assault. Davis poses the questions: why are researchers surprised by the outcome of violent actions and why do they focus on the victims of these actions instead of the perpetrators of them? In short, if aspiring to succeed in unjust systems comes at tremendous health costs, then those systems should be deconstructed. Two central public health concepts illustrate these points.

Sherman James developed The John Henryism scale of High Effort Coping (1987) to examine the health effects of social minorities aspiring to the American Dream of socioeconomic success. Defined as an inherent propensity to actively engage—with the expectation of overcoming—biased social systems, Dr. James proposes that minority social status interacts with John Henryism and socioeconomic/material success to differentially determine health. Dr. James's work confirms this proposition by demonstrating that among Black American men with high John Henryism scores, those with low socioeconomic success have significantly higher rates of hypertension than those with higher socioeconomic success. Among Black American men with low John Henryism scores, differences in hypertension rates are reduced between those with low versus high socioeconomic success. Dr. James explains that expecting, but failing, to have hard work translate into success in an unjust system is more healthy and costly than not expecting success in such a system.

Arline Geronimus (1992) developed the Weathering Hypothesis to explain US racialized differences in birth outcomes and fertility timing. Geronimus proposes that, for Black American mothers, distress from socioenvironmental exposures associated with intersecting racial, gender, and economic minority status—combined with policy-sponsored dismantling of supportive ethnic institutions—conspire to drive earlier health deterioration. The earlier onset of negative birth outcomes at younger ages for Black mothers is one result. She goes on to speculate that earlier fertility timing among Black American mothers may be a sociobiological and behavioral response to support healthy birth outcomes while facing these phenomena. Subsequent research has gone on to test and confirm the Weathering Hypothesis by demonstrating stress-mediated accelerated biological aging associated with minority social status in other populations (Geronimus et al., 2015).

These concepts and findings demonstrate the cost of resilience, how and why some populations are reliably required to exercise it, and their best efforts to mitigate these requirements. Such insights should, but unfortunately too frequently do not, inform and guide public health policy responses to improve racialized health inequity.

Health Equity

Health equity is increasingly, and often uncritically, offered as the standard response to racialized health inequity. Researchers, advocates, and activists from population health, health policy, health education, and health behavior—among others—currently engage a vibrant discourse on what health equity entails, how best to operationalize and measure it as well as notions of how to construct and deliver upon its promise. A brief review of the two concepts, generally informing health equity, economic and philosophical equity, follows.

Economic equity proposes redistributive social service programming designed to grant the financially vulnerable some form of currency transfer to alleviate material hardship (Gupta et al., 1999). These programs generally neglect human dignity, often stigmatizing recipients. Additionally, such programming fails to address the structural and institutional forces creating conditions of poverty. This observation is not suggesting that cash transfers are not helpful for economic and material hardship. Evidence, however, also suggests that simple financial redistribution fails to implicate structural mechanisms that reliably make select populations vulnerable while protecting others (Geronimus, 2000; Geronimus & Thompson, 2004; Pearson, 2008).

John Rawls's Theory of Justice (1971) represents the most referenced example of philosophical equity. Rawls proposes that tensions between notions of individual liberty and group equality were reconcilable through a contractarian conceptualization of justice. Per this perspective, just societies are reflected through social contracts, assuring fair access to resources and liberty to apply them. This "contractarian" justice is secured through two central principles. Rawls suggests a thought experiment, "The Veil of Ignorance," whereby individuals are tasked with constructing a social contract to govern a hypothetical socially diverse society. Participants are denied information on which diverse group they might represent in this society. Rawls argues that ignorance of potential social position promotes more egalitarian and equitable social construction, designed to protect vulnerable societal members. Rawls also argues that social and economic institutions should be arranged to benefit those most disadvantaged if that disadvantage is born of unfair and unjust initial social arrangements. In essence, proportional resource redistribution to disadvantaged members of society is justified in the event of socially biased primary distribution. Rawls fails to address what resources and risks matter for equity, the importance of social minority self-representation, or the mechanisms reliably (re)producing unjust societies. A range of critiques acknowledges and highlight additional shortcomings demanding resolution before a justice informed and grounded conceptualization of health equity can be constructed.

Social majorities have not proven just and fair arbiters representing the perspectives and interests of social minorities (Young, 2012). Government secured access to basic capabilities and endowments are required for all societal members to legitimately manifest their greatest possible human potential

(Nussbaum, 2003). Stratified socioeconomic inequality is inextricably linked to majority/minority identity status distinction in ways that require social minorities to alter key dimensions of themselves including cherished cultural traditions in order to access conventional success (Fraser, 1998). Notions of inherent human difference are prior to and inform norms and values translating into state sponsored and institutionally enforced differential identity construction processes (Sen, 2009).

Synthesizing and integrating concepts from these observations establishes that racialized health inequity, indeed, derives from structurally rooted multidimensional racialized social inequality. Moreover, efforts focused exclusively on individual or even institutional intervention, because they fail to address the fundamental causal nature of SSR, will be at best ameliorative and may actually exacerbate existing racialized social inequality and health disadvantage (Geronimus, 2000; Pearson, 2008; Rahman, 2018). Consequently, equity efforts to address racialized health inequity mandate just representation, respect for the integrity of diverse identity construction processes, valuation of sociocultural orientations, secure opportunities for self-determination, acknowledgment of and commitment to eliminate biased institutional mechanisms, and collaborative majority/minority planning opportunities to meet these objectives.

POLICY PROPOSALS

Systemic Structural Antiracism

Public policies to address SSR require similarly structurally rooted antiracist responses. Where racism separates, disengages, and dehumanizes BIPOCS, antiracism must aspire to rejoin, reengage, and humanize them. Intergroup Contact Theory suggests that opportunities to forge and nurture authentic relationships across social differences increase mutual understanding and regard (Pettigrew & Tropp, 2006). These opportunities are essential to developing notions of inherent human worthiness and related values that inform and influence how societies get (re)organized and (re)constructed. This process requires a collaborative negotiation between majority and minority populations on which new sets of norms and practices are developed and utilized to recognize and value diverse group-level human differences. Such valuing is essential to how public policy proposes to address the long history of unjust human relationships and construct antiracist social systems. Mechanisms promoting such interactions should sponsor multigroup insight, understanding, and a shared common interest of national well-being and health promotion. An impediment to this charge is that policy interventions proposing to alleviate problems for vulnerable subgroups are often perceived as preferential treatment. Conversely, universal policies, while broadly appealing, are often constructed using biased majority population norms—treating people situated differently as if they are the same—and are likely to increase inequality instead of alleviating it. Targeted Universalism proposes to address these challenges with a common integrative approach that supports minority needs while addressing majority interests (Powell et al., 2009).

Systemic Structural Antiracist Health Equity

In broad strokes, antiracist health equity policy should recognize and acknowledge that multiple and varied manifestations of racialized health inequity are the inevitable outcomes of dehumanizing and socially disconfirming SSR-driven racial inequality. Public policy efforts to mitigate, reduce, or undo structurally rooted racialized health inequity require similarly structurally rooted antiracist and socially confirming health equity methods, modalities, and interventions. These efforts require dialogue across social differences and recognition of what social roles and related actions hold the greatest promise for broad-based health equity.

To these ends, antiracist health equity should seek to exploit the unique experiences, knowledge, and expertise of populations occupying diverse positions in US stratified racial hierarchies. Those living lives proximal to phenomena of interest—racial minorities—understand the practical functional value of socio-behavioral responses to marginal status and should be respectfully solicited for their insight into these practices. Rigors associated with daily survival in such conditions leave precious few resources to investigate and, because of power asymmetries, little capacity to meaningfully improve more distal but fundamental causal institutional and structural mechanisms. Consequently, they should not be asked to do this work.

Conversely, majority population White Americans disproportionately occupy social positions granting access to resources sufficient to investigate, as well as power and influence to change, institutional and structural impediments constraining the lives of racial minorities. Paradoxically, despite increasing White antiracist activism, most efforts continue proposing individual behavioral change resiliency strategies targeting minorities instead of structural and institutional efforts targeting their White co-racial counterparts. To be explicit, systemic structural antiracist health equity efforts necessarily require a commitment to deconstruct and dismantle White Supremacy from majority population White partners.

Policies promoting antiracist health equity do not propose precluding or replacing individual resilience, identity group confirming, or institution altering intervention strategies. Instead, antiracist structural equity aspires to integrate and synthesize major components from these approaches with core tenets of the Social Determinants of Health and Fundamental Cause Theory. Such integration stands to inform and advance comprehensive, multidimensional, and multilevel racial identity confirming health promotion. The following details a set of core concepts and principles to aid and guide this work. Systemic structural antiracist health equity policy should:

1. Acknowledge and articulate how systemic ethno-racial White American supremacy is the fundamental causal mechanism reliably imposing minoritizing and dehumanizing oppression and domination upon BIPOCs.
2. Research and document the historical as well as contemporary multidimensional and multilevel manifestations, mechanisms, and negative health implications of SSR on BIPOCS.
3. Research and document how diverse racialized populations' historical sociocultural and behavioral responses were (a) developed to offset minoritizing oppression and domination, (b) constructed and function to help secure social well-being and health, and (c) the more contemporary dynamic and evolving manifestations of these responses.
4. Research and document how interventions designed to alter more proximal risk markers such as individual behavior change, minority resilience, redistribution of conventional economic resources, cultural change, and medical coverage have not meaningfully and consistently reduced persistent and pernicious health inequity.
5. Research and develop intervention strategies proposing to integrate this range of phenomena and perspectives into structurally rooted, multidimensional, multilevel antiracist health equity approaches designed to support and advance ethnicity-informed health promotion.

CONCLUSION

Systemic structural antiracist health equity policy entails commitment to constructing a US society recognizing, securing, and honoring the core humanity of all human populations. This humanization, in turn, requires systemic structural assessment tools and responses. New initiatives emerging from such assessments mandate a paradigm shift promoting respectful collaborative efforts between minority *and* majority groups. Essential to these efforts is that the disproportionate beneficiaries of SSR understand and accept responsibility for actively participating in deconstructing it. This is a clear departure from most current efforts proposing to teach victims of racial injustice new individual-level resilience strategies to cope with dehumanization. In simplest language, oppressed US and world populations will not benefit from more progressive liberal modalities explaining how they can best struggle to survive dehumanization. All populations, oppressors and oppressed, need instead to value the health-securing resource of working together in efforts to construct social orders and institutions that recognize and honor the fundamental truth that all peoples, by lieu of existence, are inherently worthy of and have a fundamental right to self-determination and dignified life.

REFERENCES

Abraido-Lanza, A. F., Dohrenwend, B. P., Ng-Mak, D. S. & Turner, J. B. (1999). The Latino Mortality Paradox: A Test of the 'Salmon Bias' and Healthy Migrant Hypotheses. *American Journal of Public Health* 89, 1543–1548.

Airhihenbuwa, C. O., & Liburd, L. (2006). Eliminating Health Disparities in the African American Population: The Interface of Culture, Gender, and Power. *Health Education & Behavior* 33(4), 488–501.

American Anthropological Association. (1999). American Anthropological Association Statement on Race. *American Anthropologist* 100(3), 712–713.

American Sociological Association. (2003). The Importance of Collecting Data and Doing Social Scientific Research on Race. Washington, DC: *American Sociological Association.*

Anderson, E. (2016). Durable Social Hierarchies: How Egalitarian Movements Imagine Inequality. *Insights from the Social Sciences.* https://items.ssrc.org/what-is-inequality/durable-social-hierarchies-how-egalitarian-movements-imagine-inequality/.

Ansley, F.L. (1989). Stirring the Ashes: Race, Class and the Future of Civil Rights Scholarship, *Cornell Law Review 74*(6), 994–1067.

Antecol, H., and K. Bedard. (2006) Unhealthy Assimilation: Do Immigrants Converge to American Health Status Levels? *Demography* 43(2), 337–360.

Bonilla-Silva, A., (1997) Rethinking Racism: Toward a Structural Interpretation. *American Sociological Review* 62(3), 465–480.

Braveman, P. A., Kumanyika, S., Fielding, J., Laveist, T., Borrell, L. N., Manderscheid, R., & Troutman, A. (2011). Health Disparities and Health Equity: The Issue Is Justice. *American Journal of Public Health,* 101(1), S149–S155.

Braveman P. (2011) Black-White Disparities in Birth Outcomes: Is Racism-related Stress a Missing Piece of the Puzzle? In: Lemelle, A.J., Reed, W., & Taylor, S., eds. *Handbook of African-American Health.* New York: Springer; pp. 155–163.

Brighouse, H., Ladd, H. F., Loeb, S., & Swift, A. (2018) *Educational Goods: Values, Evidence and Decision-Making.* Chicago, IL: University of Chicago Press.

Dani A. A., & Haan, A. (2008). *Social Policy in a Developmental Context: Structural Inequalities and Inclusive Institutions in Inclusive States Social Policy and Structural Inequalities.* Washington, DC: World Bank.

Collins J.W., Rankin K.M. & David R.J., (2011) Low Birth Weight Across Generations: The Effect of Economic Environment. *Maternal and Child Health Journal*, 15(4), 438–445.

Creanga A.A., Syverson C., Seed K., Callaghan W.M. (2017) Pregnancy-related Mortality in the United States, 2011–2013. *Obstetrics & Gynecology* 130, 366–373.

Davis L.A., (2014). Have We Gone Too Far with Resiliency? *Social Work Research*, 38(1), 5–6.

Dressler, W.W., Oths, K.S., & Gravlee, C.C. (2005) Race and Ethnicity in Public Health Research: Models to Explain Health Disparities, *Annual Review of Anthropology* 34 (1), 231–252.

Douglas, F. (1852, July 5) *The Meaning of July Fourth for the Negro*. Rochester, NY: Folkways Records, 1975.

Duleep, H.O., & Sanders S. (1992). Discrimination at the Top: American-Born Asian and White Men. *Journal of Industrial Relations* 31(3), 416–432.

DuBois, W. E. B., Anderson, E., & Eaton, I. (1899). *The Philadelphia Negro: A Social Study*. Philadelphia: University of Pennsylvania Press.

Feagin, J. R. (2006). *Systemic Racism: A Theory of Oppression*. Routledge.

Finch, B., R. Hummer, B. Kolody, and W. Vega. (2001). The Role of Discrimination and Acculturative Stress in Physical Health of Mexican-Origin Adults. *Hispanic Journal of Behavior Science* 23, 399–429.

Ford, C. L. & Harawa, N. T. (2010) A New Conceptualization of Ethnicity for Social Epidemiologic and Health Equity Research. *Social Science and Medicine* 71, 251–258.

Fraser, N. (1996) *Social Justice in the Age of Identity Politics*. Palo Alto, CA: Stanford University.

Frisbie, W.P., Cho, Y., & Hummer, R.A. (2001) Immigration and the Health of Asian and Pacific Islander Adults in the United States. *American Journal of Epidemiology* 153(4), 372–380.

Gee, G. C., Ryan, A., Laflamme, D. J., & Holt, J. (2006). Self-reported Discrimination and Mental Health Status among African Descendants, Mexican Americans, and Other Latinos in the New Hampshire REACH 2010 Initiative: The Added Dimension of Immigration. *American Journal of Public Health*, 96(10), 1821–1828.

Gee, G. C., Ro, A., Shariff-Marco, S., & Chae, D. (2009). Racial Discrimination and Health among Asian Americans: Evidence, Assessment, and Directions for Future Research. *Epidemiologic Reviews* 31(1), 130–151.

Gee G. & Ford. C (2011) Structural Racism: Old Issues, New Directions *DuBois Review* 8(1), 115–132.

Geronimus, A. T. (1992). The Weathering Hypothesis and the Health of African-American Women and Infants: Evidence and Speculations. *Ethnicity & Disease* 2(3), 207–221.

Geronimus, A., & Thompson, J. (2004). To Denigrate, Ignore, or Disrupt: Racial Inequality in Health and the Impact of a Policy-induced Breakdown of African American Communities. *Du Bois Review: Social Science Research on Race* 1(2), 247–279.

Geronimus A. T. (2000). To Mitigate, Resist, or Undo: Addressing Structural Influences on The health of Urban Populations. *American Journal of Public Health* 90(6), 867–872.

Geronimus, A. T., Pearson, J. A., Linnenbringer, E., Schulz, A. J., Reyes, A. G., Epel, E. S., Lin, J., & Blackburn, E. H. (2015). Race-Ethnicity, Poverty, Urban Stressors, and Telomere Length in a Detroit Community-based Sample. *Journal of Health and Social Behavior* 56(2), 199–224.

Guess, T.J. (2006) The Social Construction of Whiteness: Racism by Intent, Racism by Consequence *Critical Sociology* 32(4), 650–673.

Gupta, S., Clemnts, B.J., Gillingham, R., Schiller, C., Verhoeven, M., Alonso-Terma, R. M. & Mourmouras, A. (1998) Should Equity Be a Goal of Economic Policy. *Economic Issues* 16, 790–796.

Hamilton, T. & Hummer, B. (2011) Immigration and the Health of US Black Adults: Does Country of Origin Matter? *Social Science Medicine*, 73(10) 1551–1560.

Hicken, M.T., Ford, C., & Lee, H. (2020) *Structural Racism and Health in Black Communities*. https://www.sciline.org/disparities/racism-health-black-communities/

Hudson, D.L., Karter, A.J., Fernandez, A., Adams, A.S., Zhou, J, & Adler, N. E. (2013). Racial/Ethnic Differences in the detection and treatment of depression among patients with diabetes: The Diabetes Study of Northern California (DISTANCE). *American Journal of Managed Care* 19(5), 344–352.

Huynh, M., Parker, J.D., Harper, S., Pamuk, E., Schoendorf, K.C. (2005). Contextual Effect of Income Inequality on Birth Outcomes. *International Journal of Epidemiology* 3(4), 888–895.

Jackson, P. B., & Williams, D. R. (2006). The Intersection of Race, Gender, and SES: Health Paradoxes. In A. J. Schulz & L. Mullings (Eds.), *Gender, Race, Class, & Health: Intersectional Approaches* (pp. 131–162). San Francisco: Jossey Bass/Wiley

James, S.A, Strogatz, D.S, Wing, S.B., & Ramsey, D.I. (1987) Socioeconomic Status, John Henryism, and Hypertension in Blacks and Whites. *American Journal of Epidemiology* 126(4), 664–673.

James S.A, (1994) John Henryism and the health of African-Americans. *Culture, Medicine and Psychiatry* 18(2), 163–182.

James, S.A., (1993) Racial and Ethnic Differences in Infant Mortality and Low Birth Weight: A Psychosocial Critique, *Annals of Epidemiology* 3(2), 130–136.

Kandel, D. B. (1995). Ethnic differences in drug use: Patterns and paradoxes. In G. J. Botvin, S. Schinke, & M. A. Orlandi (Eds.), *Drug Abuse Prevention with Multiethnic Youth*. Thousand Oaks, CA: Sage.

Kaplan, G.A., Turrell, G., Lynch, J.W., Everson, S.A., Helkala, E.L., & Salonen, J.T. (2001). Childhood Socioeconomic Position and Cognitive Function in Adutlhood. *International Journal of Epidemiology* 30(2), 256–263.

Kaplan, M., & G. Marks. (1990). Adverse Effects of Acculturation: Psychological Distress Among Mexican American Young Adults. *Social Science and Medicine* 31, 1313–1319.

Krieger, N. (2021) Structural Racism, Health Inequities, and the Two-Edged Sword of Data: Structural Problems Require Structural Solutions. *Frontiers in Public Health, 9, 655447–655447.*

Link, B. G., & Phelan, J. (1995). Social Conditions as Fundamental Causes of Disease. *Journal Of health and Social Behavior, Spec No* 35, 80–94.

Leonardo Z. (2004). The Color of Supremacy: Beyond the Discourse of "White Privilege." *Educational Philosophy and Theory* 36(2), 137–152.

Lewis, O. (1966). *La Vida: A Puerto Rican Family in the Culture of Poverty*, San Juan and New York. New York: Random House

MacDorman, M.F. (2011). Race and Ethnic Disparities in Fetal Mortality, Preterm Birth, and Infant Mortality in the United States: An Overview. *Seminars in Perinatology* 35(4), 200–208.

Marks, G., Garcia, M., & Solis. J., (1990) Health Risk Behaviors of Hispanics in the United States: Findings from NHANES, 1982–1984. *American Journal of Public Health* 80. 20–26.

Moynihan, D.P. (1965). *The Negro Family, The Case for National Action.* Washington, DC: Office of Policy Planning, Research United States Department of Labor

Nazroo, J. Y. (1998) Genetic, Cultural or Socio-Economic Vulnerability? Explaining Ethnic Inequalities in Health. *Sociology of Health and Illness,* 20(5), 710–730.

Nussbaum, M. C. (2004). Beyond the Social Contract: Capabilities and Global Justice. an Olaf Palme Lecture, delivered in Oxford on 19 June 2003. *Oxford Developmental Studies*, 32(1), 3–18.

Pearson, J.A. (2008). Can't Buy Me Whiteness: New Lessons from the Titanic on Race, Ethnicity, and Health/ *Du Bois Review: Social Science Research on Race* 5(1), 27–47.

Pearson, J. A., & Geronimus, A. T. (2011). Race/Ethnicity, Socioeconomic Characteristics, Coethnic Social Ties, and Health: Evidence from the National Jewish Population Survey. *American Journal of Public Health* 101, 1314–1321.

Pearson, J.A. (2020). Structural Racism in Living While Black at Duke. https://today.duke.edu/2020/07/living-while-black-session-videos-now-available.

Peck, G.(2019). Labor Abolition and the Politics of White Victimhood: Rethinking the History of Working-Class Racism. *Journal of the Early Republic* 39(1), 89–98.

Petersen, E.E., Davis, N.L., Goodman, D., Cox, S., Syverson, C., Seed, K., Shapiro-Mendoza, C., Callaghan, W.M., & Barfield, W. (2019). Racial/Ethnic Disparities in Pregnancy Related Deaths—United States, 2007–2016. *Morbidity and Mortality Weekly Report* 68, 762–765.

Pettigrew, T. F., & Tropp, L. R. (2006). A Meta-analytic Test of Intergroup Contact Theory. *Journal of Personality and Social Psychology* 90(5), 751–783.

Petteway R. (2021). *Dreams of a Beloved Public Health: Confronting White Supremacy in Our Field.* Health Affairs Blog.

Powell, J.A., Menendian, S,, & Reece, J. (2009). *The Importance of Targeted Universalism.* Poverty & Research Action Council.

Pratto, F., Sidanius, J., Stallworth, L.M., & Malle, B. M. (1994) Social Dominance Orientation: A Personality Variable Predicting Social and Political Attitudes. *Journal of Personality and Social Psychology* 67(4), 741–763.

Pounder, C. C. H., Adelman, L., Cheng, J., Herbes-Sommers, C., Strain, T. H., Smith, L., Ragazzi, C., Corporation for Public Broadcasting. (2003). *Race: The Power of an Illusion.* San Francisco: California Newsreel

Rahman K. S. (2018). Constructing and Contesting Structural Inequality, *Critical Analysis of Law* 5, 1.

Rawls, J. (1971). *A Theory of Justice*. Cambridge, MA: The Belknap Press of Harvard University Press.

Sen, A. (2009). Chapter 2: Rawls and Beyond. In *The Idea of Justice* (pp. 52–74). London: Cambridge: The Belknap Press of Harvard University Press,

Sidanius, J., & Pratto, F. (1999). *Social Dominance: An Intergroup Theory of Social Hierarchy and Oppression*. Cambridge, UK: Cambridge University Press.

Smaje, C. (1996). The Ethnic Patterning of Health: New Directions for Theory and Research. *Sociology of Health and Illness* 18(2), 139–171.

Steele, C. (2011). *Whistling Vivaldi: How Stereotypes Affect Us and What We Can Do*. New York: W.W. Norton and Company.

Takaki, R. T. (1998). *Strangers from a Different Shore: A History of Asian Americans*. Boston: Little, Brown.

Thomas, T. (1995). Acculturative Stress in the Adjustment of Immigrant Families. *Journal of Social Distress and the Homeless* 4, 131–142.

Viruell-Fuentes, E. A., Abdul-Rahim, S. & Miranda, P. (2012). Beyond Acculturation: Immigration, Discrimination, and Health Research Among Mexicans in the United States. *Social Science & Medicine* 65(7), 1524–1535.

Whitehead, M. (1991). The Concepts and Principles of Equity and Health. *International Journal of Health Services: Planning, Administration, Evaluation* 22(3). 429–445.

Williams, D.R. (1999). Race, Socioeconomic Status, and Health: The Added Effects of Racism and Discrimination. *Annals of the New York Academy of Sciences* 896, 173–188.

Young, I.M. (2012). Chapter 1: Displacing the Distributive Paradigm. In (D. S. Allen & I. M. Young) *Justice and the Politics of Difference* (pp. 15–38). Princeton: Princeton University Press.

Chapter 6

#StopAsianHate

Examining Rising Levels of Anti-Asian Hate Crimes in the United States

Janice A. Iwama

On March 11, 2020, the World Health Organization (WHO) declared a pandemic following a rise in COVID-19 cases around the world. A few days later, former US President Donald Trump declared a state of emergency and posted a tweet that referenced the COVID-19 virus as the "Chinese" virus. Faced with accusations of spreading racism, Trump argued that the virus originated in China and insisted on tying the pandemic to the country. However, whether intentional or not, this rhetoric soon spread across the country, with other government officials using similar terminology to describe the coronavirus. Soon, the rise in COVID-19 cases was followed by a similar rise in anti-Asian hate crimes, with many victims reporting hostile language referencing the coronavirus, such as "Go back to China" or "You're the one who brought the virus here" (Gover, Harper, & Langton, 2020; Viala-Gaudefroy & Lindaman, 2020).

With the rising number of anti-Asian hate crimes, policymakers have drawn attention to this issue while arguing that the political rhetoric being used by many public leaders needs to stop, and that efforts must be put into place to prevent the spread of anti-Asian sentiment. Incidents such as the fatal attack of an eighty-four-year-old Thai man in San Francisco, the assault of a ninety-one-year-old man in Oakland's Chinatown, and the unprovoked fire set on an eighty-nine-year-old woman in Brooklyn have created ripple effects among members of the Asian community. Brutal high-profile attacks such as these have terrified the Asian community and drawn the attention and support of community and civil rights leaders. Furthermore, with the underreporting of hate crimes by individuals and law enforcement agencies, it is highly probable that there are many more attacks against individuals of Asian descent in which hate is a clear motivation given the history of anti-Asian sentiment and hate crimes in the United States (Cai, Burch, & Patel, 2021; Lah & Kravarik, 2021; Lim, 2021).

Over the last three decades, 46 states have passed hate crime legislation aimed at reducing and preventing hate crimes by prescribing enhanced penalties for hate crimes, requiring law enforcement agencies to collect data and information on hate crimes, mandating hate crime training for law enforcement personnel, and providing compensation for victims of hate crimes (Grattet et al., 1998). On the one hand, many scholars argue that hate crime laws are passed as a symbolic gesture rather than a deterrent measure to prevent hate crimes. Hate crimes have a profound impact on not only the victim but the victim's community and the targeted group, whether it is race, ethnicity, religion, gender, or gender identity. Therefore, hate crime laws are viewed as tools that send a message to the local community that bias will not be tolerated in the event of a criminal act. On the other hand, even though hate crime laws do carry a symbolic role, implementing a hate crime law is more difficult during the investigation and prosecution given the lack of tangible evidence of a bias motivation found in many reported hate crimes. Furthermore, because local level efforts vary in the implementation of hate crimes across different jurisdictions, it is difficult to tell whether they effectively prevent and reduce hate crimes (Gover et al., 2020; Shively et al., 2013).

The purpose of this chapter is to examine anti-Asian hate crimes and discuss solutions to prevent and increase the reporting of hate crimes against Asians in the United States. First, I provide an overview of major historical events that illustrate discrimination and hate crimes since the arrival of Asian immigrants at the beginning of the nineteenth century. Next, I discuss the passage of federal and state hate crime legislation in the United States. Although these policies were intended to better understand the size and scope of hate crimes across the United States, they fail to address some of the challenges with underreporting of hate crimes by Asian Americans. Past historical events can provide an understanding of why Asians are unlikely to report hate crimes. Given recent concerns with rising levels of anti-Asian sentiment and hate crimes, it is clear that new policies and practices are necessary to better assist in addressing key structural causes of hate crimes against Asians. I conclude by providing policy recommendations that may fill these gaps and encourage the reporting of hate crimes by Asian Americans through the adoption of research-based practices.

BACKGROUND

History of Hate Crimes against Asian Americans

Throughout US history, bias incidents and hate crimes against individuals of Asian descent have taken place. The first wave of Asian immigrants arriving in the United States originally came from China in the 1800s, and many began to settle in different parts of the West Coast. This rise in the Asian population was soon followed by anti-Asian sentiment and rhetoric which sought to limit the rights and opportunities of Asian Americans. For example, the 1854 California Supreme Court case, *People v. Hall*, barred Chinese people from testifying against White people in California and argued that they were an "inferior" race and, therefore, incapable of providing testimony due to their lack of intellect. By denying Chinese residents these rights, alongside Native Americans and African Americans, the California Supreme Court ensured that Chinese people were unlikely to report any crimes against their White peers. As a result, many racially motivated attacks against Asian immigrants remained undocumented, with only a handful of reports found in the local newspapers in the 19th century. The Chinese massacre in October of 1871, however, drew the nation's attention to the discrimination and hate crimes experienced by Chinese residents. Following the murder of a policeman and a local rancher in Los Angeles, California, a White mob arrived at a Chinese community to attack, rob, and murder Chinese residents in retaliation for these murders. Although it was clear that racial bias played a role in the attack of Chinese residents resulting in the murder of 19 Chinese immigrants at the end of the massacre, only a handful of individuals were charged and found to be guilty. Shortly after, these convictions were overturned on appeal due to technicalities (Gover et al., 2020; Mineo, 2021; Rouse, 2013; Zheng, 2021).

Over the next century, Asian Americans continued to experience bigotry and racism in the United States. For example, the attack on Pearl Harbor during World War II was followed by an executive order signed by the president following political pressure by leaders to incarcerate all individuals of Japanese descent in the United States due to a heightened fear of espionage. Whether they were US citizens or not, all Japanese Americans were forced into prison camps with US leaders arguing that "the Japanese race is an enemy race" (DeWitt, 1943, p. 34). Like the experiences of Chinese Americans in the 1800s, racially motivated attacks against Japanese people in the United States remained largely unnoticed and underreported due to Japanese Americans' fear of retaliation. However, the abuse and victimization of Japanese people who were forced into the World War II prison camps brought attention to the widespread prejudice against all individuals of Japanese descent in the United States. By the end of World War II, the Japanese prison camps were shut down, but several decades would pass before the US government acknowledged any wrongdoing in the incarceration of more than 120,000 individuals of Japanese descent (Burton et al., Farrell, Lord & Lord, 1999; Petrosino, 1999).

Major historical events such as the Chinese Massacre of 1871 and the internment of individuals of Japanese descent into prison camps during

World War II are examples of discrimination and hate crimes experienced by Asian people in the United States. Yet, numerous other examples of bias and discrimination against US Asians can be found at different points in time as the Asian population continued to grow. By the end of the twentieth century, the US Asian population had reached nearly 12 million residents and was projected to continue growing at a faster rate than any other racial or ethnic group by the middle of the twenty-first century. Despite the rising number of Asian Americans and other minority groups at the end of the twentieth century, federal and state hate crime legislation took several decades before being passed, leaving many new residents vulnerable to anti-Asian sentiment and hate crimes.

Evolution of Hate Crime Legislation

Early efforts to bring attention to crimes motivated by bias were led by national, state, and local advocacy and civil rights organizations during the mid-20th century. For example, the Los Angeles County Commission on Human Relations (LACCHR) began collecting data and information on hate crimes reported by both victims and witnesses in Los Angeles County and published annual reports to inform members of the community about such incidents (Los Angeles County Commission on Human Relations, 1969). Although these early efforts provided a better understanding of the nature of these events, they were restricted to information on certain types of offenses and against certain targeted groups based on organizations' constituents (Anti-Defamation League, 1992, 2001; Grant et al., 2011). Without any federal hate crime legislation at the time, the federal government viewed these incidents as isolated problems that needed to be dealt with by local law enforcement agencies. After the passage of the Civil Rights Act of 1964, however, the Federal Bureau of Investigation (FBI) began to investigate a series of violent events involving civil rights workers, members of the Ku Klux Klan, and local law enforcement agencies in the Southern states. As civil rights and labor law, the legislation prohibited unequal application of voter registration requirements and racial segregation in federally protected locations such as schools, employment, and public accommodations. Consequently, for the first time in US history, discrimination based on race, color, religion, sex, or national origin was outlawed while registering to vote (Iwama, 2018).

Soon after the assassination of Dr. Martin Luther King Jr. and the urban riots that followed in several major cities across the United States, Congress passed the Civil Rights Act of 1968, which included the first federal hate crime statute. In order to address some of the ongoing violence fueled by racism that had been taking place at the time, the statute made it a crime to use, or threaten to use, force to willfully interfere with any person because of race, color, religion, or national origin when the person is participating in a federally protected activity, such as public education, employment, jury service, travel, or the enjoyment of public accommodations, or helping another person to do so (Civil Rights Act of 1968 18 U.S.C. § 245). Additionally, the statute known as the Fair Housing Act made it a crime to use, or threaten to use, force to interfere with housing rights because of the victim's race, color, religion, sex, or national origin.

Despite the passage of federal hate crime statutes, reports of attacks motivated by bias against Asian Americans continued to make headlines across the United States. In 1982, for example, Vincent Chin was beaten to death by American workers in the auto industry, who were upset at the potential loss of their jobs due to perceived Japanese automobile competition and mistakenly believed that he was of Japanese—rather than Chinese—descent (Chen et al., 2020). Similar incidents continued to occur throughout the second half of the century, but many believed that these were infrequent incidents given the lack of data or information to support the prevalence of these incidents (Perry, 2009; Tafoya, 1991). Acknowledging that these incidents have severe and negative consequences on groups of individuals, who are being targeted and their communities, the US Commission on Civil Rights (1983) was established to study and collect information on acts of violence against racial and ethnic groups. In 1983, the Commission published a report on the nature and extent of the problem and concluded that there existed several contributing circumstances in addition to the rhetoric of hate and acts of violence. In particular, the Commission contended:

> Effective police responses to incidents of racial and religious violence are necessary to keep such incidents from spreading. If the police fail to respond or respond in ways which clearly demonstrate a lack of sensitivity, perpetrators can interpret the police inactivity to indicate official sympathy or even official sanction (US Commission on Civil Rights, 1983, p. 14).

Furthermore, the Commission encouraged federal and state governments to explore promising solutions to prevent the spread of such incidents given the nature and cause of such racism and anti-Semitism that continues to exist among some individuals and communities in the United States. For example, the Commission recommended raising education and public awareness, improving police intervention, developing policy measures to combat racial and religious terrorism, and encouraging media and public officials to pursue accurate and unbiased reporting.

In order to understand the nature and extent of the problem, members of US Congress introduced the Hate Crime Statistics Act (HCSA) in the late 1980s but were unable to pass the bill until 1990 (Marovitz, 1993; Nolan et al., 2002; Shively et al., 2013). Under this legislation, Congress was able to recognize and effectively address hate crimes in several ways. First, the HCSA established a standard definition of hate crimes to distinguish it from non-hate crimes by describing hate crimes as,

> Crimes that manifest evidence of prejudice based on race, religion, disability, sexual orientation, or ethnicity, including where appropriate the crimes of murder, non-negligent manslaughter; forcible rape; aggravated assault, simple assault, intimidation; arson; and destruction, damage or vandalism of property. (Hate Crime Statistics Act 1990, 28 U.S.C. § 534)

Second, it emphasized the importance of collecting data and information on the prevalence of hate crimes to identify any patterns and trends to help develop preventive strategies. The FBI became responsible for collecting data and information on hate crimes reported to the city, college, university, county, state, tribal, and federal law enforcement agencies using their Uniform Crime Reporting (UCR) program. The FBI also became responsible for providing support to law enforcement agencies in the investigation of these cases. Finally, the federal hate crime statute introduced enhanced penalties for crimes motivated by bias to deter individuals from committing these crimes.

Overall, the passage of the Hate Crime Statistics Act in 1990 intended to help policymakers and practitioners better understand the size and scope of hate crimes across the United States. It also encouraged state governments to require their law enforcement agencies to provide training to their officers on the identification and reporting of hate crimes to assist in the collection of hate crime data (Iwama, 2018). By the end of the 20th century, however, it was clear that there were a number of limitations with the FBI's national hate crime data collection. While the number of law enforcement agencies submitting incident reports on hate crimes to the FBI increased over time, scholars found that some law enforcement agencies failed to identify and properly classify hate crimes, which brought up concerns about the accuracy of the data (McDevitt et al., 2003). As law enforcement agencies began to develop better training on the identification and classification of hate crimes, the quality and quantity of hate crime data reported to the FBI improved. At the same time, policymakers and practitioners were encouraged to consider policies and practices that address some of the unique challenges faced by Asian people in the United States.

HATE CRIMES AGAINST ASIAN AMERICANS TODAY

By 2019, the US Asian population grew to more than 23 million residents across the United States. This population nearly doubled since the end of the 20th century, making it the fastest-growing racial or ethnic group with most individuals coming from China (23 percent), India (20 percent), Philippines (18 percent), Vietnam (9 percent), Korea (8 percent), and Japan (6 percent). A vast majority of US Asians continue to live in the Western part of the United States, with nearly one-third of the US Asian population living in California alone (Budiman & Ruiz, 2021). Asians are projected to continue growing and are expected to surpass the Latinx population by 2055 as the largest immigrant group in the United States. However, a recent spike in anti-Asian hate crimes during the COVID-19 pandemic has reinvigorated the national discussion on identifying better solutions to prevent and reduce the likelihood of hate crimes against Asians.

Hate Crime Data

Shortly after the FBI began collecting hate crime data from law enforcement agencies, there were 355 hate crimes against Asian Americans and Pacific Islanders reported. Two decades later, the number of hate crimes dropped to 115, which was the lowest number of reported hate crimes against Asian Americans and Pacific Islanders. Yet, other racially motivated hate crimes also experienced a similar decrease during this period. Over the next four years, however, the number of anti-Asian and Pacific Islander hate crimes began to increase in contrast to other racially motivated hate crimes. For example, the number of reported hate crimes against Asian Americans and Pacific Islanders increased by 7 percent between 2018 and 2019, while the number of anti-Black, anti-White, and anti-American Indian/Alaska native hate crimes decreased by about 1 percent, 13 percent, and 39 percent, respectively. Unfortunately, the FBI does not publish the annual hate crime report until the following year and, therefore, the number of reported hate crimes against Asians and Pacific Islanders in 2020 remains unknown (Federal Bureau of Investigation, 2020).

In the meantime, numerous advocacy and civil rights organizations have already started publishing their hate crime data, indicating a rise in the number of reported hate crimes against Asian Americans. For example, the Stop AAPI Hate Coalition—which was created in March of 2020 to track incidents of hate, violence, harassment, discrimination, shunning, and child bullying against Asian Americans and Pacific Islanders in the United States—reported an increase in physical assaults and online hate incidents between 2020 and 2021 based on data collected from March of 2020 to March of 2021 (Jeung et al., 2021). The *New York Times* also started to track and collect information on hate crimes using media reports from across the country and found an increase between March of 2020 and March of 2021 with clear evidence that it was race-based hate given the language the perpetrator used (Cai et al., 2021). Although limited in terms of their representation of all victims of a hate crime, it is clear that anti-Asian and Pacific Islander hate crimes have increased, but whether this is across the entire country or whether these incidents are concentrated in a few major cities remains unclear. This delay in collecting and publishing hate crime information makes it challenging to introduce policies and practices to reduce the number of reported anti-Asian hate crimes in the United States (Federal Bureau of Investigation, 2020; Iwama, 2018; Shively et al., 2013).

To address this gap in the national hate crime data collection, President Biden signed the COVID-19 Hate Crimes Act in 2021, which sought to make the reporting of hate crimes more accessible at the local and state levels by boosting public outreach and ensuring reporting resources are available online in multiple languages. It also directed the Department of Justice to designate a point person to expedite the review of hate crimes related to COVID-19 and authorize grants to state and local governments to conduct crime-reduction programs to prevent and respond to hate crimes (Sprunt, 2021). It is too early to say whether this law will prove to be effective at increasing the reporting of hate crimes and reducing the number of anti-Asian hate crimes following the anti-Asian sentiment and rhetoric associated with the COVID-19 pandemic. Nevertheless, previously cited examples of hate crimes against Asians in the United States can be used to identify effective policies to prevent and reduce hate crimes against US Asians.

POLICY RECOMMENDATIONS

Over the last decade, policymakers, practitioners, and scholars have identified responses to prevent and reduce outbreaks of racial violence. Recommendations from advocacy and civil rights organizations, government commissions, and scholars have included better training for law enforcement agencies, responding to cultural and language barriers, modifying school curricula, and raising public awareness. Although there is no easy or quick solution to address the persistence of racism in the United States, as shown throughout history, there are initiatives that can be taken to deter individuals from committing hateful acts. Below are a series of recommendations to provide insight to policymakers and practitioners to identify and develop inclusive and beneficial reforms for individuals of Asian descent and their communities.

Law Enforcement Training

While many states require law enforcement agencies to provide mandatory hate crime training, there is little instruction on the type of training needed to improve the reporting and classification of hate crimes in their communities. Law enforcement agencies need to consider training that helps build critical community partnerships, foster trust, enhance the reporting and identification of cases, and improve the data collection, reporting, analysis, and use of the hate crime data to guide investigations and prosecutions. First, training that focuses on building critical community partnerships is best suited to address hate crimes against individuals of Asian descent. By collaborating with local community partners, agencies can discuss the major problems faced by Asian Americans and Asian immigrants in their communities and identify potential areas that increase their chances of being victimized. For example, numerous individuals of Asian descent who own small businesses have been targeted in violent attacks by local residents, who blame them for the COVID-19 pandemic, and experienced significant losses in their revenue due to stay-at-home restrictions (Ramachandran, 2021). In order to address these problems, the training should focus on describing the potential types of victimization faced by Asian Americans and Asian immigrants due to the anti-Asian rhetoric associated with the pandemic. Second, training should encourage agencies to engage in outreach activities to foster trust and encourage local residents, business owners, and community leaders to identify and report any hate crimes in the community. Finally, training should bring officers' attention to the challenges local residents face in relation to recent events, such as the COVID-19 pandemic, and better inform officers using the hate crime data to identify any patterns and trends in attacks against Asians.

Training can be developed in conjunction with national law enforcement organizations such as the International Association of Chiefs of Police (IACP) or the Police Executive Research Forum (PERF), which have made hate crimes a priority issue for their members in the past. Additionally, the Department of Justice's (DOJ) Hate Crimes Prevention and Enforcement Initiative—which includes the DOJ's Civil Rights Division, the Community Relations Service (CRS), the US Attorney's Offices, the FBI, the Office of Community Oriented Policing Services (COPS), and other agencies in the Office of Justice Programs, such as the Office for Victims of Crime (OCV) and the Bureau of Justice Statistics (BJS)—seeks to build law enforcement agencies capacity by providing assistance in training to prevent and respond to hate crimes. These initiatives and professional organizations can provide law enforcement agencies with guidance in developing training that addresses concerns with anti-Asian hate crimes while considering the local context of the agency.

Culture and Language Barriers

With the Asian population projected to increase to 46 million in 2060, policymakers and practitioners should consider the culture and language barriers that some individuals face to prevent and reduce anti-Asian hate crimes.

For example, policymakers can require law enforcement agencies to engage in cultural awareness training, which includes members of the local community as part of their training. Community leaders from the Asian community could talk about their culture, experiences as immigrants, the structure and role of law enforcement in their home country, and their perceptions of police. At the same time, agencies can raise awareness to communities about hate crime legislation, how to report a hate crime, and inform communities on how hate crimes are handled. This kind of training would be helping officers and community members better understand the experiences of potential victims, educate community members about hate crimes, and help to build partnerships with members of Asian and immigrant communities.

Another issue to consider with Asian American communities is the language barrier, which can deter individuals from reporting a hate crime. According to the 2019 US Census data, less than three-quarters of all US Asians were proficient with the English language. Although most Asian Americans reported as being proficient with the English language, only about one-half of foreign-born Asians reported as proficient (Budiman & Ruiz, 2021). When dealing with a victim who does not speak English, police officers, particularly those from smaller law enforcement agencies, may not have the ability to bring an officer or translator who speaks the victim's language. Based on information collected from participating law enforcement agencies for a study on hate crimes against immigrants, a police officer noted that officers may try to ask the victim's child or neighbor to interpret or translate for them if they are unable to communicate with the victim in some cases (Shively et al., 2013). However, this may deter victims from reporting hate crimes due to privacy concerns and the sensitive nature of the crime. As a result, some law enforcement agencies are utilizing online or phone services to reach interpreters or translators that are available all day. Other agencies have also returned to the victim at a later time with an interpreter to get the details of the victimization depending on the situation. While law enforcement agencies have been encouraged to recruit Asian officers, Asian Americans only make up about 2 percent of the nation's law enforcement officers (Contreras, 2021). Given the widening gap in the demographic makeup of communities and their local police officers with agencies facing challenges in recruiting officers from Asian communities, it is unlikely to change in the near future (Leatherby & Oppel, 2020). Nevertheless, agencies need to consider addressing language barriers given the rising Asian population in some communities and available options in their community.

School Policies

According to the FBI's national hate crime data collection, educational institutions are the third most frequent location where hate crime incidents take place, following incidents that occurred in or near residences or homes, and on highways, roads, alleys, streets, or sidewalks. In 2019, nearly one in every ten reported hate crimes occurred at an educational institution, which includes schools, colleges, and universities (Federal Bureau of Investigation, 2020). Because many hate crimes occur in educational institutions, school officials should establish a protocol for reporting bias incidents and hate crimes that target any of their students, parents, and/or school personnel. School officials should identify an official role for an individual—whether it is a School Resource Officer or other school personnel—and ensure that the individual is trained as suggested earlier in identifying and gathering information on hate crimes. Furthermore, schools may adopt a revised version of the FBI's two-tier process to report and investigate hate crimes as recommended by law enforcement agencies (Iwama, 2018). According to the two-tier process, any hate crime incident report made to an official would begin with a search for keywords involving any biased language, such as racial, ethnic, or homophobic slurs that might describe a bias motivation. If any language associated with bias were identified, the incident report would be forwarded to a hate crime official for a second review. While many law enforcement agencies include a check-off box in their incident report for the responding officer to indicate whether or not the incident is bias motivated, some officers may not remember to check the box in all incidents or fail to identify any bias motivation following their review of the incident. By adopting the FBI's two-tier process, the agency ensures that incident reports are carefully reviewed at two different points in the process and reduces the discretion of the responding officer to determine whether or not they believe that incident was bias motivated. Although schools may not necessarily need to create a unit for this second review, they should consider appointing a person to this position to ensure that all incoming reports are reviewed carefully.

Public Awareness

In 1981, the US Commission on Civil Rights recommended increasing education and public awareness on hate crimes. The Commission suggested that shedding light on previous incidents involving hate crimes, such as the harsh treatment of Japanese during World War II, can help public members to better understand the dangers of racial violence. Forty years later, advocacy and civil rights groups, as well as government agencies, continue to encourage communities to engage in education and public awareness campaigns to shed light on the negative effects of racial violence. For example, a recent study on the impact of COVID-19-related anti-Asian racism found that Asian Americans who reported being discriminated also experienced greater depression, anxiety, and stress as well as physical complaints (Liu et al., 2021). While some existing community-policing programs engage in outreach activities to help identify and report hate crime incidents, agencies should consider partnering with other groups such as mental health advocates, given the effects of anti-Asian discrimination on the immigrant and Asian communities. In a study on anti-immigrant hate crimes, hate crime experts participating in a focus group suggested also partnering with local churches or service providers, utilizing cable news stations that cater to immigrants or Asians, and establishing special sessions of citizen police academies that target immigrants or Asian community members to provide assistance in reporting hate crime incidents and support for members of the community experiencing negative effects from these incidents (Shively et al., 2013).

CONCLUSION

Overall, the challenges faced with preventing and reporting hate crimes are well known. The passage of the COVID-19 Hate Crimes Act of 2021 acknowledges that the main issue is the delayed publication of vital information that can better assist, train, and fund areas with many hate crimes. The limitations in hate data collection, legislation, and research raise more questions than scholars are currently able to answer. Yet, the prevalence of anti-Asian hate crimes deserves our attention given the widespread growth of anti-Asian and anti-immigrant sentiment following the COVID-19 pandemic that could readily translate into increasing acts of violence given the rise in the Asian population closely linked to the increasing positive cases of COVID-19. This chapter addresses this by advancing our knowledge regarding hate crimes against Asians despite the current limitations in the available hate crime data. While it encourages further examination into the topic, this chapter represents a comprehensive examination of the past, present, and future of anti-Asian hate crimes and provides recommendations for best practices and research-based solutions to #STOPASIANHATE.

REFERENCES

Anti-Defamation League. (1992). *1991 Audit of anti-Semitic incidents.* New York: Anti-Defamation League.
Anti-Defamation League. (2012). *Statement by anti-defamation league senate judiciary subcommittee on constitution, civil rights and human rights on hate crimes and the threat of domestic extremism.* Accessed 15 September 2016. Available

at: http://www.adl.org/assets/pdf/combating-hate/Senate-Judiciary-Subcommittee-HCPA-statement.pdf.

Budiman, A., & Ruiz, N. G. (2021). *Key facts about Asian Americans, a diverse and growing population*. Washington, DC: Pew Research Center. Accessed June 28, 2021. Available at: https://www.pewresearch.org/fact-tank/2021/04/29/key-facts-about-asian-americans/.

Burton, J., Farrell, M., Lord, F., & Lord R. (1999). *Confinement and ethnicity: An overview of World War II Japanese American relocation sites*. Accessed June 28, 2021. Available at: https://www.nps.gov/parkhistory/online_books/anthropology74/index.htm.

Cai, W., Burch, A. D. S., & Patel, J. K. (2021). Swelling anti-Asian violence: Who is being attacked where. *New York Times*. Accessed June 23, 2021. Available at: https://www.nytimes.com/interactive/2021/04/03/us/anti-asian-attacks.html.

Chen, H. A., Trinh, J., & Yang, G. P. (2020). Anti-Asian Sentiment in the United States. *American Journal of Surgery*, 220: 556–557.

Contreras, R. Percentage of Asian American police officers lag behind need as hate crimes rise. *Yahoo News*. Accessed June 28, 2021. Available at: https://www.yahoo.com/lifestyle/percentage-asian-american-police-officers-093040778.html.

DeWitt, J. L. (1943). *Final report: Japanese evacuation from the West Coast*. Washington, DC: Government Printing Office.

Federal Bureau of Investigation. (2020). *2019 Hate Crime Statistics*. Accessed June 28, 2021. Available at: https://ucr.fbi.gov/hate-crime/2019.

Gover, A. R., Harper, S. B., & Langton, L. (2020). Anti-Asian hate crime during the COVID-19 pandemic: Exploring the reproduction of inequality. *American Journal of Criminal Justice*, 45: 647–667.

Hate Crime Statistics Act 1990, H.R. 1048. 101st Congress (1989-1990), viewed 16 September 2016, https://www.congress.gov/bill/101st-congress/house-bill/1048/text.

Iwama, J. (2018). "Hate crimes." In Martinez, R., Hollis, M. E., & J. I. Stowell (Eds.), *The handbook of race, ethnicity, crime and justice*. New York: John Wiley & Sons, Inc., 87–104.

Jeung, R., Yellow Horse, A.J., & Cayanan, C. (2021). *Stop AAPI Hate National Report*. San Francisco, CA: Stop AAPI Hate. Accessed June 28, 2021. Available at: https://stopaapihate.org/wp-content/uploads/2021/05/Stop-AAPI-Hate-Report-National-210506.pdf.

Lah, K. & Kravarik, J. Family of Thai immigrant, 84, says fatal attack 'was driven by hate.' *CNN News*. Accessed June 28, 2021. Available at: https://www.cnn.com/2021/02/16/us/san-francisco-vicha-ratanapakdee-asian-american-attacks/index.html.

Leatherby, L. & Oppel, R.A. (2020). Which police departments are as diverse as their communities? *New York Times*. Accessed June 28, 2021. Available at: https://www.nytimes.com/interactive/2020/09/23/us/bureau-justice-statistics-race.html.

Lim, D. (2021). Shocking video shows 91-year-old man senselessly pushed to ground in Oakland's Chinatown. *ABC 7 News*. Accessed June 28, 2021. Available at:

https://abc7news.com/man-pushed-to-ground-in-oakland-violence-chinatown-robberies/10311111/.

Liu, C., Liu, T., Chang, J., Koh, A., Huang, L., Shu Fu, R., Noh, R., & Yang, A. (2021). *Stop AAPI hate mental health report*. San Francisco, CA: Stop AAPI. Accessed June 28, 2021. Available at: https://stopaapihate.org/wp-content/uploads/2021/05/Stop-AAPI-Hate-Mental-Health-Report-210527.pdf.

Marovitz, W.A. (1993). "Hate or bias crime legislation." In Kelly, R.J. (Ed.), *Bias crime: American law enforcement and legal responses*. Chicago, IL: Office of International Criminal Justice.

Martin, S.E. (1995). A cross-burning is not just an arson: Police social construction of hate crimes in Baltimore County. *Criminology* 33(3): 303–326.

Martinez, Jr, R. (2008). The impact of immigration policy on criminological research. *Criminology* 7(1): 53–58.

McDevitt, J. & Iwama, J. (2016). "Challenges in measuring and understanding hate crime." In Bynum, T.S. & Huebner, B.M. (Eds.), *The handbook of measurement issues in criminology and criminal justice*. Hoboken, NJ: John Wiley & Sons, Inc.

McDevitt, J. & Balboni, J. (2003). "Hate crimes victimization: a comparison of bias and nonbias-motivated assaults." In Sgarzi, J.M. & McDevitt, J. (Eds.), *Victimology: A study of crime victims and their roles*. Upper Saddle River, NJ: Prentice Hall.

McDevitt, J., Balboni, J.M., Bennett, S., Weiss, J.C., Orchowsky, S., & Walbolt, L. (2000). *Improving the quality and accuracy of bias crime statistics nationally: an assessment of the first ten years of bias crime data collection (executive summary)*. Boston, MA: The Center for Criminal Justice Policy Research, Northeastern University.

McDevitt, J., Cronin, S., Balboni, J., Farrell, A., Nolan, J., & Weiss, J. (2003), *Bridging the information disconnect in bias crime reporting*. Washington, DC: Bureau of Justice Statistics, U.S. Department of Justice.

McVeigh, R., Welch, M.R. & Bjarnason, T. (2003). Hate crime reporting as a successful social movement outcome. *American Sociological Review* 68: 843–867.

Mineo, L. (2021). The scapegoating of Asian Americans. *The Harvard Gazette*. Accessed June 28, 2021. Available at: https://news.harvard.edu/gazette/story/2021/03/a-long-history-of-bigotry-against-asian-americans/.

Nolan, J.J., Akiyama, Y. & Berhanu, S. (2002). The hate crime statistics act of 1990: developing a method for measuring the occurrence of hate violence. *American Behavioral Scientist* 46: 136–153.

Olzak, S. (1990). The political context of competition: lynching and urban racial violence, 1882-1914. *Social Forces* 69(2): 931–961.

Perry, B. (2009). *Hate crimes: understanding and defining hate crime*. Westport, CT: Praeger Publishers.

Petrosino, C. (1999). Connecting the past to the future: Hate crime in America. *Journal of Contemporary Criminal Justice* 15(1): 22–47.

Ramachandran, V. (2021). Asian-owned businesses say they're reeling from hate and violence, operating in fear. *PBS News Hour*. Accessed June 28, 2021. Available at:

https://www.pbs.org/newshour/economy/asian-owned-businesses-say-theyre-reeling-from-hate-and-violence-operating-in-fear.

Rouse, W. (2013). *People v. hall. Defining documents: Manifest destiny and the new nation (1803-1860)*. Ipswich, MA: Salem Press/EBSCO Publishing.

Shively, M., McDevitt, J., Farrell, A., & Iwama, J. (2013). *Understanding trends in hate crimes against immigrants and Hispanic Americans*. Washington, DC: National Institute of Justice.

Sprunt, B. (2021). Here's what the new hate crimes law aims to do as attacks on Asian Americans rise. *NPR News*. Accessed June 28, 2021. Available at: https://www.npr.org/2021/05/20/998599775/biden-to-sign-the-covid-19-hate-crimes-bill-as-anti-asian-american-attacks-rise.

Tafoya, W. (1991). "Rioting in the streets: Deja vu?" In Taylor, N. (Ed.), *Bias crime: The law enforcement response*. Chicago, IL: Office of International Criminal Justice.

US Commission on Civil Rights. (1983). *Intimidation and violence: racial and religious bigotry in America*. Washington, DC: U.S. Commission on Civil Rights.

US House of Representatives. (2009). *Departments of transportation and housing and urban development, and related agencies appropriations act, 2010* (House Report 111-366). Washington, DC: U.S. Government Printing Office.

Valcore, Viala-Gaudefroy, J. & Lindaman, D. (2020). Donald Trump's 'Chinese virus': The politics of naming. *The Conversation*. Accessed June 23, 2021. Available at: https://theconversation.com/donald-trumps-chinese-virus-the-politics-of-naming-136796.

Zheng, M. (2021). *Current controversies: Hate crimes*. San Diego, CA: Greenhaven.

Chapter 7

Complexity and Possibility
Black Public Opinion on Immigration
Niambi M. Carter

This past year, America has faced dual pandemics. COVID-19 on the one hand and a racial reckoning on the other. Of course, these issues seemed to be separate matters, but like most things in America, race became the tie that bound these two seemingly different things together. Very early in our experience with COVID-19, the racial disparities in contracting the virus and fatalities from the virus became apparent. That Black and other minoritized communities faced a unique set of circumstances that made them more susceptible to the virus helped to expose the deeper fissures of an already broken health care system.

On top of all of this, high-profile deaths of Black people at the hands of White vigilantes and police officers created an unbearable situation that bubbled over into the summer. The summer and fall of 2020 saw Black Lives Matter protests in almost every part of this country and in countries around the globe, from Ghana to Australia. Advocates for racial justice were focused on the societal conditions that lead to the dehumanization of Black lives, such as inadequate medical care, poor education, environmental injustice, and the like. At the same time, we had a government—helmed by Donald J. Trump—that racialized the coronavirus, calling it the "China virus" and, at other times, "kung flu." Tethering the virus to Asian people and equating calls for racial justice with terrorism created a racially hostile environment where Asian people saw themselves being attacked and Black people were painted as enemies of the state and a threat to the safety of all people.

In the year since the first appearance of the coronavirus and the steady drumbeat of a government that was more interested in racializing the virus than combatting it, there has been an uptick in anti-Asian hate crimes and sentiment. Of particular note have been cases where the alleged attackers were Black—raising, once again, the specter of Black anti-Asian sentiment, which featured prominently during the Los Angeles Uprisings of 1992. Though many of these attacks have been one-on-one acts of violence, the mass shooting in Georgia by a White assailant finally got the country to pay attention to anti-Asian hate crimes. Yet, there does not seem to be the same hand wringing about dangerous White men who attack Asian people. However, according to the Department of Justice, most hate crimes in this country are perpetrated by White people, particularly White men. Moreover, White people are the only group with a documented history of carrying out coordinated attacks against civilians and governmental authorities (Giroux, 2017). Whether we are talking about the January 6 riot in Washington, DC, attempting to circumvent the 2020 presidential election or the 1898 Wilmington Race Riot to overthrow a duly installed government, the face of mass violence in America is White (Cecelski & Tyson, 1998; Fox et al., 2020; McWhirter, 2012; Messer, 2011). According to the NAACP, from 1883 to 1968, there were approximately 4,743 *recorded* lynchings in America; a majority of the victims of these crimes were Black, but there were also lynching victims of Mexican descent, Asian descent, and indigenous Americans (Beck 2015; Seguin & Rigby 2019). Despite this documented history, the narrative we hear and see is that Black people are the primary threats to American tranquility and more likely to commit acts of violence against others.

This tells us something about the perverse way that race operates in America. Fears of White perpetrators of violence, given the historical record, would be totally rational, but Black people have been made the face of anti-immigrant violence. But how does this portrayal square with what Black people actually feel about immigration? More importantly, what is it that Black people actually *do* about immigration or immigrants? The historical and contemporary records tell us that Black people have lots of opinions about immigration, but are far more ambivalent when it comes to acting on behalf of or against immigrant communities (Carter, 2019). In short, Black people, in general, are not the enemies of immigrants—despite long-standing tropes of anti-immigrant Black people that we see in the news. This is not to diminish individual acts of bigotry. Rather, it is a necessary intervention into the narrative of hostile, anti-immigrant Black people, which does not hold up to scrutiny despite its popularity.

In this chapter, I argue that Black people have a fairly nuanced set of ideas when it comes to immigration. What is more, they do not feel any particular hostility to one group or another. Rather, what they are feeling is more protectionist over their groups' interests and seek a political representation that will promote their interests, not undercut the needs of others vis-à-vis immigration restriction. This does not mean, however, that Black people are supportive of immigration at all times. Rather, Black people do not see immigration restriction as a viable path forward for their social mobility.

IMMIGRATION AND AMERICAN IDENTITY

Black people have been excluded from full citizenship for most of their time in America. Therefore, when discussing immigration, much of what we know comes from theorizing about the attitudes and behaviors of White people (Carter, 2019). In *Who Are We?: The Challenge to America's National Identity*, Samuel Huntington (2004) argues that America, and American identity by extension, is changing because of non-European immigrants—driven largely by Mexican immigration—who resist assimilation in terms of their acquisition of English language and adoption of prevalent American (i.e., Eurocentric) cultural values. Huntington perceives this as a negative for native-born Americans because American culture is being altered in ways that make it indistinguishable from our neighbors to the South. While Huntington is only one voice, he does express a common belief that immigrants are in the country without sufficient allegiance to the symbols of America. Of course, this presumes that America is a singular experience for all people who call themselves Americans (Carter & Pérez, 2016). That type of unitary America has never existed and Huntington's discussion of it as such affirms a notion of America as a racially White country (Devos & Banaji, 2005).

Although Americans worried about Germans and Irish immigrants in times past, these fears dissipated as these groups were incorporated into Whiteness (Ngai, 1999). Due to changes in immigration policy in 1965, immigrants today are from non-European countries and these groups cannot "become" racially White as immigrants of the past (Jacobson, 2001). This is not only because immigrants do not necessarily want to approximate Whiteness, but because the administration of White identity in this country has hardened the boundaries of Whiteness (Nobles 2000). Consequently, much of the contemporary conversation of immigration focuses on whether one is in the country with authorization or without. This focus on who is "legal" or "illegal" is an attempt to elide the racialized nature of our immigrant attitudes in this country by focusing on the rule of law and notions of fairness (Pantoja, 2006; Pérez, 2016). The post-9/11 immigration regime has attempted immigration enforcement as a matter of national security. Although the regulation of the Mexican border is framed as a way to make Americans safer, there is not the same attention paid to the Canadian border, which is far larger and porous. To wit, there is virtually no discussion of undocumented immigrants coming into the United States from Canada (Short & Magaña, 2002).

Another example includes Californian's direct democracy initiatives to push anti-immigrant propositions. Propositions 187 and 227 were attacks on the Latino people residing in the state using fears of undocumented immigration as a cover. Proposition 187 was particularly harsh and made it illegal for undocumented children to go to school and prevented hospitals from providing health care services to someone suspected of being undocumented. Moreover, undocumented persons were denied the provision of any social services, including nonemergency medical treatment. In addition, teachers, law enforcement, and other first responders were to survey and report on those they believed to be undocumented. This legislation was devised to make the lives of undocumented persons so precarious that they disappeared from public life and from this country altogether. Proponents of the measure framed this as pro-American legislation that would keep those who had broken the law by coming to this country from usurping goods and services meant for citizens. The racism of the measure was right under the surface.

Proposition 187 passed with 59 percent of the vote, and while the legislation was never allowed to proceed, it demonstrated how direct democracy could be used to violate the civil rights of non-White people. Ballot measures like Propositions 187 and 227 became the favored tools of states and localities across the country trying to prevent immigrants from gaining a foothold in their communities (Tolbert & Hero, 1996). Like Proposition 187, Proposition 227, dubbed the English Language in Public Schools Statute, sought to end English as a Second Language (ESL) and other such programs that would transition children with limited English proficiency into English language learning. This kind of bilingual education was judged as a failure by 227 supporters who saw bilingual education as a hindrance and as "a refusal to participate in an English-dominant society" (HoSang, 2010, p. 210). Because White Californians felt that immigrants were changing their communities, they responded by creating a climate that would be inhospitable to newcomers. Although overtly racial language was not used, it was clear that the world was changing and while demographics may not be destiny, California was not going to remain as it had been when White people were firmly ensconced in power (Sonenshein, 1993).

While racist language was never used in either case, it was clear that what was being experienced in California was also happening in other places. Couched as concerns for fairness and equitable access to resources, these efforts did little to deflect attention away from the racist intent of these kinds of anti-immigrant ballot measures. Most recently, we have seen similar measures in places that are not traditional immigrant gateways, but have become new receiving contexts, like Alabama and Pennsylvania (Johnson, 2011; McKanders, 2007). Much of the conversation around racial threats has been driven by White fears. There has been far less discussion of Black opinions regarding immigration. While Black people around the country have also been skeptical of what these new demographic changes mean for them, they have not necessarily materialized in the types of mobilization efforts seen on the part of White people in California and other states (Anderson, 2003; Carter and Pérez, 2016).

Contextualizing Black Opinion on Immigration

In general, Black people have not spearheaded or supported efforts to curtail immigration, whether documented or undocumented (Carter, 2019). It is more usual that Black people stay above the political fray rather than put their electoral support behind such measures. In California, for example, African Americans comprised 10 percent of the voting coalition that passed Proposition 187 (Morris, 2000). This was essentially a measure pursued and supported by an overwhelmingly White population. Whether in California in the 1990s or the 2016 presidential election, Black people have demonstrated a disinterest in the electoral restriction of immigrants (Carter & King-Meadows, 2019).

This sense that immigrants are not to be targets of Black political agendas or policy efforts is separate from their feelings about immigrants, which are more ambivalent. On the one hand, Black people have generally left the immigration question off of their political agenda. For example, in the 6th Annual Black Women's Roundtable/ESSENCE Power of the Sister Vote poll (2020) only 2 percent of Black women cited immigration reform as a priority for them; in 2017 and 2018, only 3 percent of Black women cited immigration as a priority. They cited racism and a rise in hate crimes against Black people, criminal justice reform, and health care as their most important issues. Similarly, the 2020 American Election Eve Poll found that most Black voters support a pathway to citizenship, but do not consider immigration among their top issues. Of course, the pandemic played an outsized role in our 2020 election cycle, but this is not uncommon for Black voters. In the 2018 American Election Eve Poll, only 11 percent of Black respondents selected immigration reform/DACA[1] as their most important issue. While immigration has made an episodic appearance in conversations involving Black people—like we see now in current discussions of Black-on-Asian violence—immigration is not as salient an issue for Black people as it is for other communities.

Taking a longer view, if we look at Black behaviors from a historical perspective, this pattern holds. For example, the Immigration Act of 1924, also called the Johnson-Reed Act (1924), had its origins in the chauvinistic nationalism of the period (Carter & Pérez 2016). The Immigration Act introduced quotas to prevent the immigration of southern and eastern Europeans and excluded Asian immigration. These provisions remained in place until 1965, after civil rights organizers were successful in getting the Civil Rights Act (1964) and the Voting Rights Act (1965) passed. In 1924 when the immigration law was signed, the country was preoccupied with devising a eugenic immigration program that would prevent "lesser" immigrants from entering the country and damaging its standing as a "first-order nation" (Baynton, 2005). The law turned scientific racism into national policy and was sold as a way to control the slide of the country toward oblivion by disallowing those deemed to be morally, intellectually, culturally, and racially deficient from gaining entrance to America.

Parallel to contemporary conversations about "reverse racism," the real motivator for creating the Immigration Act of 1924 was a fear of anti-American, anti-White discrimination. Sen. David Reed (R-PA), one of the bill sponsors, argued that the quotas in 1921 were unfair to the American population because the quotas were based on Census data that overrepresented the foreign born. Reed and his colleagues argued the quotas needed revising because, by employing either the 1910 or 1920 Census, the immigration caps would favor those immigrants from southern and eastern Europe to the disadvantage of "native stocks" (Ngai, 2004; Trevor, 1924).[2] Consequently, quotas for northern Europeans would be lowered and this threatened to fundamentally alter the racial identity of America.

An unanticipated consequence of this moment was the recognition of Black people in the language of citizenship (Ngai, 1999). The chief architects of this law argued that Black people were being grandfathered as American citizens because of the Fourteenth Amendment (1868), but this was a "gratuitous gesture to the former slaves," not a real attempt at opening the borders to people of African descent or any other group that was not constructed as racially White (Ngai, 1999, p. 81). There were only 300 visas slotted for each of the African nations that were acknowledged by the Immigration Act of 1924 (i.e., Ethiopia, Liberia, and South Africa). Because South Africa was a settler colony, their 100 visas went to White South Africans, leaving only about 200 visas for Africans racialized as Black (Ngai,1999). By acknowledging Black people, and not their heritage in the formation of these quotas, the statute made it clear Black people literally did not count. While the Johnson-Reed Act held up Black people as evidence of American openness, Black people were not considered fully incorporated members of the body politic. If they were, in fact, considered as contributors to the nation it is estimated that "the African nations from which they originated would have received 9 percent of the total immigration quota, resulting in 13,000 fewer slots for Europeans" (Ngai, 1999, p. 72). As a result, Black people—who were rightly concerned about what immigration meant for their prospects at upward social mobility—were less sanguine about immigration restriction as being a useful tool to achieve their goals (Hellwig, 1981).

This was for two reasons. First, if America closed its borders to immigrants for the sake of protecting American interests, it was probably a safe way to wager that Black people and their interests were not being factored into this notion of American interests. The same nativism that excluded immigrants had its roots in the White supremacy that oppressed Black people. Therefore, pursuing Black equality on the backs of immigrants did not hold much promise for Black people (Hellwig, 1981). Secondly, if Black people supported immigration restrictions, they were, in essence, supporting arguments for their continued exclusion. As a people seeking self-determination, if they "opposed welcoming other minorities, they might strengthen doctrines used against themselves" (Hellwig, 1981, p. 111). Consequently, Black people were very reluctant to cast their lot with the racist, xenophobic rhetoric of the time.

W.E.B. Du Bois, one of the most noted Black intellectuals of his time, argued in *The Crisis*[3] that federal immigration policy was bigoted and with a preference for western and northern Europe.[4] For Du Bois, immigration policy was not about enriching the nation, but about creating a situation whereby Whiteness was the only metric for admission to the United States. Not only did this discriminate against those from non-European countries, it further solidified the identity of America as a White man's country. While America is "at times heartily ashamed even of the large number of "new" White people whom her democracy has admitted," Du Bois argues America is staunchly committed to barring Black sociopolitical incorporation (465). He states "against Negroes she can and does take her unflinching and immovable stand," and "trains her immigrants to this despising of 'niggers' from the day of their landing" (465). Du Bois was highlighting the many ways that anti-Black bias was used by newly arriving immigrants to approximate a White American identity. And while these newer groups of European immigrants were treated as provisional White people, their enforcement of the racial status quo was a way to become fully American (Jacboson, 2001).

These systemic, racist practices aimed at Black people that Du Bois articulates undercuts the idea that America was unified in its treatment of immigrants. Black people had made overtures to immigrant communities but found themselves abandoned by these same groups when they recognized there were more benefits to being in league with White supremacy rather than working with Blacks to combat this oppression (Ferreira, 1999). Nevertheless, Black people were never served by these racist immigration laws and they were certainly not voters by and large. Thus, they were never going to be beneficiaries of this type of legislation. What this legislation did do, however, demonstrate the many ways that Black citizens were not being served by the state. This did not mean that Black people would not or could not see some benefits from immigration restriction. One area where Black people were particularly concerned was in competition for employment (Gay, 2006; Posadas, 1982; Shihadeh & Barranco, 2010). This was not necessarily because of ill feelings toward immigrants, but because of sentiments about how those immigrants might be used to displace Black workers. While there is some evidence that this fear was not unfounded (Borjas, 2016; Posadas, 1982), immigration historically has not been at the top of Black political agendas and that remains true in the present. This is because the country's temperature on immigration often paralleled the country's efforts to stall Black progress. This is no less true in the present with respect to immigration.

WHAT'S HAPPENING NOW? CONTEMPORARY BLACK OPINIONS ON IMMIGRATION

The rise of Donald J. Trump in 2016 as the Republican presidential nominee, and eventual winner of the 2016 election, raised Black concerns given the hostile racial climate he created. Donald Trump tried to get Black people to support his campaign by using anti-immigration rhetoric, but this did not work for the vast majority of Black people (Carter & King-Meadows 2019). While Trump was successful in garnering some Black voters, and improving his vote share with Black men in 2020, his particular rhetoric was soundly rebuked by Black voters. From the Muslim ban to building the wall at the Mexican border to the separations of children from their parents with no clear plan for tracking and reuniting families, Donald Trump's attempts to use immigration as an inducement for Black voters were not persuasive. While these issues have received support from his base, these policies have been derided as xenophobic and racist. Historically, Black people have not been persuaded by these kinds of "us" against "them" tropes, Trump was operating from a discriminatory playbook that in language and deed has moved White voters, but has proven far less successful with Black voters.

Coalition and competition models have long been the dominant frames for understanding how Black people get along, or do not get along, with other racially and ethnically distinct communities (Bobo & Hutchings, 1996; McClain et al., 2006; Pastor & Marcelli, 2003). The competition model argues that when immigrants and native-born communities see themselves as vying for the same, albeit limited, opportunities—like job opportunities or political positions—they will view immigration more negatively (Citrin et al., 1997; Gay, 2006). This is particularly true for the most vulnerable native-born citizens who have the fewest skills and are in more direct struggle with undocumented persons for the slim opportunities that exist (Catanzarite, 2000; Waldinger, 1997). For native-born Black people, this sense of competition can be especially acute given their proximity to immigrants spatially and in terms of skill levels (Betancur, 2005; Shihadeh & Barranco, 2010).

In the area of employment, there is some evidence that the presence of newcomers depresses Black employment prospects (Borjas, 2016; Shihadeh & Barranco, 2010). This, of course, is only part of the story as immigrants are not hiring themselves. Powers (2005) shows that employer preferences for immigrant labor are racialized as justifications for why they prefer immigrant employees. Employers want to hire immigrants because they are deemed as easier to exploit because of their citizenship status, but use racial stereotypes about native-born Black workers as lazy and difficult to justify these hiring decisions. In short, the old language of immigrants "taking jobs" obscures the ways in which decisions are made that actively change the life circumstances of both the native-born and newcomers. Moreover, research suggests immigrants and native-born Black people and White people are not generally in the same job markets. Within the same industry, low-skilled Black and White employees are placed in different positions and have stopped doing the lowest-wage, lowest-skilled work where immigrants commonly find themselves (Betancur, 2005; Torres et al., 2006).

Cleavages over jobs are only one axis of competition. Racial group threat becomes activated as groups live in proximity to others. Gay (2006) demonstrates Black people are more likely to live closer to immigrants and, as such, view their position as more precarious in relation to immigrants and have more negative opinions of immigrants and immigration. Nteta (2013) also finds working-class Black people were most supportive of identification cards, creating an immigrant database, and decreasing the numbers of immigrants allowed into the county. These feelings of threat and insecurity cannot be separated from innumeracy. To the extent that a group *overestimates* the presence of "the other" there is a tendency to feel more threatened by that out-group (Key & Heard, 1984; Rocha & Espino, 2009). Generally speaking, individuals are not proficient at estimating the presence of others and this often leads to exaggerating the presence of "others," which can heighten feelings of insecurity (Brader et al., 2008).

Despite these findings, there is evidence that Black people are less hostile toward immigrants than their White counterparts (Cummings & Lambert, 1997; Thornton et al., 2012). Coalition theories posit that shared minority status will cause Blacks and other minoritized communities to see themselves as more alike than different and unify around their shared minority status. This collective remedy to the social problem of exclusion has been seen under certain circumstances. As a starting point, Thornton and Mizuno (1999) show that Black people view themselves as being more akin to immigrant groups (i.e., non-White people) than to fellow White citizens. Further, Black people are not generally in favor of immigrant restriction despite their belief they face the most competition from immigrants (Diamond, 1998). Likewise, Morris (2000) demonstrates that closeness to Asians and Latinos either reduced or had no effect on Black support for anti-immigrant ballot measures in the state of California. This suggests that there is far less hostility on the part of Blacks than popularly considered. Where the opinions of Black people and White people have been explicitly compared, Black people "are, in fact, consistently more permissive on immigration than White people," which suggests a need to consider group identity rather than individual self-interest (Brader et al., 2010,

p. 1). In sum, Black people and White people have not had the same experiences in America and there is no reason to believe their responses to immigration will be the same. While both Black and White people can all be considered Americans, each group's experiences with America have diverged greatly.

In considering the uniqueness of Black politics, it is important to bear in mind how important group identity is to individual group members. Indeed, Black people do not often get the opportunity to be seen as individuals; the racial group is central to how Black people are seen and how they see themselves. Dawson (1995) argues *linked fate*, or seeing one's future prospects as tied to the well-being of other in-group members, is a cognitive shortcut for deciding political matters. Using group well-being as a proxy for individual interest helps Black individuals make political decisions. Given the range of issue domains that Black people have to consider, it would stand to reason that those with high levels of linked fate (i.e., group identity) would apply that to the question of immigration as well. Hurwitz et al. (2015) find that Blacks and Latinos both see their fates as intertwined, as both groups face discrimination and disadvantage—which provides fodder for coalitional politics. This makes sense given that much of the language of immigration is rooted in racialized and racist notions of belonging (Carter & Pérez 2016; Devos & Banaji, 2005). So much so, the term "immigrant" is often thought to apply only to communities of color and has become hyper-identified with Latino-identified people.

McCabe et al. (2021) find that when people are asked about "undocumented" Latino immigrants *before* being asked about Latino immigration more generally, their attitudes are more negative. This confirms earlier work by Pérez (2010) that finds that "implicit attitudes toward Latino immigrants shape preferences for illegal and legal immigration polity net of other measures of intolerance" (536). In short, racial attitudes matter a great deal in how people think about immigration, and this is especially true of Latino immigrants who consistently draw more negative attitudes. And when their attitudes are compared, we find that Whites who demonstrate strong, chauvinistic national attachments are more likely to be more hostile to all immigrant groups, except for White immigrants (Carter & Pérez, 2016). This hostility is also exhibited in White people with strong racial identities. On the other hand, Black people who demonstrate strong national attachments are *less* hostile to all immigrants regardless of racial identity. In instances where Black people stake out a more exclusionary national identity, they are equally negative in their opinions of *all* groups, including African immigrants. And, unlike White people, an allegiant identity to their racial group does not influence Black peoples' attitudes about immigrants.

Consequently, it is difficult for Black people to tie their group consciousness with this racist rhetoric rooted in White supremacist notions of superiority. This is not because Black people are always altruistic so much as they do not want to align themselves with a worldview that subjugates their group (Carter, 2019; Carter & King-Meadows, 2019; Carter & Pérez, 2016). In short, the racial logic that leads people to treat those presumed to be immigrants with a level of suspicion because they are not "real Americans" is the same racial logic that suggests Black people are bracketed Americans and not entitled to the same protections under the law (Carter, 2019; Carter & Pérez, 2016; Kim, 1999).

This can be dangerous for native-born Black people *and* immigrant Black people (Morgan-Trostle et al., 2016). There is evidence to suggest that immigrant Black people are not generally seen as different from native-born Black people for longer than a generation (Waters, 2009). This means those Black immigrants who may enjoy preliminary benefits because they are seen as "better" than native-born Black people cannot transfer those benefits to their children. Similarly, because Black communities are surveilled to a greater degree than others, it is also the case that unauthorized immigrants are more likely to be adversely affected by aggressive policing and immigration enforcement regimes (Morgan-Trostle et al., 2016). Black people have more engagements with the police; the extent local authorities are allowed to function as quasi-immigration officials can have disastrous consequences on the health and safety of Black people, both immigrant and native-born (Armenta, 2016; Lawston & Escobar, 2009; Wallace, 2018). In this way, Black resistance to supporting immigration restrictions may be less about being in solidarity with immigrants and more about resisting being political bedfellows with potential bigots.

Discussion

Trump recycled many of the lessons Black people have learned over their centuries-long engagement with the American project. It was common for Black people to look at American stances on immigration as a proxy for where the country might stand with regard to their rights (Hellwig, 1981). In moments when the United States took a more restrictionist posture toward immigration, it was also avoiding affirmative action on domestic issues, like lynching, that were imperative for its Black citizens.[5] This is partly why immigration reform should be recognized as a significant part of civil rights reforms in the 1960s. When America closed its borders to "outsiders" they were also forestalling the rights of native-born Black people despite their status as citizens.

This sense of racial pessimism among Black people extends to other groups as well. One of the key ideas of this chapter is that Black people have not had the quintessential "American experience." Black people have had to fight for their citizenship, their right to vote, and simply their right to exist as part of this country. Black people recognize that their treatment in America is conditioned by their race. Therefore, they remain displeased with their treatment in this country but are also cognizant of what other communities, like immigrants, have had to endure. Therefore, Black people do not see immigrants and immigration as enemies to their progress.

Ambivalence has been the default position for Black people on the issue of immigration. While Black people recognize and support the idea of self-determination for immigrants, they also recognize their group's upward mobility has not been realized. Indeed, some may even believe that the presence of immigrants may diminish Black's life chances. What the research demonstrates is these fears do not automatically lead to a hardening of Black opinion on immigration (Carter, 2019). In general, Black people do not see immigration as an issue of chief importance. Although they have opinions about immigration, it is not an issue where they expend a lot of political capital. In short, I argue, Black people recognize the struggles of immigrant groups but are neither rushing to attack those groups nor are they going out of their way to help them. What seems most likely is Black people may feel some affinity for these other marginalized groups because of the discrimination they face, even if they do not mobilize around the issue of immigration. This suggests that Black public opinion on immigration is far less rigid than we may perceive and that Black politics is flexible enough to incorporate the struggles of other minoritized groups because they have similar, *not the same*, struggles. Where the issue of immigration is concerned, it has not inspired the majority of Black people to be either for or against this issue (Cohen, 1999; McClain et al., 2006; Thornton et al., 2013; Thornton & Mizuno,1999).

NOTES

1. Deferred Action for Childhood Arrivals (DACA) is a program that allows undocumented immigrants brought to the United States as children to defer deportation and the ability to work in the United States. Those who fit the DACA criteria are able to apply for naturalization. To learn more about DACA see the US Citizenship and Immigration Services page at https://www.uscis.gov/humanitarian/consideration-of-deferred-action-for-childhood-arrivals-daca.

2. According to Ngai (1999) "native stock" was a term used to refer to those descended from the White population of the United States from an earlier period. All those not considered White in 1790 could not properly be considered Americans. This definition excluded native Americans, Black people, Irish, Italians, Jewish people, and Asian people who were barred from becoming citizens. This understanding of what it meant to be a so-called American made eighteenth century whiteness a requirement to be considered an American. Using this understanding also meant Northern and

Western Europeans would receive the majority of slotted positions because they were considered prototypical Americans. In short, this act was an attempt to preserve a very particular definition of who was White.

3. *The Crisis* is the news magazine of the NAACP.

4. There was an Emergency Quota Act of 1921. This act is significant because it imposed the first limits on immigration and used quotas based on national origins to determine how this finite number of visas would be distributed. Because the Emergency Quota Act used 1910 census data, the immigration quotas favored southern and eastern Europeans. The Johnson-Reed Act was devised as an improvement over the Emergency Quota Act because it would be a permanent federal act and did not rely on census data that gave too much consideration to those who were not western European. It was believed that western Europeans were the true progenitors of American and they deserved top billing when it came to devising immigrant quotas.

5. Concurrent with attempts to revise immigration law the Dyer Bill (1922), a federal anti-lynching bill, passed in the House of Representatives and filibustered in the Senate despite enjoying significant senatorial support. Successive attempts to pass federal anti-lynching legislation failed throughout the 1950s. In 2020, the Emmitt Till Anti-Lynching Act that would specify lynching as a hate crime was passed in the United States House and is currently stalled in the Senate by Sen. Rand Paul (R-KY) who prevented the bill from being passed with unanimous consent.

REFERENCES

Armenta, A. (2016). Between public service and social control: Policing dilemmas in the era of immigration enforcement. *Social Problems*, *63*(1), 111–126.

Baynton, D. C. (2005). Defectives in the land: Disability and American immigration policy, 1882–1924. *Journal of American Ethnic History*, *24*(3), 31–44.

Beck, E. M. 2015. Judge Lynch denied: Combating mob violence in the American south, 1877–1950. *Southern Cultures*, *21*(2), 117–139.

Betancur, J. J. (2005). Framing the discussion of African American-Latino relations: a review and analysis. In A. Dzidzienyo & S. Oboler (Eds.), *Neither enemies nor friends: Latinos, Blacks, Afro-Latinos* (pp. 159–172). Palgrave Macmillan US.

Bobo, L., & Gilliam, F. D. (1990). Race, sociopolitical participation, and Black empowerment. *American Political Science Review*, *84*(2), 377–393. doi: 10.2307/1963525

Borjas, G.J. (October 2016). Yes, immigration hurts American workers. *POLITICO Magazine*. https://tinyurl.com/a8f45474.

Brader, T., Valentino, N. A., & Suhay, E. (2008). What triggers public opposition to immigration? Anxiety, group cues, and immigration threat. *American Journal of Political Science*, *52*(4), 959–978. doi: 10.1111/j.1540-5907.2008.00353.x

Carter, N. M. (2019). *American while black: African Americans, immigration, and the limits of citizenship*. Oxford University Press, Inc.

Carter, N. M., & King-Meadows, T. (2019) Perceptual knots and Black identity politics: Linked fate, American heritage, and support for Trump era immigration policy. *Societies* 9(1), 11–38. doi: 10.3390/soc9010011.

Carter, N. M., & Pérez, E.O. (2016) Race and nation: How racial hierarchy shapes national attachments: Race and nation. *Political Psychology, 37*(4), 497–513. doi: 10.1111/pops.12270.

Catanzarite, L. (2000). Brown-collar jobs: Occupational segregation and earnings of recent-immigrant Latinos. *Sociological Perspectives, 43*(1), 45–75. doi: 10.2307/1389782.

Citrin, J., Green, D. P., Muste, C., & Wong, C. (1997). Public opinion toward immigration reform: The role of economic motivations. *The Journal of Politics, 59*(3), 858–881.

Cohen, C.J. (1999). *The boundaries of blackness: AIDS and the breakdown of Black politics*. The University of Chicago Press.

Cummings, S., & Lambert, T. (1997). Anti-Hispanic and Anti-Asian sentiments among African Americans. *Social Science Quarterly, 78*(2), 338–353.

Dawson, M. C. (1995). *Behind the mule: Race and class in African-American politics* (1st pbk printing). Princeton University Press.

Diamond, J. (1998). African-American attitudes towards United States immigration policy. *International Migration Review, 32*(2), 451–470.

DuBois, W. (1920). *Darkwater: Voices from within the veil*. Harcourt Brace and Company.

Ferreira, P. (1999). All but "a black skin and wooly hair": Frederick Douglass's witness of the Irish famine. *American Studies International, 37*(2), 69–83.

Fox, J. A., Gerdes, M., Duwe, G., & Rocque, M. (2020). The Newsworthiness of Mass Public Shootings: What Factors Impact the Extent of Coverage? *Homicide Studies*, 25(3), 239–255. 108876792097441. doi: 10.1177/1088767920974412.

Gay, C. (2006). Seeing difference: The effect of economic disparity on Black attitudes toward Latinos. *American Journal of Political Science, 50*(4), 982–997. doi: 10.1111/j.1540-5907.2006.00228.x.

Giroux, H. A. (2017). White nationalism, armed culture and state violence in the age of Donald Trump. *Philosophy & Social Criticism, 43*(9), 887–910.

Hellwig, D. J. (1981). Black leaders and United States immigration policy, 1917–1929. *The Journal of Negro History, 66*(2), 110–127. doi: 10.2307/2717281.

Hero, R. E., & Tolbert, C. J. (1996). A racial/ethnic diversity interpretation of politics and policy in the states of the U.S. *American Journal of Political Science, 40*(3), 851–871. doi: 10.2307/2111798.

HoSang, D. (2010). *Racial propositions: Ballot Initiatives and the making of postwar California*. University of California Press.

Huntington, S. P. (2004). *Who are we?: The challenges to America's national identity*. Simon & Schuster.

Hurwitz, J., Peffley, M., & Mondak, J. (2015). Linked fate and outgroup perceptions: Blacks, latinos, and the U.S. Criminal Justice System. *Political Research Quarterly, 68*(3), 505–520.

Jacobson, M. F. (2001). *Whiteness of a different color European immigrants and the alchemy of race*. Harvard University Press.

Johnson, K. R. (2011). Sweet home Alabama: Immigration and civil rights in the New South. *Stanford Law Review Online, 64*, 22–28.

Key, V. O., and Alexander Heard. 1984. *Southern politics in state and nation*. New ed. Knoxville: University of Tennessee Press.

Kim, C. J. (1999). The racial triangulation of Asian Americans. *Politics & Society, 27*(1), 105–138. doi: 10.1177/0032329299027001005.

Lawston, J. M., & Escobar, M. (2009). Policing, detention, deportation, and resistance: Situating immigrant justice and carcerality in the 21st century. *Social Justice, 36*(2), 1–6.

McCabe, K. T., Matos, Y., & Walker, H. (2021). Priming legality: Perceptions of Latino and undocumented Latino immigrants. *American Politics Research, 49*(1), 106–113.

McClain, P. D., Carter, N. M., DeFrancesco-Soto, V. M., Lyle, M. L., Grynaviski, J. D., Nunnally, S. C., Scotto, T. J., Kendrick, J. A., Lackey, G. F., & Cotton, K. D. (2006). Racial distancing in a southern city: Latino immigrants' views of Black Americans. *The Journal of Politics, 68*(3), 571–584. doi: 10.1111/j.1468-2508.2006.00446.x.

McKanders, K. M. (2007). Welcome to Hazelton-Illegal immigrants beware: Local immigration ordinances and what the federal government must do about it. *Loyola University of Chicago Law Journal, 39*, 1–49.

McWhirter, C. (2012). *Red summer: The summer of 1919 and the awakening of Black America*. St. Martin's Press.

Messer, C. M. (2011). The Tulsa race riot of 1921: Toward an integrative theory of collective violence. *Journal of Social History, 44*(4), 1217–1232.

Montoya, C. M., Bejarano, C., Brown, N. E., & Gershon, S.A. (2021). "The intersectional dynamics of descriptive representation." *Politics & Gender*, FirstView, 1–30. doi: 10.1017/S1743923X20000744.

Morgan-Trostle, J., K. Zheng, A. Das, and C. Lipscombe. 2016. *The State of Black Immigrants 2016*. New York: New York University School of Law and Black Alliance for Just Immigration.

Morris, I. L. (2000). African American voting on proposition 187: Rethinking the prevalence of interminority conflict. *Political Research Quarterly, 53*(1), 77. doi: 10.2307/449247.

Ngai, M. M. (1999). The Architecture of Race in American Immigration Law: A Reexamination of the Immigration Act of 1924. *The Journal of American History, 86*(1), 67. doi: 10.2307/2567407.

Ngai, M. M. (2005). *Impossible subjects: Illegal aliens and the making of modern America*. Princeton University Press.

Nobles, M. (2000). *Shades of citizenship: Race and the census in modern politics*. Stanford University Press.

Nteta, T. (2013). United we stand? African Americans, self-interest, and immigration reform. *American Politics Research, 41*(1), 147–172. doi: 10.1177/1532673X12452909.

Pantoja, A. (2006). Against the tide? Core American values and attitudes toward US immigration policy in the mid-1990s. *Journal of Ethnic and Migration Studies, 32*(3), 515–531. doi: 10.1080/13691830600555111.

Pastor, M., & Marcelli, E. (2003). Somewhere over the rainbow?: African Americans, unauthorized Mexican immigration, and coalition building. *The Review of Black Political Economy, 31*(1–2), 125–155.

Pérez, E. O. (2010). Explicit evidence on the import of implicit attitudes: The IAT and immigration policy judgments. *Political Behavior, 32*(4), 517–545.

Posadas, B. M. (1982). The hierarchy of color and psychological adjustment in an industrial environment: Filipinos, the Pullman company, and the brotherhood of sleeping car porters. *Labor History, 23*(3), 349–373.

Powers, R. S. (2005). Working it out in North Carolina: Employers and Hispanic/Latino immigrants. *Sociation Today, 3*(2), 1–23.

Rocha, R. R., & Espino, R. (2009). Racial threat, residential segregation, and the policy attitudes of Anglos. *Political Research Quarterly, 62*(2), 415–426.

Seguin, C., & Rigby, D. (2019). National crimes: A new national data set of lynchings in the United States, 1883 to 1941. *Socius, 5*, 1–9. doi: 10.1177/2378023119841780.

Short, R., & Magaña, L. (2002). Political rhetoric, immigration attitudes, and contemporary prejudice: A Mexican American dilemma. *The Journal of social psychology, 142*(6), 701–712.

Shihadeh, E. S., & Barranco, R.E. (2010). Latino employment and Black violence: The unintended consequence of U.S. immigration policy. *Social Forces, 88*(3), 1393–1420. doi: 10.1353/sof.0.0286.

Sonenshein, R. J. (1993). *Politics in black and white: Race and power in Los Angeles.* Princeton University Press.

Song, M. (2004). Introduction: Who's at the bottom? Examining claims about racial hierarchy. *Ethnic and Racial Studies, 27*(6), 859–877.

Thornton, M. C., & Mizuno, Y. (1999). Economic well-being and Black adult feelings toward Immigrants and Whites, 1984. *Journal of Black Studies, 30*(1), 15–44.

Thornton, M. C., Taylor, R. J., & Chatters, L. M. (2013). African American and Black Caribbean mutual feelings of closeness: Findings from a national probability survey. *Journal of Black Studies, 44*(8), 798–828.

Torres, R. M., Popke, E. J., & Hapke, H. M. (2006). The South's silent bargain: Rural restructuring, Latino labor and the ambiguities of migrant experience. In H. A. Smith & O. J. Furuseth (Eds.), (pp. 37–67). *Latinos in the New South: Transformations of place.* Burlington, VT: Ashgate.

Trevor, J. B. (1924). An Analysis of the American Immigration Act of 1924. *International Conciliation, 10*, 370–443.

Waldinger, R. (1996). From Ellis Island to LAX: Immigrant prospects in the American city. *International Migration Review, 30*(4), 1078–1086.

Wallace, D. (2018). Safe routes to school? Black Caribbean youth negotiating police surveillance in London and New York City. *Harvard Educational Review, 88*(3), 261–286.

Waters, M. C. (2009). Social science and ethnic options. *Ethnicities, 9*(1), 130–135.

Chapter 8

Legacy of Good Trouble

The Next Frontier for Voting Rights

Candice C. Robinson, LaTeri McFadden, and J. Nicole Johnson

In a *New York Times* opinion article published after his death on July 30, 2020, Civil Rights Pioneer John Lewis told the public: "Voting and participating in the democratic process are key. The vote is the most powerful nonviolent change agent you have in a democratic society" (Lewis, 2020). The United States saw the power of the vote as a nonviolent change agent with the election of President Joseph R. Biden over the incumbent in the November 2020 presidential election, the first national election following Lewis's death. The months after the election saw increased discussions on the fragility of democracy and a need for voting reform in the United States.

Despite being an American civil right, voting continues to be a battlefield for state's rights and between political parties, often in an attempt to mask the underlying racialized issues. In January 2021, Congress updated the previously titled John Lewis Voting Rights Act of 2020 (H.Con.Res.107)[1] to the For the People Act of 2021. After John Lewis's death, Congress renamed the original act the "Voting Rights Advancement Act of 2019" as a tribute to his dedication to challenging voting inequalities in the name of "good trouble." Key components of the act protect voters by amending the Voting Rights Act of 1965. It aims to make it easier to vote in federal elections, end congressional gerrymandering, and strengthen campaign rules for implementation in the November 2022 general election—all issues that impact the voting power of communities of color. Representative John P. Sarbanes introduced it into the House on January 4, 2021 (H.R.1)[2] and it passed on March 3, 2021. After passing the House, Senator Jeff Merkley introduced the bill to the Senate (S.1)[3] on March 17, 2021.

The S.1 version of the For the People Act of 2021 was delayed due to the lack of support from Republican senators and Democratic Senator Joe Manchin. Senator Manchin stated that he did not support a voting reform bill that is not bipartisan and restricts states' rights (DeBonis, 2021; Manchin, 2021). It was then edited and reintroduced to the Senate (S.2093)[4] after Senator Manchin proposed a compromised version of the bill. In June 2021, the S.2093 version of the For the People Act of 2021 failed due to the lack of support from Republican senators. Essentially, party lines hindered reform that provides access to voting equality.

Meanwhile, Republican-led states and politicians push for more restrictive voting reform based on unfounded claims of voter fraud in the November 2020 election. From January to May 2021, 14 state legislatures approved 22 new laws to restrict voting, including everything from registration to casting a ballot (Boschma, 2021; Viebeck, 2021). Only two states with these new laws, Kentucky and Kansas, have split party control: Republican-led legislatures and Democratic Governors. The federal government's voting laws expand voters' rights, but these newly established voting laws restrict voting. These laws (a) shorten the window to apply for and deliver a mail-in ballot, (b) reduce early voting opportunities, (c) limit absentee voting lists, (d) tighten and impose voter identification requirements, (e) ban volunteers from passing out snacks and water to voters in line, and (f) reduce polling locations and hours to name a few. Notably, these laws target voters of color who disproportionately lack identification, experience longer lines than White voters, and have fewer polling locations (American Civil Liberties Union [ACLU], 2017; Morris, 2021). Politicians, including Texas State Senator Bryan Hughes and Georgia Governor Brian P. Kemp, argue that their laws provide more voting integrity. They believe that the states should determine their own voting rules (Blount, 2021; Corasaniti, 2021). Thus, recent voting reform is an issue masked as states' rights. In opposition, the Brennan Center for Justice, an independent, nonpartisan law and policy organization, and other critics argue that these laws are some of the most restrictive since the Jim Crow era (Weiser et al., 2021). Remembering that the similar Jim Crow Laws disproportionately targeted Black Americans, the history of race in America compounds voting reform.

In this chapter, we unpack the various parts of voting reform, giving attention to current racial inequities in voter registration, voting, the strength of citizen's votes, and recent legislation. First, we provide a brief history of the disparities in the vote, including the history of Jim Crow voting laws. Next, we discuss the twenty-first century assault on voting rights, including (a) blocking voter registrations through felony disenfranchisement and roll purging; (b) adding barriers to voting with limits on absentee and early voting, voting locations, and requirements of identification; and (c) impacting the strength of votes through gerrymandering and the electoral college. We also include a brief discussion of the fight against suppression. Finally, we call for individuals and organizations to apply pressure to the government to protect citizen's right to vote as a way of ensuring that individual solutions to voter suppression—such as increased voter drives and getting people to the polls—are accompanied by state and national government policy changes.

HISTORY OF RACIAL DISPARITIES IN VOTING

The right to choose our representation and make decisions through voting is a cornerstone of American democracy and arguably the most consistent public marker of civic engagement (Tocqueville, 1835; Putnam, 1999; Robinson, 2019; Skocpol & Fiorina, 2004). The US Constitution ratification in 1789 solidified voting as an essential part of democracy but did not federally mandate it. States, then and now, determine the requirements for voting within their borders. Soon after the constitution's ratification, early state legislatures restricted voting to property-owning and tax-paying White men. Several states explicitly excluded or discouraged non-enslaved Black Americans from voting (Klinghoffer & Elkis, 1992). Until the mid-19th century, the US system of democracy predicated on exclusion rather than inclusion.

The nineteenth century introduced the Thirteenth (1865), Fourteenth (1868), and Fifteenth (1870) Amendments to the US Constitution, which outlined the rights of persons and citizens within the United States. The Thirteenth Amendment[5] abolished slavery. The Fourteenth Amendment[6] granted citizenship to formerly enslaved persons, to all persons born within the United States, and, therefore, all citizens' rights. Finally, the Fifteenth Amendment[7] granted the right to vote regardless of race or former enslavement, removing the ability for states to discriminate against citizens based on their race when voting. The Nineteenth Amendment[8] removed voting discrimination based on sex fifty years following the Fifteenth Amendment. Despite the 1920 passage of the women's vote, states continued to disenfranchise Black women.

Following the Civil War, Black Americans were actively represented in Congress. In 1870, Senator Hiram Revels of Mississippi and Representative Joseph Rainey of South Carolina became the first Black American to serve in the US Congress. However, White supremacist backlash overshadowed the success of the Thirteenth, Fourteenth, and Fifteenth amendments. In conjunction with the increase of Black Americans in the US Congress came the onset of Jim Crow Laws, such as literacy tests and fees, that specifically disenfranchised generations of Black voters (Barker et al., 1999). States actively created barriers to voting based explicitly on race. Former Confederate states, including Alabama, Arkansas, Georgia, Louisiana, Mississippi, North

Carolina, South Carolina, Tennessee, Texas, and Virginia, overwhelmingly instated poll taxes and reading requirements for voter registration. These requirements disproportionately impacted Black Americans due to their higher rates of impoverishment and illiteracy at the time. In the Northern States, disenfranchisement often appeared as gerrymandering, the act of politicians deliberately redrawing legislative district lines to benefit one party over others (Martis, 2008; McGhee, 2020).

Representative George Henry White of North Carolina was the last Black American to serve in Congress during this era, ultimately leaving office in 1901. As he left Congress, he presented a speech titled *Defense of the Negro Race-Charges Answered*, where he expressed several concerns regarding education, jobs, and voting. At the time, there was no formal collection of voting rates for Black Americans; however, White (1901) notes:

> It is an undisputed fact that the negro vote in the State of Alabama, as well as most of the other Southern States, have been effectively suppressed, either one way or the other—in some instances by constitutional amendment and state legislation, in others by cold-blooded fraud and intimidation, but whatever the method pursued, it is not denied, but frankly admitted in the speeches in this House, that the black vote has been eliminated to a large extent.

As the United States enacted equitable reform in the mid-nineteenth century, they were met with repression by the end of the century, impacting voting rates and diverse and equal representation for decades. Black Americans were not represented in the US Congress again until Representative Oscar De Priest of Illinois joined Congress in 1929.

The Voting Rights Act

It was during the beginning of the 20th century, with the rise of voter disenfranchisement, that historically Black fraternities and sororities and civil rights organizations—including the National Council of Negro Women, National Urban League (NUL), National Association for the Advancement of Colored People (NAACP) Southern Christian Leadership Conference (SCLC), Student Nonviolent Coordinating Committee (SNCC), Brotherhood of Sleeping Car Porters, and the Congress of Racial Equality (CORE)—actively incorporated voting as one of the critical components of their fight for equality through the law (Hall, 2005; Parks, 2008; Parks & Hughey, 2020). The early 20th-century work of Black Americans and civil rights mobilizations paved the way for the 1950s and 1960s. The Civil Rights Movement brought in legislative changes that led to equal protections for all Americans under the law. The Voting Rights Act originated in part with the Civil Rights

Act of 1964, which outlawed discrimination based on race, color, religion, sex, and national origin. Expressly, it prohibited unequal voter registration requirements. However, it did not ensure that states and local municipalities enforced the Civil Rights Act.

Following March 7, 1965, known as "Bloody Sunday," US federal legislators finally prioritized protecting the vote. On this date, the Dallas County Voters League, SCLC, and SNCC—led by Martin Luther King Jr. and John Lewis—organized a march from Selma, Alabama, to Montgomery, Alabama. Police attacked organizers and marchers who crossed the Edmund Pettus Bridge. John Lewis notoriously suffered a skull fracture on this day that resulted in a scar on his head for the rest of his life. As a result of this use of force, Lyndon B. Johnson introduced the Voting Rights Act to a joint session of the US Congress on March 15, 1965. Supporters hoped the Voting Rights Act enforced equal access to voting and protected Black voters.

The Voting Rights Act of 1965 was passed with overwhelming support in Congress (Senate 79–18; House of Representatives 328–74) and was signed on August 6, 1965, by President Lyndon B. Johnson.[9] This legislation applied a nationwide ban against literacy tests and allowed the federal government to oversee any jurisdiction (state or county) that practiced voter disenfranchisement (Department of Justice, 2017). The federal government determined that states practiced voter disenfranchisement if (a) they used tests restricting the vote, (b) less than 50 percent of the voting-age population was registered to vote on November 1, 1964, or (c) less than 50 percent of voters voted in the 1964 presidential election (Department of Justice, 2020b). Furthermore, the jurisdictions in violation of the Voting Rights Act could not make any changes related to voting without the Attorney General or US District Court for the District of Columbia ensuring the change was not discriminatory (Department of Justice, 2017). Ultimately, the US government took over "covered jurisdictions" in the entire states of Alaska, Georgia, Louisiana, Mississippi, South Carolina, and Virginia and counties in Arizona, Hawaii, Idaho, and North Carolina (Department of Justice, 2020b). Analysts herald the Voting Rights Act of 1965 and its enforcement provisions as a success of equality in American democracy and civic engagement. As part of a swath of Civil Rights Legislation throughout the 1960s, the Voting Rights Act provided legislative protections against racial and ethnic discrimination in access to voter registration and voting.

The legislative protections provided by the Voting Rights Act led to increased participation in voter registration and voting for people of color. From 1966 to 1968, Black American voter registration increased from 60.2 percent to 66.2 percent (US Census Bureau, 2021). The NAACP estimates that voting participation doubled following the Voting Rights Act despite the lack of formal census data for voting by race before 1964. In 1968, Black

Americans voted at their highest rate of 57.6 percent. This voting rate was followed by a decrease in voter participation until voting once again reached a high of 60.8 percent in 2008.

While the Civil Rights Act of 1964 and Voting Rights Act of 1965 are some of the most influential laws of the 21st century, they did not fulfill their promise of full protections for access to voter registration and voting nor did they lead to more equity. With continued problems of voting equity, Presidents Richard Nixon, Gerald Ford, Ronald Reagan, Bill Clinton, and George W. Bush all amended and extended the Voting Rights Act in 1970, 1975, 1982, 1992, and 2006, respectively (Department of Justice, 2017, 2020a). These amendments included additional opportunities to register to vote for citizens through their state's motor vehicle agency, public assistance offices, mail-in voting, and bilingual options (Laney, 2008). The current amended Voting Rights Act signed in 2006 affords protections until 2032. Unfortunately, there are long-standing unintended consequences that exacerbate the racial inequities in voting despite the Voting Rights Act and the amendments' aim for equity. The decline in voter registration and voter turnout for Black Americans in subsequent decades following the Voting Rights Act shows the dark side of this reform. Below we further discuss the impact of voting rights and fallout in the twenty-first century.

VOTER SUPPRESSION IN THE 21ST CENTURY

The voter suppression of the twenty-first century coincides with the impacts of four historic presidential elections (2000, 2008, 2016, 2020)—each for different reasons—that were impacted by people of color's access to and inclusion in voting. The 2000 and 2016 elections brought to the forefront the importance of paying attention to the electoral college. The 2008 elections proved the impact of the Black and person of color vote. In 2008, Black Americans registered and voted for Obama in unprecedented numbers—65.5 percentwere registered to vote and 60.8 percent voted (US Census Bureau).

Voter suppression tactics appeared more aggressively following President Barack Obama's historic wins. The US Supreme Court struck down previous provisions of the Voting Rights Act of 1965 in *Shelby County v. Holder* in a 5–4 Court Decision. This 2013 decision eliminated conditions that required states to obtain preclearance from the US government before making changes to their voting laws or practices. It inadvertently allowed states to create stricter voter laws. The lack of voter protections and stricter voter laws disproportionately impacted communities of color, leading to lower turnout for voters of color. The effects of voter suppression were seen in the 2016 election of Donald Trump as the 45th president of the United States, an individual who was prejudiced during his campaign. Suppression then appeared again on the state level in the 2018 Georgia Governor Election. Democratic Candidate Stacey Abrams, a Black woman, lost to the Republican candidate, Brian Kemp, Georgia Secretary of State at the time. The conclusions of the 2016 presidential election, 2018 midterm congressional elections, and 2018 Georgia Gubernatorial Election in favor of Republican candidates resulted from weakening protections for voters of color.

In the face of these twenty-first century elections, below, we discuss further the themes related to voter suppression and access that the Voting Rights Act failed to protect. Given these elections and their results, scholars have observed voter disenfranchisement and suppression through three broad areas: limiting voter registrations through disenfranchisement of felons and purging of rolls; adding barriers to casting a ballot through limits on absentee and early voting, voting locations, and identification requirements; and diluting the strength of predominantly people of color voting blocs through gerrymandering and the electoral college (Ansolabehere & Hersh, 2014; Highton, 2017; Brater et al., 2018; Darrah-Okike et al., 2020; Biggers & Smith, 2020). Given these areas, many contemporary voting laws discriminate against people of color in a way that is like the Jim Crow Laws of the early twentieth century.

Limiting Voters and Voter Registration

Limiting voters and voter registration can appear in two ways that disproportionately impact communities of color's initial access to voting. The purging of the rolls is the first significant route of voter suppression related to the voter registration of Black Americans. Purging refers to state or local officials maintaining their records with routine removal of registrants who are ineligible to vote. Officials can remove people if (a) their name appears multiple times, (b) there is a change of address, (c) they are deceased, (d) they fail to vote over a specified time, (e) they are deemed mentally incapacitated, (f) or they are convicted of a disenfranchising crime (Ansolabehere & Hersh, 2014). There is no regulation of when and how purging occurs. Individuals are not notified of their status if the system or official purges them; the onus is on them to continue to confirm their registration.

People of color, specifically Black people, are more likely to be removed, even when they do not meet the above parameters (Darrah-Okike et al., 2020; Biggers & Smith, 2020; Brater et al., 2018). This issue is challenging because 29 states have voter registration deadlines before election day (NCSL, 2020a); therefore, if a citizen does not confirm their registration status, is purged, and misses the registration deadline, they are unable to vote on election day.

The second limitation of voters and voter registration is through disenfranchisement of formerly incarcerated individuals. Many states exclude current and formerly incarcerated individuals. Eleven states have permanent disenfranchisement for at least some criminal convictions unless the government approves restoration. An additional 16 states restore voting rights upon completion of a sentence, including parole and probation. Connecticut and Louisiana allow formerly incarcerated individuals to regain voting rights after prison and discharge from parole, allowing those on probation to vote. Only 19 states automatically restore voting rights after release from prison. As of March 2021, Maine, Vermont, and Washington, DC, are the only places with no disenfranchisement for people with criminal convictions (Brennan Center for Justice, 2021). These laws trace back to the amendments immediately following the Civil War.

The Thirteenth, Fourteenth, and Fifteenth amendments had historical impacts on citizenship in the United States; however, the Thirteenth Amendment in particular blocks part of American citizens' full protections. The Thirteenth Amendment left the distinctive phrase that there is "neither slavery nor involuntary servitude, except as a punishment for crime." This language has recently received attention (Blackmon, 2009; Kelly, 2017) given that it allows states to revoke citizens' rights and freedoms as a punishment for a crime. Immediately, this clause impacted Black voters.

Before he was appointed Treasury Secretary, Carter Glass stated in 1902 that the plan of criminal disenfranchisement laws would "eliminate the darkey as a political factor in [Virginia] in less than five years" (Brennan Center, 2018). Glass and other Southern strategists used these laws to disenfranchise Black voters intentionally. Thus, the rise in early disenfranchisement laws correlated with the rise of Black Americans in the criminal justice system (Uggen et al., 2012; Kelly, 2017). Considering the disproportionate numbers of Black Americans in the criminal justice system and with felony convictions—approximately 8 percent of all adults and 23 percent of African American adults—1 out of 13 Black Americans is excluded from voting. In fact, felony disenfranchisement is the first-way voter registration is limited (Shannon et al., 2017: 1814; Brennan Center for Justice, 2018). The Voting Rights Act of 1965 argued for more protections for Black voters, but it did not account for this form of disenfranchisement. Blocking voters through voter registration is just the first step in the obstacles Black Americans encounter to participate in the political process. If citizens can get past steps to voter registration, they often face barriers to casting a ballot.

Barriers to Casting a Ballot

In addition to access to actual voter registration, there are other barriers to casting a ballot on election days. These barriers first appear through limits on absentee and early voting. There has been little consideration of Americans who are not available to vote on election day. The United States first introduced absentee ballots as a solution for unavailable voters during the Civil War. They created the absentee option as a way for military voters to cast ballots despite being away from their homes. In 1986, federal law required states to send absentee ballots to military and overseas voters for federal elections (NCSL, 2020b). Now, 34 states and Washington, DC, offer a "no excuse" absentee and mail ballot voting. Sixteen states still require that individuals provide an excuse to be approved for absentee voting. Arkansas only approves absentee ballot excuses for citizens out of their county on election day and for illness or disability. The other 15 states allow absentee ballots for reasons that include out of the county on election day, illness or disability, and one or more of the following as a valid reason: individuals over a certain age (60+ or 65+), work shift during voting hours, student living out of the county, election work, religious belief, Address Confidentiality Program participant, incarcerated but still qualified to vote, and jury duty.

Beyond restricting absentee mail-in ballots, barriers to early voting are ongoing. For example, six states do not offer Pre-Election Day in-person voting options: Connecticut, Kentucky, Mississippi, Missouri, New Hampshire, and South Carolina (National Center for State Legislatures, 2020). Restrictions to absentee/mail-in ballots and early voting are particularly impactful to people who have jobs or other responsibilities that make it difficult to vote in person on the day of an election. This is particularly impactful for people of color.

An additional limitation to casting a ballot is the moving of voting locations. Voting locations typically are in an area that is accessible for a citizen's particular district. Some districts move voting locations with short notice, particularly in areas serving people of color and those living in poverty. This practice is often cumbersome, making it difficult to locate the necessary information to plan (McInerney, 2020). Indeed, when officials move polling locations, there is a drop in voter turnout (Brady and McNulty, 2011; Cantoni, 2020; Joslyn et al. 2020). If citizens can arrive at their necessary location, they may still encounter roadblocks to voting.

Lastly, voter identification laws are a barrier to casting a vote. As early as 2006, Indiana and Georgia were the first states to enforce voter identification laws (Highton, 2017). These laws require voters to have some form of identification to cast a vote. Now, 36 states have required some form of identification to cast a ballot that is categorized as "strict" or "non-strict" laws and photo ID or non-photo ID laws (NCSL, 2021). Seven states have "strict" photo ID laws; 3 states have "strict" non-photo ID laws; 11 states have "non-strict" photo ID laws; and 15 states have "non-strict" non-photo ID laws. Suppose a voter in a state with "strict" laws does not have valid identification. In that case, they will need to vote on a provisional ballot and take additional steps to ensure that their votes are counted. In a state with "non-strict" laws, voters without valid identification can cast a ballot that will be calculated without additional steps for the voter.

Acceptable forms of identification can vary between states but often include any valid state or federal government-issued photo ID, such as a driver's license, US passport, US military photo ID, or tribal photo ID. In Arkansas, Kansas, and Tennessee—strict photo ID states—and the non-strict photo ID state of Texas, officials will accept a concealed carry, handgun, or weapon license/permit. Of these states, only Kansas will accept a student ID (Arkansas Secretary of State, 2021; Kansas Secretary of State, 2021; NCSL, 2021; Tennessee Secretary of State, 2021; Texas Secretary of State, 2021)

Despite several politicians suggesting there is support for voter identification laws, ACLU, the Brennan Center for Justice, NCLS, and other civil rights organizations oppose these laws. One reason they oppose these laws is due to the accessibility and costs related to obtaining documents. As many as 11 percent of US citizens do not have government-issued photo identification. A second reason is that voter identification laws "skew democracy in favor of whites and those on the political right" (Hajnal et al., 2017: 366). Additionally, Republican-led states are more likely to enact these laws. The third reason for opposition to voter identification laws is because they disproportionately impact people of color given that this population disproportionately lacks the accepted form of identification. For instance, 25 percent of Black American citizens do not have a government-issued photo ID compared to only 8 percent of White Americans (Gaskin & Iyer, 2017). Lastly, states enact these laws when the size of Black and Latino population increases based on historical trend data (Biggers & Hanmer, 2017). This negatively impacts racial and ethnic minorities' participation in elections. The data clearly indicate that voter identification laws, as a reform measure, do not improve voter integrity, but negatively and disproportionately impact communities of color (Hajnal et al., 2017: 366).

As described in this section, narrowed absentee and early voting options and voter identification laws each negatively impact voters of color. If a person of color can overcome the individual barriers of voter registration and casting a ballot to vote, structural barriers may still impact them. Specifically, the electoral college, redistricting, and gerrymandering all threaten the strength of their votes.

Impacting the Strength of Voting

Voting blocs are equally essential to understanding the limitations of voter protections for communities of color. The first impact on voting strength happens through the electoral college. Under the electoral college system, each state receives electoral votes based on their senators and number of representatives in Congress. Unfortunately, the electoral college does not equal one vote for each person (Brennan Center for Justice, 2018). In 2000, Republican candidate Texas Governor George W. Bush ran against Democratic candidate, Former Vice President Al Gore. In 2000, the country was faced with the most widely contested election since the 1876 election of Rutherford B. Hayes. Specifically, not only was there a discrepancy between the popular vote and the electoral college, but the outcome of the election was ultimately not decided by voters. The US Supreme Court at the time reversed the Florida State Supreme Court's request for a selective manual recount, which awarded the 25 electoral votes to Bush, deeming him the winner. This electoral college problem appeared again in the 2016 presidential election. Hilary Clinton, the first woman presidential candidate, received the most votes; however, Donald Trump received the most electoral votes. Hillary Clinton won 48 percent of the popular vote with 65,853,625 ballots cast but received 232 electoral votes. Donald Trump won 45.9 percent of the vote with 62,985,106 votes; however, he received 306 electoral votes, which resulted in his win (*New York Times*, 2017). Ultimately, the electoral college becomes one of the forms of repression by following the decisions of "states" rather than most citizens.

Other suppression tactics impacting voter strength include redistricting and gerrymandering. Redistricting of congressional seats occurs every ten years based on population changes identified by the census. In 2021, there were 13 states with changes in their population and, therefore, changes in the number of congressional seats. Texas gained two seats; North Carolina, Florida, Colorado, Oregon, and Montana gained one seat; California, New York, Pennsylvania, Illinois, Ohio, Michigan, and West Virginia each lost one seat (Wadington & Santucci, 2021; Cai & Epstein, 2021; US Census Bureau, 2021). To account for the increase or decrease in population, states will need to redraw district lines so that all citizens can be accurately represented (redistricting). Redistricting in Republican-led states could exasperate voter disenfranchisement because it often coincides with gerrymandering. Gerrymandering is the act of manipulating the boundaries of a region to favor one political party (Martis, 2008; McGhee, 2020). As Republican-led states redraw their boundaries in favor of themselves, they can ensure that they will have little to no pushback to enacting laws restricting voting. Currently, communities of color can only combat these problems if they vote in large numbers. Given the above voter suppression tactics, which disproportionately impact people of color, there needs to be voter reform. Fortunately, there is hope through individual and organizational efforts to fight continued suppression.

FIGHTS AGAINST VOTER SUPPRESSION IN THE 21ST CENTURY

John Lewis's (2020) statement in the *New York Times* encouraged individuals to get involved in making a change, as Americans have done throughout its history: "Ordinary people with extraordinary vision can redeem the soul of America by getting in what I call good trouble, necessary trouble." Citizens and organizations have several approaches to fight for access to voting in the twenty-first century. The first set focuses on the individual responsibility to vote. ACLU, Black Voters Matter, Fair Fight, NUL, and other civil rights organizations assist individuals by driving voter awareness. These organizations have hosted events, trainings, webinars, and hashtags (#reclaimourvote; #enoughisenoughvote) to spread individual voter awareness. These efforts have encouraged citizens to register to vote, check their voter registration status, register friends and family, sign up as poll workers, and utilize early and mail-in voting options. Black Voters Matter has fought over the last decade to remove voting inequalities and rose to prominence during the 2017 Alabama United States Senate Race. In 2018, Stacey Abrams highlighted the importance of voting rights and the problem of purging rolls through her organization Fair Fight.

National Voter Registration Day, a nonpartisan holiday, was first celebrated in 2012 and emphasizes voter awareness; it continues to be recognized annually on the fourth Tuesday in September. The holiday aims to highlight the importance of voting to those who would not vote otherwise. Additionally, it seeks to ensure that people do not miss the opportunity to register to vote by advertising registration deadlines, therefore, increasing access to voting (National Voter Registration Day, 2020). National Voter Registration Day reinforces the importance of making a plan to vote, something that places responsibility on individual voters.

During the 2020 election, concerns about the potential spread of COVID-19 led the above organizations to increase awareness about the alternative ways to vote. They highlighted absentee and early voting opportunities for people who may have been sick or concerned about their health but still wanted the chance to cast their ballots. Many states removed typical voting barriers by expanding access to absentee, mail-in, and early voting. Notably, there was a 25 percent increase in Black voters in the state of Georgia from 2016 to 2020 (Noe-Bustamante & Budiman, 2020). Pew Research Center argues that the increase in Georgia and 7 percent increase in voter turnout nationally in 2020 was due in part to the steps states took to expand their voting options (Desilver, 2021). We argue that these changes should remain in place along with other institutionalized approaches to combating voter suppression outlined in the 2021 voter advancement acts.

2021, For the People Act, and Moving Forward

2021 began with an attempted coup at the Capitol. The events that took place on January 6, 2021, were an additional effort to disenfranchise voters and override the voices of the many who voted for Biden and Harris with the voices of the few who wanted Trump to remain in office. At that moment, many Americans realized the fragility of democracy through the attempted eradication of people's votes through intimidation. In the shadow of that event, increased voter suppression bills were introduced in over 44 states. As a response to ongoing voter suppression efforts, President Joseph R. Biden signed an executive order promoting voting rights on March 7, 2021—56 years after "Bloody Sunday." The order explicitly expands access to voter registration and election information. This expansion includes directing federal agencies to create a strategic plan, boosting automatic voter registration, and increasing access to voting for incarcerated people (Sonmez & Gardner, 2021)—all of which are in line with this century's push for voter protections.

As discussed at the beginning of this chapter, Congress has finally begun to actively discuss the For the People Act of 2021 (H.R.1, S.1, and S.2093). The act was initially known as the Voting Rights Advancement Act and passed in the House on December 9, 2019. Unfortunately, the Senate did not move the bill forward in 2019, nor 2020 when it was renamed the John Lewis Voting Rights Act of 2020. In 2021, members of Congress, voters' rights activists, and President Biden gave this iteration of the voters' rights act renewed support. The For the People Act of 2021 combines individual-level solutions to voter registration, absentee and mail-in voting, and voter access with structural support. It is important to stress that this reform only addresses some approaches of the many voter suppression tactics that disproportionately impact communities of color. Citizens need to continue applying pressure to their state officials to remove barriers to the right to vote and fully erase voter suppression.

We close here in the same way John Lewis (2021) completed his final article:

> When historians pick up their pens to write the story of the 21st century, let them say that it was your generation who laid down the heavy burdens of hate at last and that peace finally triumphed over violence, aggression and war. So I say to you, walk with the wind, brothers and sisters, and let the spirit of peace and the power of everlasting love be your guide.

NOTES

1. US Congress, House, *Directing the Clerk of the House to make a correction in the enrollment of H.R. 4.*, H.Con.Res.107, 116th Cong. 2nd sess., introduced

in House July 27, 2020, https://www.congress.gov/116/bills/hconres107/BILLS-116hconres107rds.xml.

2. USUS Congress, House, *For the People Act of 2021*, H.R.1, 117th Cong. 1st sess., introduced in House January 4, 2021, https://www.congress.gov/117/bills/hr1/BILLS-117hr1eh.xml.

3. USUS Congress, Senate, *For the People Act of 2021*, S.1, 117th Cong. 1st sess., introduced in the Senate March 17, 2021, https://www.congress.gov/117/bills/s2093/BILLS-117s1is.xml.

4. USUS Congress, Senate, *For the People Act of 2021*, S.2093, 117th Cong. 1st sess., introduced in the Senate June 16, 2021, https://www.congress.gov/117/bills/s2093/BILLS-117s2093pcs.xml.

5. Exact Phrasing of Thirteenth Amendment Section 1: Neither slavery nor involuntary servitude, except as a punishment for crime whereof the party shall have been duly convicted, shall exist within the United States, or any place subject to their jurisdiction.

6. Exact Phrasing of Fourteenth Amendment Section 1: All persons born or naturalized in the United States and subject to the jurisdiction thereof are citizens of the United States and of the state wherein they reside. No State shall make or enforce any law which shall abridge the privileges or immunities of citizens of the United States; nor shall any State deprive any person of life, liberty, or property, without due process of law; nor deny to any person within its jurisdiction the equal protection of the laws.

7. Exact Phrasing of Fifteenth Amendment Section 1: The right of citizens of the United States to vote shall not be denied or abridged by the United States or by any State on account of race, color, or previous condition of servitude.

8. Exact phrasing of the Nineteenth Amendment: The right of citizens of the United States to vote shall not be denied or abridged by the United States or by any State on account of sex. Congress shall have power to enforce this article by appropriate legislation.

9. "The Voting Rights Act of 1965, August 6, 1965." General Records of the US Government [Online Version, https://www.archives.gov/legislative/features/voting-rights-1965/vra.html, June 15, 2021].

REFERENCES

American Civil Liberties Union (ACLU). (2017). "Oppose Voter ID Legislation – Fact Sheet." *American Civil Liberties Union.* https://www.aclu.org/other/oppose-voter-id-legislation-fact-sheet.

Ansolabehere, S., & Hersh, E. (2014). Voter Registration: The Process and Quality of Lists. In Burden, B. C. and Stewart, C. (eds.), *The Measure of American Elections* (pp. 61–90). New York: Cambridge University Press.

Arkansas Secretary of State. (2020). Elections. Accessed June 15, 2021. Available at: https://www.sos.arkansas.gov/elections/voter-information/voter-registration-information.

Barker, L. J., Jones, M. H., & Tate, K. 1999. *African Americans and the American Political System*, 4th (fourth) Edition. Prentice Hall.

Biggers, D. R., & Hammer, M. J. (2017). "Understanding the Adoption of Voter Identification Laws in the American States." *American Politics Research* 45(4): 560–588. doi:10.1177/1532673X16687266.

Biggers, D. R., & Smith, D. A. (2020). Does Threatening Their Franchise Make Registered Voters More Likely to Participate? Evidence from An Aborted Voter Purge. *British Journal of Political Science* 50(3): 933–954. doi:10.1017/S0007123418000157.

Blackmon, D. A. (2009). *Slavery by Another Name: The Re-enslavement of Black Americans from the Civil War to World War II*. Anchor Books.

Blount, M. (2021). "Governor Kemp Responds to President Biden's Attack on Election Integrity Legislation." Press release, March 26, 2021. https://gov.georgia.gov/press-releases/2021-03-26/governor-kemp-responds-president-bidens-attack-election-integrity.

Boschma, J. (2021). "Fourteen States Have Enacted 22 New Laws Making It Harder to Vote." *CNN*. Accessed June 16, 2021. https://www.cnn.com/2021/05/28/politics/voter-suppression-restrictive-voting-bills/index.html.

Brady, H. E., & McNulty, J. E. (2011). Turning Out to Vote: The Costs of Finding and Getting to the Polling Place. *The American Political Science Review* 105(1): 115–134.

Brater, J., Morris, K., Pérez, M., & Deluzio, C. (2018). *Purges: A Growing Threat to the Right to Vote*. 34.

Brennan Center for Justice. (2018). *Democracy: An Election Agenda for Candidates, Activists, and Legislators*. https://www.brennancenter.org/our-work/policy-solutions/democracy-election-agenda-candidates-activists-and-legislators.

Brennan Center for Justice. (2021). *Criminal Disenfranchisement Laws Across the United States|Brennan Center for Justice*. https://www.brennancenter.org/our-work/research-reports/criminal-disenfranchisement-laws-across-united-states.

Cai, W., & Epstein, R. J. (2021). "Which States Will Gain or Lose Seats in the Next Congress." *The New York Times*, April 26, 2021, sec. US https://www.nytimes.com/interactive/2021/04/26/us/politics/congress-house-seats-census.html.

Cantoni, Enrico. 2020. "A Precinct Too Far: Turnout and Voting Costs." *American Economic Journal: Applied Economics* 12(1): 61–85. doi:10.1257/app.20180306.

Corasaniti, N. (2021). "Texas Senate Passes One of the Nation's Strictest Voting Bills." *The New York Times*, May 29, 2021, sec. US https://www.nytimes.com/2021/05/29/us/politics/texas-voting-bill.html.

Darrah-Okike, J., Rita, N., & Logan, J. R. (2020). The Suppressive Impacts of Voter Identification Requirements. *Sociological Perspectives* 0731121420966620. doi:10.1177/0731121420966620.

DeBonis, M. (2021). "Manchin Outlines Demands on Voting Legislation, Creating an Opening for Potential Democratic Compromise." *Washington Post*, June 16, 2021. https://www.washingtonpost.com/politics/manchin-narrows-his-demands-on-voting-legislation-bringing-democrats-closer-to-unity/2021/06/16/f588093e-cec4-11eb-8014-2f3926ca24d9_story.html.

Department of Justice. (2017). "History of Federal Voting Rights Laws." Accessed online at https://www.justice.gov/crt/history-federal-voting-rights-laws, June 22, 2021.

Department of Justice. (2020a). "National Voter Registration Act of 1993 (NVRA)" Accessed online at https://www.justice.gov/crt/national-voter-registration-act-1993-nvra, March 1, 2021

Department of Justice. (2020b). "Section 4 of the Voting Rights Act." Accessed online at https://www.justice.gov/crt/section-4-voting-rights-act#formula, June 22, 2021.

Desilver, D. (2021, January 28). Turnout Soared in 2020 as Nearly Two-Thirds of Eligible US Voters Cast Ballots for President. *Pew Research Center.* https://www.pewresearch.org/fact-tank/2021/01/28/turnout-soared-in-2020-as-nearly-two-thirds-of-eligible-u-s-voters-cast-ballots-for-president/.

Gaskins, K., & Iyer, S. (2019). The Challenges of Obtaining Voter Identification. Brennan Center for Justice at New York University School of Law. https://www.brennancenter.org/sites/default/files/2019-08/Report_Challenge_of_Obtaining_Voter_ID.pdf.

Hajnal, Z., Lajevardi, N., & Nielson, L. (2017). "Voter Identification Laws and the Suppression of Minority Votes." *The Journal of Politics* 79(2): 363–379. doi:10.1086/688343.

Hall, Jacquelyn Dowd. (2005). "The Long Civil Rights Movement and the Political Uses of the Past." *Journal of American History* 91(4): 1233–1263. doi:10.2307/3660172.

Henderson, John A., Hamel, Brian T., & Goldzimer, Aaron M. (2018). "Gerrymandering Incumbency: Does Nonpartisan Redistricting Increase Electoral Competition?" *The Journal of Politics* 80(3): 1011–1016. doi:10.1086/697120.

Highton, B. (2017). Voter Identification Laws and Turnout in the United States. *Annual Review of Political Science* 20(1): 149–167.

Joslyn, Nick, Bilbo, Andrew, Arndt, Jack, Berger, Heidi, & Joslyn, Mark. (2020). "Distance Traveled to Polling Locations: Are Travel Costs Imposed Equally on Party Members?" *The Social Science Journal* 57(1): 14–25. doi:10.1016/j.soscij.2018.12.006.

Kansas Secretary of State. (2021). Photo ID. https://sos.ks.gov/elections/photo-id.html.

Kelly, E. (2017). "Racism and Felony Disenfranchisement: An Intertwined History." *Brennan Center for Justice.* https://www.brennancenter.org/our-work/research-reports/racism-felony-disenfranchisement-intertwined-history.

Klinghoffer, J. A., & Elkis, L. (1992). "The Petticoat Electors": Women's Suffrage in New Jersey, 1776-1807. *Journal of the Early Republic* 12(2): 159–193. doi:10.2307/3124150.

Laney, G. P. (2008). *The Voting Rights Act of 1965, As Amended: Its History and Current Issues.* 60.

Lewis, J. (2020, July 30). Opinion | John Lewis: Together, You Can Redeem the Soul of Our Nation. *The New York Times.* https://www.nytimes.com/2020/07/30/opinion/john-lewis-civil-rights-america.html.

Manchin, J. (2021). "Joe Manchin: Why I'm Voting against the For the People Act." *Charleston Gazette-Mail*, June 6, 2021. https://www.wvgazettemail.com/opinion/op_ed_commentaries/joe-manchin-why-im-voting-against-the-for-the-people-act/article_c7eb2551-a500-5f77-aa37-2e42d0af870f.html.

Martis, Kenneth C. 2008. "The Original Gerrymander." *Political Geography* 27(8): 833–839. doi:10.1016/j.polgeo.2008.09.003.

McGhee, Eric. (2020). "Partisan Gerrymandering and Political Science." *Annual Review of Political Science* 23(1): 171–185. doi:10.1146/annurev-polisci-060118-045351.

Morris, K. (2021, June 11). "Testimony of Kevin Morris." Hearing on Voting in America: The Potential for Polling Place Quality and Restrictions on Opportunities to Vote to Interfere with Free and Fair Access to the Ballot Before the Committee on House Administration, Subcommittee on Elections in the United States House of Representatives. June 11, 2021. https://www.brennancenter.org/our-work/research-reports/congressional-testimony-voting-america-potential-polling-place-quality.

Morris, K., & Dunphy, P. (2019). *AVR Impact on State Voter Registration*. 35.

NCSL (National Conference of State Legislatures). (2020a). Same Day Voter Registration. https://www.ncsl.org/research/elections-and-campaigns/same-day-registration.aspx.

NCSL (National Conference of State Legislatures). (2020b). Voting Outside the Polling Place: Absentee, All-Mail and other Voting at Home Options. https://www.ncsl.org/research/elections-and-campaigns/absentee-and-early-voting.aspx.

NCSL (National Conference of State Legislatures). (2021). Voter Identification Requirements | Voter ID Laws. https://www.ncsl.org/research/elections-and-campaigns/voter-id.aspx#ftn%206.

National Voter Registration Day. (2020). About National Voter Registration Day | National Voter Registration Day. https://nationalvoterregistrationday.org/about/

New York Times. (2017, August 9). 2016 Presidential Election Results. *The New York Times*. https://www.nytimes.com/elections/2016/results/president.

Noe-Bustamante, L., & Budiman, A. (2020). Black, Latino, Asian Adults Key to Georgia Registered Voter Increase Since 2016. *Pew Research Center*. https://www.pewresearch.org/fact-tank/2020/12/21/black-latino-and-asian-americans-have-been-key-to-georgias-registered-voter-growth-since-2016/.

Parks, Gregory. (2008). *Black Greek-Letter Organizations in the Twenty-First Century: Our Fight Has Just Begun*. University Press of Kentucky.

Parks, Gregory S., & Hughey, Matthew W. (2020). *A Pledge with Purpose: Black Sororities and Fraternities and the Fight for Equality*. New York: New York University Press. http://ebookcentral.proquest.com/lib/pitt-ebooks/detail.action?docID=6120843.

Putnam, R. D. (1999). *Bowling Alone: America's Declining Social Capital*. New York: Palgrave Macmillan.

Robinson, C. C. (2019). (Re)theorizing Civic Engagement: Foundations for Black Americans Civic Engagement Theory. *Sociology Compass* 13(9): e12728. doi:10.1111/soc4.12728.

Shannon, S. K. S., Uggen, C., Schnittker, J., Thompson, M., Wakefield, S., & Massoglia, M. (2017). The Growth, Scope, and Spatial Distribution of People with Felony Records in the United States, 1948–2010. *Demography* 54(5): 1795–1818. doi:10.1007/s13524-017-0611-1.

Skocpol, T., & Fiorina, M. P. (2004). *Civic Engagement in American Democracy.* Brookings Institution Press.

Sonmez, F., & Gardner, A. (2021, March 7). Biden Signs Executive Order Promoting Voting Rights on 56th Anniversary of 'Bloody Sunday.' *Washington Post.* https://www.washingtonpost.com/politics/biden-voting-bloody-sunday-order/2021/03/07/ce45b082-7f60-11eb-9ca6-54e187ee4939_story.html.

Tennessee Secretary of State. (2021). What ID is Required When Voting? Accessed June 15, 2021. Available at: https://sos.tn.gov/products/elections/what-id-required-when-voting.

Texas Secretary of State. (2021). Required Identification for Voting In Person. Accessed June 15, 2021. Available at: https://www.votetexas.gov/register-to-vote/need-id.html.

Tocqueville, A. de. (1835). *Democracy in America: The Complete and Unabridged Volumes I and II.* Bantam Classics (2000).

US Census Bureau. (2021). "2020 Census Apportionment Results." Accessed online at https://www.census.gov/data/tables/2020/dec/2020-apportionment-data.html on June 15, 2021.

Uggen, C., Shannon, S., & Manza, M. (2012). "State-Level Estimates of Felon Disenfranchisement in the United States, 2010. *The Sentencing Project.* https://www.sentencingproject.org/wp-content/uploads/2016/01/State-Level-Estimates-of-Felon-Disenfranchisement-in-the-United-States-2010.pdf.

US Census Bureau. (2012). "Reported Voting and Registration by Race, Hispanic Origin, Sex, and Age Groups: November 1964 to 2018 (NOTE: Voting rates corrected February 2012)." Accessed online at www.census.gov/library/visualizations/time-series/demo/voting-historical-time-series.html on March 1, 2021.

Viebeck, E. (2020). "Here's Where GOP Lawmakers Have Passed New Voting Restrictions around the Country." *Washington Post*, June 2, 2021, sec. Politics. https://www.washingtonpost.com/politics/2021/06/02/state-voting-restrictions/.

Wadington, K., & Santucci, J. (2021). "Texas Will Gain 2 Congressional Seats. Seven States to Lose 1 Seat, Census Bureau Data Shows." *USA TODAY*, April 27, 2021. https://www.usatoday.com/story/news/politics/2021/04/26/census-bureau-release-population-totals-congress-apportionment/7381180002/.

Weiser, W. R., Weiner, D. I., & Erney, D. (2021). Congress Must Pass the 'For the People Act.' https://www.brennancenter.org/our-work/policy-solutions/congress-must-pass-people-act.

White, G. H. (1901). Defense of the Negro Race—Charges Answered. Speech of Hon. George H. White, of North Carolina, in the House of Representatives, January 29, 1901. Retrieved March 20, 2021, from https://docsouth.unc.edu/nc/whitegh/whitegh.html.

Chapter 9

Searching for a Racial Justice Agenda in High Poverty Settings

How Title I Reform's Data Blindness Limits Its Educational Effectiveness for Black and Latinx Students

Charisse Southwell and Michael Hudson-Vassell

Colorblindness is a race-neutral ideology that overlooks the role of racism as a deciding factor in society, its institutions' outcomes, and the imposed disadvantages people of color struggle against (Neville et al., 2000). Colorblindness, as a function of racism, has reproduced social inequalities in society and schools, ensuring maximum benefit for non-minority people while in school and upon leaving it (Hollins, 2011). Examples of colorblindness operating in specific areas where race is acknowledged in theory (but is categorically overlooked as a deciding factor) include (a) the achievement gaps produced by culturally biased testing, (b) learning opportunities denied through tracking practices that restrict marginalized children from challenging courses, and (c) a preponderance of marginalized students being assigned underqualified (or minimally qualified) teachers in schools where teachers with more experience also work (Darling-Hammond, 2006; Ezeanya-Esiobu, 2019). For this reason, education scholars problematize the underperformance of Black and Latinx (BLX) students as an example of the racial status quo in society being entrenched by the decisions adults make in schools. Further, their scholarship has shown that the ongoing underperformance of BLX students cannot be explained culturally, as it remains inconsistent with the norms and priorities of communities with heroes who risked death in pursuit of educational opportunities. These examinations remove the burden that mainstream dialogue places on parent lifestyles and community values to rationalize BLX students' academic struggles. These faulty rationalizations are particularly dangerous, as they produce personal responsibility arguments that ignore how systems (and the behaviors they incentivize) thwart individual efforts. Such distortions absolve government institutions of their critical contributions to systemic racism and to the inequalities that result.

Even still, race-conscious examinations and discipline shifts have failed to push federal policy's approach toward a more racially forward agenda. Currently, there is even national debate about whether critical positions (like critical race theory) should be excluded from programs that receive federal funding altogether. That such discussions can be entertained reflects the longstanding tradition of negating justice-responsibility that has informed US public education since Reconstruction (Anderson, 1988).

Nevertheless, because they functioned as early sites for colonial domination, schools are sites we must assume are governed by the logic from the colonial project (Spring, 2016). This perspective is particularly informed by the endurance of differential outcomes across student subgroups. For instance, a multifactor analysis by Reardon et al. (2016) provided evidence that school segregation predicted larger achievement gaps between Black students and their White peers. Additionally, Hung et al. (2020) found a strong relationship between academic (math and English) achievement gaps and both economic inequality and segregation. This underscores the important collusion of social barriers in determining academic disparities for marginalized children.

COLORBLINDNESS AND DATA BLINDNESS

Despite the potential of racially conscious examinations to inform appropriate policy reforms, policymakers decouple their improvement-focused intentions from racially realistic actions and instead favor colorblind commitments that will never undo entrenched inequalities in schools (Egalite et al., 2017; Freeman, 2005). When applied to US education policy, colorblindness is accurately described as a signature application of racism that systematically downplays the practical consequences of racial hierarchies. Thus, it enables racial domination to continue under the pretense that it is nonexistent or of little import to the business of schooling. As it relates to Title I of the Elementary and Secondary Education Act (ESEA), colorblindness characterizes the national- and state-level incentivization of efforts that target racially marginalized students without ever addressing the instructional priorities, educational interventions, and schooling goals that uphold their racial domination (Wells, 2014).

Colorblindness also drives the policy mandates surrounding research planning and data use. In such mandates, these investigative functions are mistakenly treated as singular, general processes that exist beyond the reach of racialization. As such, guidance for data activities—decision making supports to appropriately address Title I children's needs—ignore the proximal existence of racism. This omission is woven into the very methodologies that—like policy—reduce the experiences of BLX children to a single story (or overlook the nuances across their stories) when searching for existing needs to prioritize.

Herein lies the problem of data blindness, which we have conceived as race-neutral methodologies that support culturally invalid techniques (e.g., selected data points, posed research questions, sought-after bodies of knowledge, etc.); these problematic techniques preserve a eugenics-esque relationship between those studied, the knowledge produced about them, and, ultimately, the decisions made about what is to be done to them. The development of this current situation can be tracked in the history of Title I law as it responded to social conflicts.

Our goal in writing this chapter is to extend thinking around Title I policy for social justice and to examine what possibilities might scale racial benefit for BLX students if they could occupy a high priority in explicit racial research agendas that support data process mandates at the LEA and state levels. To accomplish this task, we begin with a brief description of present-day academic outcomes for BLX students and the role of Title I policies in shaping those outcomes. We then provide a historical overview of Title I policy as a federal mandate, paying special attention to how the use of colorblind rhetoric in its creation has served to entrench racial inequality in schools. We then examine Title I policy through its needs assessment and accountability provisions, focusing on how colorblindness and data blindness constrain research questions and processes that harm BLX students. Finally, we provide recommendations for reforming Title I research and evaluation practices to inform programs that effectively serve the needs of BLX students.

TITLE I AND BLX STUDENT PERFORMANCE

Title I is the primary funder for education at the federal level and a suitable place to explore the possibilities for how education reform can benefit BLX students explicitly. The grant provides money to school districts with high concentrations of children from low-income families and, historically, has targeted issues of "poverty, delinquency, unemployment, illiteracy, and school dropouts" as threats to the nation's competitiveness as an advanced and just society (US Department of Health, Education & Welfare, 1969). Today, the program remains a part of the national agenda to close gaps in achievement by ensuring each child has a "significant opportunity to receive a fair, equitable, and high-quality education" (Every Student Succeeds Act 2015, Sec. 1001).

Title I treats gaps in achievement as funding opportunities, allotting additional aid to schools enrolling higher proportions of students on free and/ or reduced lunch (ranges start from 50.1 percent). Additionally, the funding provides a secondary lever for support at the district level, wherein special allocations ("set-asides") target vulnerable subgroups of children (e.g., delinquent students, homeless students) through supplementary interventions linked to academic achievement (Snyder et al., 2019).

Whether at the school level or at the district level, Title I settings tend to be overpopulated with students from racially marginalized groups. To date, Title I funding has served over 26 million children in nearly 56,000 public schools (US Department of Education, 2018). From 2008 to 2017, Latinx children who attend Title I schools have received the largest proportions of Title I support at the school level, followed by White children, Black children, and other children of color (The Annie E. Casey Foundation, 2018). These figures do not include students served by the aforementioned set-asides.

By and large, the funding that Title I provides at the local level is marginal compared to the operational budget districts have to meet students' academic needs (Michelman, 2016). Because Title I dedicates its school-level funding to the poorest schools, schools struggling with similar issues that fail to meet the minimum poverty cutoff do not have access to the additional funding. Nevertheless, educators' ability to use this funding to circumvent the educational obstacles marginalized children face holds great promise for engraining best practices to close achievement gaps at the local level. This is particularly true for BLX students, who are overrepresented among marginalized students and in Title I schools. More generally, successful practices for addressing these needs may then extend to how public education is deployed to all children within districts, where BLX students exist in higher proportions as well (National Center for Education Statistics, 2019).

Further, Dynarski and Kainz (2015) reported that districts allocate their Title I spending in areas (e.g., teacher professional development, technology, etc.) that have not demonstrated an impact on the outcomes of Title I students. Title I evaluations have denoted this as well, as researchers have found that the impacts of funded initiatives diminish over time, particularly for children who may have needed additional remediation for factors beyond just being poor (e.g., language/cultural differences) (Borman & D'Agostino, 1996; Kainz, 2019). This suggests a functional gap for educational leaders in determining areas most worthwhile for additional funding. This functional gap exists despite government-mandated needs assessments and data reporting requirements that must precede allocation decisions at the local and state levels, measures that were added to Title I policy as a way to encourage systematic decision making (Boyle & Lee, 2015; Every Students Succeeds Act, 2015).

These challenges and their disparate impacts on BLX students are not exclusive to Title I-funded settings. Public education has struggled to demonstrate that its financial decisions have driven improvement in the academic performance of marginalized students. Because most children in public schools are from marginalized groups (BLX students are especially overrepresented), the above implications of Title I spending and programmatic performance as broadscale equity and improvement opportunities are hard to ignore. Further, current education policy fails to adequately address the learning disparities affected by the overrepresentation of racially oppressed students in Title I schools. For this reason, successfully implementing Title I-funded programs can be valuable to inform a racially conscious restructuring of education laws, funding policies, and data processes.

TITLE I IN THE 1960S: NATIONAL DEVELOPMENT DURING AN ERA OF RACIAL UNREST

In the 1950s and early 1960s, race, racism, and wariness of federal control were central issues in the discussion of public funding for education. The Soviet Union's launch of Sputnik in 1957 triggered the belief that American technology was falling behind due to racial unrest and systemic inequalities in states' educational programs. Extending access to quality education for marginalized groups was a way to advance the nation's technological outputs and preserve democracy against communism. Colorblindness, performed to downplay racism's role in the US's "inability" to keep pace with the Soviet Union, can be seen in President Lyndon B. Johnson's administration's approach to this task. The administration canvassed the experiences of Black people in Northern urban cities, specifically using the experiences of Black people who migrated from the South to the North to blame Blackness (instead of ongoing racial unrest in a conflict-ridden society) as the cause for the nation's urgency. By the end of 1965, ESEA was signed into law by Lyndon B. Johnson as part of the broader War on Poverty.

Because of the ruling stereotypes about marginalized people's intellectual inferiority, the public readily accepted the common belief that, through schooling, BLX children (and all children of color) could escape the intergenerational "culture of poverty." This belief, resembling earlier eugenics-era ideas regarding the inherent vices of poverty, was merged with existing deficit-oriented narratives about the cultural inferiority of BLX people (ideas such as those informing the "cultural deprivation" theory of the 1966

Coleman Report) and deployed in this context to position Black communities as the site of national failure. The "culture of poverty" concept turned out to be a very influential rhetorical strategy, leading to a bevy of additional legislation across various programs at the federal level, such as food assistance and health programs.

To this extent, this propaganda categorically ignored the democratic impacts of racial unrest by downplaying the educational performance of White students in the 1960s, which featured about a 40 percent graduation rate for both males and females over twenty-five years old (Snyder, 1993). Propaganda also attempted to link federal response to the government's ongoing interest in helping families through the Great Depression, which largely impacted poor Southern Whites. Southern Whites also received the most federal relief through the racially-specific social policies instituted during and after the Great Depression that ensured White people's access to aid (Kirby, 1986).

Here begins the colorblind education ethic, wherein redressing issues plaguing marginalized people is normed as rhetoric, not action. Title I would become no exception to this phenomenon, as it has been shown to largely benefit poor, White males in and outside of urban school districts, even though the gap between minority and non-minority has been steadily increasing (Gillborn, 2008).

Instead of the pro-justice improvement it has been positioned to be, Johnson's administration sought to assuage White anxieties by framing the country's position as one brought on by Black need, namely, that of Black poverty and failing urban schools (Jeffrey, 1978). The poster issue for federal intervention in education in social justice was thus Black and Brown people's enduring victimization at the hands of an oppressive society. This colorblind stance on naming racism as a social dynamic would continually undermine social progress through schooling efforts for some time to come. Particularly, Southern schools resisted federal involvement because it threatened the practice of school segregation and the control states and local districts had over school curriculum (Casalapsi, 2017; Kaestle, 2001). These concerns rose to prominence in the years between *Brown v. Board of Education* and the Civil Rights Act of 1964, as Adam Clayton Powell—the first Black chairman of the Committee on Education and Labor—added his *Powell Amendment* to major pieces of legislation. The amendment would allow the federal government to withhold funding from segregated schools, treating segregation as the specific activity that denied BLX students access to rigorous education.

Eventually, this amendment was removed from federal education bills when the senate refused to approve Title I legislation with the amendment, leading to a stalemate in expansive and progressive federal legislation in education (Hanna, 2005). With the passage of the Civil Rights Act of 1964, conversations about federal responsibility in social justice died, and federal monetary aid in segregation in schools was cut short (Hanna, 2005; Jeffrey, 1978). Here, though, is where the social justice needs of the Black community were distorted yet again, and instead used to cover how federal involvement would increase support for poor White communities.

Those adopting a colorblind logic would argue that these moments were a step in the right direction because the policies helped to shed light on the interests of BLX people and created room for meeting that need as a national agenda. However, through the lens of critical race theory, we can see that upending racism for the benefit of BLX people has not existed as a federal priority, but rather as a direct instance of interest convergence. According to Derrick Bell, interest convergence asserts that "the interest of blacks in achieving racial equality will be accommodated only when it converges with the interests of whites" (Brown & Jackson, 2013, 17). Interest convergence will continue to undermine Title I's effectiveness as long as Title I remains a policy that evades racial differences in experiencing poverty, and as long as it evades the centrality of power at the intersection of poverty and race for children in Title I-funded settings. These two conditions are characteristic of colorblind racial ideology, which safeguards educational institutions from addressing the demographic-specific needs of school-aged children (Wells, 2014). This mundane form of racism leads to the under-serving of BLX children by omitting important structural considerations from the discussion—hindering attempts at critical discourse among educational decision makers (like school leaders, school boards, local government officials), who divorce their actions from the social inequalities that occur in their jurisdictions (Perlow, 2017). Framing such approaches as beneficial to BLX children would be false, as time has shown that BLX people have not been the primary beneficiaries (if at all, in some cases) of such legislation, including Title I (Boteach et al., 2014; Gillborn, 2008).

In what would become a series of early reauthorizations focused on creating the idea that educational deprivation is inextricably tied to family income, increased emphasis on particular subgroup performance emerged as the terms "educationally deprived" and "children from low-income families" were used interchangeably (Stein, 2004). To this end, Stein (2004) asserts that in the early congressional debate texts from 1965, the *culture* of the children being served by Title I was addressed three times more than the *academic skills* of children. Such norms established a primary focus on the necessity of shifting children away from cultural deprivation, but the resulting legislation never addressed *how* the program would ensure that children developed the skills needed to do so. This lack of specificity and nuance has contributed to Title I's decreased effectiveness in meeting the original reform goal of closing achieving gaps between BLX children who are targeted by programs that tend to be culturally alienating and culturally deficit-oriented in nature (e.g., Ladson-Billings, 2006; Goodman & West-Olatunji, 2010).

TITLE I IN THE 1980S AND EARLY 2000S: NEEDS ASSESSMENTS AND FUNDING ACCOUNTABILITY

From its inception in 1965 to the present, ESEA incorporated requirements for districts to demonstrate the effectiveness of programs and services purchased using Title I funds. At first, this was driven by a funding management focus wherein property taxes served as the primary source of school funding. The idea was to eradicate the role that high concentrations of BLX people going to high poverty schools played in worsening need—a move that addressed segregation and quieted the calls from civil rights leaders to take concrete measures to provide equal educational opportunities (Stein, 2004).

Further, Title I eligibility requirements depended on a basic grant formula that considered the number of families with incomes below the low-income factor of $2,000 (adjusted to $16,585.22 in today's value after inflation). The $2,000 threshold relied on outdated census data, and larger shares of funds were distributed to wealthier states which were depicted as "an unquestioned hard core of poverty" (Elementary and Secondary Education Act, 1965; Congressional Research Service, 2017). In the early years of the program, funds reached children who were not disadvantaged, exacerbating disparities in education funding between wealthy and poor areas (Jeffrey, 1978).

The formula created several issues. First, dollars were allocated based on the number of disadvantaged children multiplied by the state's typical allocation per student divided by two. Under this formula, it was estimated that 95 percent of the counties in the United States would receive funding (Jeffrey, 1978). Second, due to demographic shifts between 1960 and 1965, the formula benefitted states with declining or highly mobile concentrations of poverty.

Despite this infusion of federal monetary support, early examinations on the outcomes of disadvantaged children showed that improvement was hindered by the lack of federal follow-up in the form of monitoring spending practices. Namely, it was discovered that there were broadscale disproportionate appropriations of funds across low-poverty and high-poverty schools, and educators tended to have difficulties selecting programs and services that worked. These problems were coupled with districts' illegal use of funds, education leaders' selection of inadequate programs, state failures to monitor the program, weak federal enforcement of the law, and little to no parent or family engagement (Vinovskis, 1999; Washington Research Project, 1969).

A report titled "A Nation at Risk: The Imperative for Education Reform," released in 1983, led to an increased focus on accountability by highlighting declines in Scholastic Aptitude Test (SAT) performance, science achievement scores, and overall achievement scores since the 1960s (National Commission on Excellence in Education, 1983). The Hawkins-Stafford Elementary and Secondary School Improvement Amendments of 1988 brought about requirements for local educational agencies to develop improvement plans in cases where children served by Title I funding demonstrated inadequate improvement or declines in performance.

These conditions gave rise to the inclusion of needs assessments as a component of financial mandates in the 1980s, when program evaluation emerged as a public accountability activity (Boyle & Lee, 2015; Patton, 2008; Paul, 2016). Eventually, Title I's emphasis on the distribution of funds as the key lever in resolving the achievement gap would follow, expanding to an interest in improving transparency in how monies are spent and demonstrating substantial evidence for these directions through ongoing evaluation activities.

By 1994s Improving America's Schools Act (IASA), effectiveness issues persisted, with the act acknowledging that "although the achievement gap between disadvantaged children and other children has been reduced by half over the past two decades, a sizable gap remains, and many segments of our society lack the opportunity to become well educated" (Improving America's Schools Act of 1994, 1144). The 2001 No Child Left Behind Act included requirements for student data to be disaggregated by subgroups—to further target student groups that were not making adequate progress—along with accountability measures to ensure those gaps were closed (Boyle & Lee, 2015; Hess & Petrilli, 2005).

Notably, IASA and Goals 2000: Educate America Act of the 1990s allowed states to develop their own accountability standards and required that states and districts "turn around" low-performing schools. IASA also added requirements for districts and schools to develop a parent-involvement policy, integration provisions to expand the programs available through partnerships with other education programs, and standardized assessment requirements for math and reading (Paul, 2016; Improving America's Schools Act, 1994).

The most recent reauthorization of the ESEA, the Every Student Succeeds Act (ESSA) brought about increased flexibility for states to set accountability goals and non-academic indicators of educational progress for disadvantaged youth, such as student engagement, graduation rates, postsecondary readiness, school climate, and progression of English Language Learners (Every Student Succeeds Act, 2015). Under ESSA, biennial evaluation plans are submitted by the Institute of Education Sciences to study topics under categories such as accountability and school improvement, student support and academic achievement, and choice and parent engagement. The state and district roles in this appear to be limited to providing data that has been critiqued for its restrictiveness by education researchers. Although it introduced various metrics for demonstrating effectiveness, ESSA has been less clear about what supporting "effectiveness" through Title I evaluations means within local contexts and looks like when performing at optimal efficiency.

NARROW MEASURES AND SINGLE STORIES

One issue with narrowly defined student performance as a single indicator of effectiveness is that it frequently highlights the achievement gap. Focusing on this gap as a deficit problem belonging to BLX students shifts the attention to the individual instead of programmatic and systemic schooling environments and overlooks ready avenues for actionable change. The gap also implies that White achievement is the standard that BLX and other students of color should aspire to reach (Quinn, 2020). There is also empirical evidence that entrenched achievement gap discourse foregrounds expectations of BLX student performance. In such scenarios, educators perpetuate racial stereotypes when their internal narratives about at-risk students' academic outcomes inform harmful practices (Quinn, 2020).

The following sections explore our concept of data blindness as a function of colorblindness and racism. They also review a bevy of research techniques to solve the challenges of effectiveness and needs assessment standards. These have been previously overlooked by the Title I program in prior approaches to eradicating social inequality. Because discourse and action surrounding the educational and social experiences of BLX people must account for their commodification as objects in the perennial colonial structure and must interpret outcomes through the logic of racism, the following section purposefully centers on the community benefit BLX children and people can receive (Milner, 2007).

DATA BLINDNESS: HOW COLORBLINDNESS HARMS TITLE I COMMUNITIES THROUGH PROBLEMATIC RESEARCH AND EVALUATION NORMS

Data blindness is a term that has been used to describe the systemic overlooking of alternative data that exists. As big data continues to evolve, this term often reflects views on how information technology and computer science might create more informative ways for mining deep data. Our position is much different. In conceptualizing data blindness, we connect it to colorblindness in that it extends its obscurement of the impacts of race to accepted/

destructive research norms. We have conceived data blindness as race-neutral methodologies that lend the perception of rigor to culturally unsuitable (and thus invalid) techniques for studying social phenomena. It includes selected data points, posed research questions, sought-after bodies of knowledge, and so on that emerged from scientific racism and currently works to preserve colonial ideologies about those studied. The material implications of data blindness are found in its support of decisions that recolonize people of color and their children (Zuberi, 2001). For example, a signature feature of data blind processes is that they allow for translation (or follow-up actions like decisions about education interventions) to be made without the consent or endorsement of the communities they impact most (Zuberi & Bonilla-Silva, 2008; Zuberi, 2001).

Data blindness highlights the researcher's burden in addressing racism, which operates across all systems, including the sciences. Like all human-run processes, data blindness can be solved by attending to the agency (or choice) that local level researchers have to explore marginalized students' experiences while also paying attention to racially sensitive constructs that are better suited for understanding their experiences in culturally consistent and trustworthy ways. For instance, the following excerpt outlines technical guidance Florida districts received for providing baseline data in its 2019 application for parent and family engagement (a Title I set-aside):

What are the LEA's points of strength and opportunities for improvement? Based on what data source(s)?

- Use both quantitative data (e.g., summative student achievement [e.g., FSA], local formative student achievement, teacher evaluation) and qualitative data (e.g., perception surveys, focus groups), as applicable to the Area of Focus. For example, qualitative data is particularly useful in regard to parent and family engagement.
- Be sure to look for patterns and trends in the data.
- Remember, the most recently available data must be used.

What are the underlying causes of underperformance? (p. 13).

The above approach privileges methods over methodology. The former concerns itself with data collection tools only (e.g., quantitative vs. qualitative), disconnecting them from the types of systematic justification (methodology) which requires that tools are suitable for the phenomenon under study and appropriate for the goals of the research (e.g., using critical race theory-quantitative methodology to select culturally relevant variables that are needed to understand what is contributing to BLX student performance in high poverty schools) (Zuberi & Bonilla-Silva, 2008; Walter & Andersen, 2013).

As another example, Washington State's 2019 Title I program guide discusses data and evaluation outright:

1. Has the Title I, Part A program been effective?
2. What has worked well in the Title I, Part A program?
3. What has not worked well in the Title I, Part A program?
4. How should the Title I, Part A program be refined?

> The data are analyzed and the results of these analyses are used as the source of evidence to determine the answers to the four questions.
> Information is collected in the form of formative and summative student performance data; surveys; attendance data; and other data from students, teachers, and administrators.
> As necessary and appropriate, the results of the analysis are shared with Title I, Part A staff, Title I, Part A building classroom teachers, principals, LEA administrators, parents, and other stakeholders to determine necessary and important changes that should be made to the Title I, Part A program to better survey its students.
> The results of the evaluation, including information about any changes to the Title I, Part A program, are shared with LEA and school officials and distributed to all Title I, Part A families in Title I, Part A schools. (pp. 15–16)

Though the above identified different ways that data could be used, it too does not present methodological guidance on how research specific to their educational experiences, needs, and responses should drive the construction of the evaluation process, the determinants of success, and how implementation occurs. Nor is there specific language on sharing findings with the community so that community members can collaborate in deciding what to (dis)continue. This too would be informed by the methodology. Data blindness, conceived here as an extension of colorblindness in how data, research, and evaluation are treated in Title I policy, produces myriad harms. However, its primary violence is that it preserves racial inequities by renaming, ignoring, or denying the proximal existence of racism in the evidence used to substantiate what interventions are worthwhile. This creates a cycle wherein persistent BLX student underperformance is subject to the mundanity mentioned above. Specifically, it contributes to stereotypes of people of color's intellectual inferiority that leave us incurious about why after almost sixty years of public investment, BLX students have not yet caught up to their White peers. In colorblindness ideology, researchers have shown how such cycles leave people of color burdened with proving that structural racism is not a myth (to institutional actors that largely benefit from the status quo). It also leaves people of color to contend with the notion that their oppressors (both individuals and institutions) are unintentionally so, and therefore free of blame or responsibility (Bonilla-Silva, 2014).

DECOLONIZING RESEARCH TECHNIQUES AS A TITLE I RACIAL JUSTICE AGENDA

Effectiveness is at the heart of Title I, and its promise lies in connecting social equity to outcomes and funding. Previous conceptualizations of the policy shrouded this, however, as—in practice—import was given to funding concerns and adequate spending by the fiscal year's end. Today, funding eligibility discourse is not linked to demonstrable use of outcomes data to drive decision making, hindering the ability of data-conscious leadership to reflectively inform assessments of programs' suitability for adoption/continuation/improvement. In other words, there are no levers for ensuring that Title I program decisions are vetted in advance of funding requests at the school, district, or state levels. This could be improved by establishing clear evidentiary guidelines for Title I program adoption, which would align well with Title I legislation's existing provisions for evaluations of program effectiveness. However, as it stands, program data and program adoption information tend to be reported simultaneously; this incentivizes a compliance stance, reducing data-driven decision making to paper justifications instead of requiring demonstrated systematicity.

Decolonizing research techniques are a catalog of racially centered, emancipatory dispositions, questions, analyzes, and discourses that are intentionally suited for upending racism (King, 2005; Smith, 2013; Walter & Andersen, 2013). Members of marginalized communities have used these techniques in research to aid decolonizing efforts. For example, racial healing through data/research work has been done with indigenous communities around the world. Of note, the Maori Education Movement in New Zealand used, in part, research and data findings to de-weaponize the curriculum against non-White children and restructure power relations between the once-colonized indigenous people, their communities, and government-controlled institutions (Mahrooqui & Asante, 2012; Smith, 2013). A rigorous and scientifically strong approach, these techniques make the connection between hegemony and research explicit. This approach stands in contrast to the historical presence of researchers at the start of the colonial effort; their silence, poor methods, and intentional misleading played an intrinsic role in the creation of (a) the data we have easy access to today and (b) the prevalence of research methods that can do little more than repeat stories of failure and deficiency for BLX students.

The act of research and evaluation can be deployed as a critical justice activity to interrupt racism in schools and erase it as a schooling outcome for

BLX students. To accomplish this, emphasis must be placed on updating the concept of needs so that it reflects contemporary, justice-oriented methods. Such methods counter the colonizing story of status quo data, which pathologizes BLX students and obscures their inherent strengths at the individual and community levels. Policy should amplify these strengths, so that power is shifted back into the hands of BLX people and their communities, and so that the education process intertwines seamlessly with their way of life.

Overall, Title I needs a policy-driven system that supports improvement and enhances the translational strength of the data districts use to inform academic interventions for BLX students. The following are examples of how this could be established using a decolonizing research approach to Title I research and evaluation:

- Using metrics that are culturally consistent with the ways that BLX people define educational success
    - As a matter of validity, it is prudent that policy makers work in authentic concert with researchers who are subject matter experts in justice-oriented education practices across content areas. Such intentional collaborations would allow them to broker the translation of community-based assets and educational priorities into measurable phenomena that will address the academic needs of BLX children.
- Prioritizing the use of qualitative research as an equally valuable research methodology
    - In keeping with the above, policy makers should engage with qualitative research(ers) to consider the hyperlocal nuances that might be helped or harmed by the policies they put forth. Additionally, policy makers should allow room for qualitative research to be used in needs assessments and outcomes reporting—as the flawed concept that quantitative research is any more rigorous or less subjective than qualitative research has been debunked in the scientific community.
- Requiring transparent attention to rigor in explanations of evaluation and research plans that are submitted to the state
    - Policy makers should account for rigor in program evaluation design as a point of policy. Currently, there appear to be no readily accessible standards concerning what counts as program evaluation, and this aspect remains one of the more under-conceptualized components of the legislation.
    - To this end, policy makers should separate the ask for needs assessments from intervention proof of concept, which could require explicit description of who the intervention impacted and whether those students were a part of the target population. It could also require the use of formative check-ins that use the same rigorous standards as end-of-year evaluations.

CONCLUSION

Current discussions on the link between data and educational policy tend to reflect the nuances and opportunities that big data has brought to social science fields. However, the goal of this chapter is to suggest an affirmative research agenda that targets BLX students' strengths and needs as an explicit matter of policy and one upon which funding for school improvement is contingent. This suggestion is not in line with NCLB's attempt to couple student performance with Title I funding, which unduly penalized schools serving BLX students (Manna, 2010). Instead, this suggestion points to a research agenda that can lift the needs of BLX students and bring them to scale as a central concern. Such an agenda can ensure that the infrastructure and operation of a rigorous research-to-practice program targeting BLX student performance in Title I-funded settings is a requirement, not merely an idea.

ESSA is currently due for reauthorization. If reauthorized during the Biden-Harris administration, a reconceptualization of data infrastructure support as a means of performing fiscal responsibility would ensure that educational services that can help BLX children and decrease educational inequities are given the proper emphasis. The COVID-19 pandemic could serve as an object lesson of what could have been. Urgencies shifted schooling's focus away from assessment and accountability measures to myriad other factors. Attention went to securing meals for children in distance learning, obtaining one-to-one technology for all students, and broadening internet access—all existing issues that were brought to the forefront because the pandemic impacted a larger proportion of children (Ujifusa, 2020). These issues are express manifestations of how BLX students—for whom being poor is a compounding (not single, explanatory) factor—have experienced poverty. These truths exist throughout education research, but districts have still used lunch status as the guiding measurement of poverty, which works as the primary explanatory variable for looking at the effects of poverty. Had these variables been integrated into how poverty research is conducted as a standard within districts, districts and municipalities may have been able to meet the current moment with a clearer idea of what contributions are needed, now that more families are represented below the poverty line.

The opportunity still remains, and it is due time for policymakers to incorporate data utilization and evaluation practices that are inclusive and beneficial to disadvantaged families and youth as a point of Title I policy moving forward. The recommendations highlighted above could improve the role that Title I policy plays, enabling it to move beyond passive monitoring of data and reporting of achievement gaps, and allowing decision makers to actively use data to select (and subsequently evaluate) services targeted to improve educational outcomes for BLX students.

REFERENCES

Anderson, J. D. (1988). *The Education of Blacks in the South, 1860-1935*. University of North Carolina Press.

Annie E. Casey Foundation. (2018). *Children in Title I Schools by Race and Ethnicity in the United States* [Infographic]. https://datacenter.kidscount.org/data/line/8418-children-in-title-i-schools-by-race-and-ethnicity?loc=1and loct=1#1/any/false/1603,1539,1381,1246,1124,1021,909,857,105/asc/167,168,133,3,185,107/17042.

Bonilla-Silva, E. (2006). *Racism without Racists: Color-Blind Racism and the Persistence of Racial Inequality in the United States*. Rowman and Littlefield Publishers.

Borman, G. D., & D'Agostino, J. V. (1996). Title I and student achievement: A meta-analysis of federal evaluation results. *Educational Evaluation and Policy Analysis, 18*(4), 309–326.

Boteach, M., Stegman, E., Baron, S., Ross, T., & Wright, K. (2014). *The War on Poverty: Then and Now. Applying Lessons Learned to the Challenges and Opportunities Facing a 21st-Century America*. Center for American Progress. https://www.americanprogress.org/issues/poverty/reports/2014/01/07/81661/the-war-on-poverty-then-and-now/.

Boyle, A., & Lee, K. (2015). Title I at 50: A Retrospective. *American Institutes for Research*. https://www.air.org/sites/default/files/downloads/report/Title-I-at-50-rev.pdf.

Brown, K., & Jackson, D. D. (2013). The history and conceptual elements of critical race theory. In M. Lynn and A. D. Dixon (eds.), *Handbook of Critical Race Theory in Education*, 9–22. Routledge Handbooks Online.

Casalaspi, D. (2017). The making of a" legislative miracle": The elementary and secondary education act of 1965. *History of Education Quarterly, 57*(2), 247.

Congressional Research Service. (2017). History of the ESEA Title I-A Formulas. https://www.everycrsreport.com/files/20170717_R44898_9eea86370068f3561f7b1c876ec02ba0f48a1bee.pdf.

Dynarski, M., & Kainz, K. (2015). Why federal spending on disadvantaged students (Title I) doesn't work. *Evidence Speaks, 1*(7), 1–5.

Darling-Hammond, L. (2006). Securing the right to learn: Policy and practice for powerful teaching and learning. *Educational Researcher, 35*(7), 13–24.

Egalite, A. J., Fusarelli, L. D., & Fusarelli, B. C. (2017). Will decentralization affect educational inequity? The every student succeeds act. *Educational Administration Quarterly, 53*(5), 757–781.

Elementary and Secondary Education Act of 1965, Pub. L. 89-10, 64 Stat. 1100, codified as amended at 20 USC. §§236-244 (1965). https://www.govinfo.gov/content/pkg/STATUTE-79/pdf/STATUTE-79-Pg27.pdf.

Every Student Succeeds Act, 20 USC. § 6301 (2015). https://www.congress.gov/114/plaws/publ95/PLAW-114publ95.pdf.

Ezeanya-Esiobu, C. (2019). Research, innovation, indigenous knowledge and policy action in Africa. In *Indigenous Knowledge and Education in Africa*. Springer.

Freeman, E. (2005). No child left behind and the denigration of race. *Equity and Excellence in Education, 38*(3), 190–199.

Florida Department of Education. (2018). *2018-19 Title I, Part A Application Companion Guide. A Report.*

Gillborn, D. (2008). *Racism and Education: Coincidence or Conspiracy?* Routledge.

Goodman, R. D., & West-Olatunji, C. A. (2010). Educational hegemony, traumatic stress, and African American and Latino American students. *Journal of Multicultural Counseling and Development, 38*(3), 176–186.

Hanna, J. (2005). The Elementary and Secondary Education Act: 40 Years Later. *Harvard Graduate School of Education.* https://www.gse.harvard.edu/news/05/08/elementary-and-secondary-education-act-40-years-late.

Hess, F. M., & Petrilli, M. J. (2005). The politics of no child left behind: Will the coalition hold? *Journal of Education, 185*(3), 13–25.

Hollins, E. R. (2011). The meaning of culture in learning to teach: The power of socialization and identity formation. In Ball, A. F., and Tyson, C. A. (eds.), *Studying Diversity in Teacher Education.* Rowan and Littlefield.

Hung, M., Smith, W. A., Voss, M. W., Franklin, J. D., Gu, Y., & Bounsanga, J. (2020). Exploring student achievement gaps in school districts across the United States. *Education and Urban Society, 52*(2), 175–193.

Improving America's Schools Act of 1994, Pub. L. 103-382, 108 Stat. 3518. (1994). https://www.congress.gov/103/statute/STATUTE-108/STATUTE-108-Pg3518.pdf.

Jeffrey, J. R. (1978). *Education for Children of the Poor. A Study of the Origins and Implementation of the Elementary and Secondary Education Act of 1965.* Ohio University Press.

Kainz, K. (2019). Early academic gaps and Title I programming in high poverty, high minority schools. *Early Childhood Research Quarterly, 47*, 159–168.

Kaestle, C. F. (2001). Federal aid to education since World War II: Purposes and politics. *The Future of the Federal Role in Elementary and Secondary Education. A Collection of Papers.* Center on Education Policy.

King, J. E. (ed.). (2006). *Black Education: A Transformative Research and Action Agenda for the New Century.* Routledge.

Kirby, J. T. (1986). *Rural Worlds Lost: The American South, 1920-1960.* LSU Press.

Ladson-Billings, G. (2006). From the achievement gap to the education debt: Understanding achievement in US schools. *Educational Researcher, 35*(7), 3–12.

Mahrooqi, R., & Asante, C. (2012). Revitalizing the Maori language: A focus on educational reform. *Pertanika Journal of Social Sciences and Humanities, 20*(4).

Milner IV, H. R. (2007). Race, culture, and researcher positionality: Working through dangers seen, unseen, and unforeseen. *Educational Researcher, 36*(7), 388–400.

National Commission on Excellence in Education. (1983). A nation at risk: The imperative for educational reform. *The Elementary School Journal, 84*(2), 113–130.

National Center for Education Statistics. (2019). Concentration of public school students eligible for free or reduced-price lunch.

Neville, H. A., Lilly, R. L., Duran, G., Lee, R. M., & Browne, L. (2000). Construction and initial validation of the color-blind racial attitudes scale (CoBRAS). *Journal of Counseling Psychology, 47*(1), 59.

Office of Superintendent of Public Instruction. (2019). Title I, Part A Program Guide: Tools and Tips for Title I, Part A Directors. Office of Superintendent of Public Instruction, State of Washington. https://www.k12.wa.us/sites/default/files/public/titlei/TitleI%20Guide%2019-20%20MASTER.pdf.

Patton, M. Q. (2008). *Utilization-Focused Evaluation*. Sage Publications.

Paul, C. A. (2016). Elementary and Secondary Education Act of 1965. *Social Welfare History Project*. Retrieved from http://socialwelfare.library.vcu.edu/programs/education/elementary-and-secondary-education-act-of-1965/.

Perlow, O. (2017). Getting' free: Anger as resistance to white supremacy within and beyond the academy. In Perlow, O. N., Wheeler, D. I., Bethea, S. L., and Scott, B. M. (eds.), *Black Women's Liberatory Pedagogies: Resistance, Transformation, and Healing Within and Beyond the Academy*. Palgrave Macmillan.

Quinn, D. M. (2020). Experimental effects of "achievement gap" news reporting on viewers' racial stereotypes, inequality explanations, and inequality prioritization. *Educational Researcher, 49*(7), 482–492.

Reardon, S. F., Kalogrides, D., & Shores, K. (2019). The geography of racial/ethnic test score gaps. *American Journal of Sociology, 124*(4), 1164–1221.

Smith, L. T. (2013). *Decolonizing Methodologies: Research and Indigenous Peoples*. Zed Books Ltd.

Snyder, T. D. (1993). 120 Years of American Education: A Statistical Portrait. US Department of Education, Office of Educational Research and Improvement, National Center for Education Statistics.

Snyder, T. D., Dinkes, R., Sonnenberg, W., & Cornman, S. (2019). Study of the Title I, Part A Grant Program Mathematical Formulas. Statistical Analysis Report. *National Center for Education Statistics*. https://nces.ed.gov/pubs2019/titlei/.

Spring, J. (2016). *Deculturalization and the Struggle for Equality: A Brief History of the Education of Dominated Cultures in the United States*. Routledge.

Stein, S. J. (2004). *The Culture of Education Policy*. Teachers College Press.

Stovall, D. (2006). Forging community in race and class: Critical race theory and the quest for social justice in education. *Race Ethnicity and Education, 9*(3), 243–259.

Ujifusa, A. (2020). How will ESSA Hold up During COVID-19? Pandemic Tests the Law's Resilience. https://www.edweek.org/policy-politics/how-will-essa-hold-up-during-covid-19-pandemic-tests-the-laws-resilience/2020/11.

US Department of Health, Education, and Welfare Office of Education. (1969). History of Title I ESEA. https://files.eric.ed.gov/fulltext/ED033459.pdf.

US Department of Education. (2018). Improving Basic Programs Operated by Local Educational Agencies (Title I, Part A). https://www2.ed.gov/programs/titleiparta/index.html.

Vinovskis, M. A. (1999). Do federal compensatory education programs really work? A brief historical analysis of Title I and Head Start. *American Journal of Education, 107*(3), 187–209.

Walter, M., & Andersen, C. (2013). *Indigenous Statistics: A Quantitative Research Methodology*. Left Coast Press.

Washington Research Project, W. D., and National Association for the Advancement of Colored People, N. Y. N. (1969). Is It Helping Poor Children? Title I of ESEA. A Report.

Wells, A. S. (2014). Seeing Past the 'Colorblind' Myth of Education Policy: Why Policymakers Should Address Racial/Ethnic Inequality and Support Culturally Diverse Schools. *National Education Policy Center*. https://nepc.colorado.edu/publication/seeing-past-the-colorblind-myth.

Zuberi, T. (2001). *Thicker than Blood: How Racial Statistics Lie*. University of Minnesota Press.

Zuberi, T., & Bonilla-Silva, E. (eds.). (2008). *White Logic, White Methods: Racism and Methodology*. Rowman and Littlefield Publishers.

Conclusion
Tyrell Connor and Daphne M. Penn

The current political and social climate provides strong evidence that our nation is at another pivotal crossroads toward racial equity and justice. Our nation's leaders are in a constant tug-of-war about how to move forward with policies that have the potential to produce racial equity. On the one hand, the country witnessed overwhelming bipartisan support to recognize and acknowledge Juneteenth as a federal holiday. On the other hand, we have witnessed many of those same Congress members simultaneously denounce the use of critical race theory within our education system. These competing sociopolitical views leave many citizens wondering how to move forward.

Historically, federal policy has benefited, but mostly burdened, communities of color. People of color have experienced long-lasting effects of policy reform, from the benefits gained during the civil rights era to the burdens of oppressive immigration and criminal justice practices. Trump-era politics have only exacerbated the racial tensions and undertones present within this country. Therefore, it becomes critical to assess the current state of policy and the role of race in policy outcomes. Past (and current) neglect of applying an antiracist perspective when forming policy has left many communities of color oppressed and resource-deprived. Racial equity can only be achieved if race is at the forefront of every policy discussion.

This volume provides a forward-thinking blueprint on how we should address policy using a racial equity lens. The 14 contributors in this book have eloquently written compelling arguments on how we can move forward as a country. These scholars have offered valuable insights on a number of policy issues, ranging from the racist practices of the criminal justice system to matters of voter suppression and immigration policy. Within this text are clear considerations and suggestions about how race must be explicitly recognized within any policy discussion.

KEY TAKEAWAYS

Criminal justice policy and practices are some of the leading causes of racial inequality in the United States. Our current criminal justice system is a modern-day manifestation of the past racist practices of slavery and Jim Crow philosophies. This has been visible from high-profile cases like Michael Brown, Breona Taylor, and George Floyd. Currently, activists and advocates have intensified their demand for major criminal justice reform that adopts an antiracist perspective. The contributors of this volume highlighted the disproportionate burden that structurally disadvantaged people face within our criminal justice system and outlined the specific ways in which racial inequity must be addressed. For example, gun control policy is proposed as a way to reduce gun violence in this country. However, as discussed by Daniel Semenza and Brian Wade, most suggestions around gun control have focused on mass shootings using assault rifles and suicides (a White burden) and not on homicides and handguns (a Black burden).

In relation to recent calls to defund the police, Jalila Jefferson-Bullock and Jelani Jefferson Exum suggested this demand has not been well received because the public does not necessarily view policing as punishment. When defunding the police is properly situated within sentencing reform, it aligns with the general public's view of suitable ways to address the policing problems experienced by marginalized people in the United States. Angela S. Murolo tackled the exclusion of communities of color from cannabis-related financial revenue stemming from the growing US movement to legalize cannabis for recreational use. Furthermore, Emily Tucker revealed how surveillance technology used to assist law enforcement officers has increased racial disparities in the criminal justice system due to algorithmic bias. If the issues raised by the authors in this volume are not seriously considered during policy conversations, communities of color will continue to bear the burden of punitive policies and never reap the benefits of reforms aimed at reducing harm.

Trump-era policies and rhetoric have led to an increase in policy discussions around immigration and xenophobia—issues addressed in this volume. Janice A. Iwama highlighted the ways in which the hateful language used during the onset of the COVID-19 pandemic has increased hostility toward the Asian community. There have also been attempts to create tensions between the Black and Asian communities while both groups work to combat heightened oppression. However, as Niambi M. Carter argued, racial hostility toward immigrants is a direct consequence of White rage fueled by White supremacy—not Black political attitudes of indifference toward immigration policy. In response to attempts to create discord between the Black and Asian communities, it is important to emphasize that racial progress for either group would be a step toward equity for all. Additionally, it is important to further understand how communities of color, specifically Black Americans, experience and view immigration as policy discussions continue to progress. Otherwise, policymakers may continue to perpetuate xenophobia and racism within immigration policy without fully including perspectives from various racial groups.

This volume also explored racial disparities within the field of education and health care. These disparities have been well documented and can be attributed to the long-lasting effects of systemic racism. As it relates to racialized health disadvantage, political conversations surrounding health care and access have neglected to mention the impact of the social determinants of health on the Black community. As Jay Pearson noted in chapter 5, communities of color will not reap the benefits of any health care policy if policy makers do not recognize how systemic racism contributes to vast health disparities. With regard to education, Charisse Southwell and Michael Hudson-Vassell demonstrated how data blindness—a race-neutral approach used in educational spaces—has perpetuated inequalities and lessened the chances of educational success for Black and Brown youth. Given the ongoing educational disparities related to colorblind strategies, it is abundantly clear that race must be prioritized and recognized within educational policy discussions.

Finally, Candice C. Robinson, LaTeri McFadden, and J. Nicole Johnson tackled the issue of rising voter suppression efforts in the United States. The right to vote for Black and Brown Americans has been one of the most effective practices to enforce racial equity in the United States. Voting gives citizens the authority to demand and provide resources for their local communities. However, Black Americans were historically denied voting rights using poll taxes, literacy tests, grandfather clauses, and criminal convictions. The lack of democratic participation denied the Black community access to public goods and resources for educational and economic achievement, with repercussions that have lasted for generations. The 2020 presidential election surprised most Americans when Latinx voters in Arizona and Black voters in Georgia and Pennsylvania flipped Republican strongholds to democratic victories for President Joe Biden. Since then, states throughout the country have quickly begun to implement laws that strategically suppress the votes for Black and Brown American citizens. Therefore, voting reform and protections for communities of color are once again at the political forefront. Congress has yet to pass the For the People Act of 2021 to protect the right to vote for citizens of all backgrounds. The racial implications on voting rights will be highly damaging to our democracy if protections are not granted at the federal level.

Important Lessons

Overall, each chapter in this volume addresses a unique policy dilemma for communities of color. Although each chapter focused on a different policy, three common themes emerged within each policy interrogation. First, historic systemic racism was at the heart of each policy dilemma. The pervasive history of racist practices in the United States still has significant ramifications on today's policy issues—including criminal justice reform, education policy, drug prohibition, immigration, and racialized health disadvantage. Understanding this history provides a clearer picture of what mistakes to avoid moving forward. This can be compared to the way a physician approaches her treatment for a patient. To develop the best medical plan, the doctor must first understand the patient's medical history. The doctor must know of any allergies, past surgeries or illnesses, and certain lifestyle behaviors in order to prescribe a treatment that does not cause additional harm. The same approach should be considered for policies designed to advance racial equity. We must understand the errors of the past to prescribe a better and more equitable future.

Second, present-day policies continue to reproduce racial inequalities. Although the civil rights era was a significant step toward racial equity, most post-civil rights reforms have simply repackaged racism. Due to the implicit nature of contemporary racist practices, it becomes more challenging to identify racial oppression compared to previous explicit forms of racism. The information presented in these chapters provides evidence that the United States is far from a post-racial society. This means that activists and advocates must continue to diligently investigate the racial impacts of policy—even if they perceive the reform as a promising approach to achieving equity. Building on the previous example, a physician may feel hopeful about a newly developed drug to help her patient with a serious disease. However, if that doctor prescribes the drug without diligently researching its side effects, she risks causing serious harm to her patient. As citizens, activists, advocates, and educators, we must continue to check for the racial side effects of any policy that will potentially impact the lives of communities of color.

Finally, each chapter impressively provides a roadmap for the future. Each contributor offers enlightening considerations through their exploration of how past and contemporary policies have shaped racial inequality. The threat of reproducing racial inequality remains even within some of the most progressive policy ideas. It is abundantly clear that racism was used to build this country and it cannot be ignored when trying to heal it. In his 2019 book, *How to be an Antiracist*, Ibram X. Kendi compared racism to metastatic cancer. Referring back to our example of a physician treating a patient, most people would find it troublesome if a health provider prescribed cough medicine as the primary treatment for a cancerous tumor. The United States has continuously ignored the "metastatic racism" embedded within our public policies (Kendi, 2019, p. 237). The best way forward is to recognize that racism is the core issue and develop policies to lessen, and eventually, eradicate its effects.

Our current political climate, albeit polarizing at times, still has a bright future. Ongoing policy discussions about universal health care, defunding the police, cannabis legalization, and gun control are now commonplace topics within political discourse. In fact, Americans increasingly support these policy changes, as evidenced by recent polling (Barry et al., 2020; Cusick, 2021; Manchester, 2018). Therefore, we remain hopeful that we are not too far from realizing the potential of inclusive and equitable social policy. To turn this dream into reality, we must continue to be diligent about centering racial equity in policy conversations and remain steadfast in our efforts to organize around issues that disproportionately impact structurally disadvantaged communities. The contributors of this volume have challenged us to move beyond simply critiquing policy and toward imagining progressive solutions that remedy the harms associated with racist policy. The more we recognize, name, and challenge racism across public policy domains, the closer we get to racial equity for all.

REFERENCES

Barry, C. L., Han, H., Presskreischer, R., Anderson, K. E., & McGinty, E. E. (2020). Public Support for Social Safety-Net Policies for COVID-19 in the United States, April 2020. *American journal of public health*, *110*(12), 1811–1813. doi: 10.2105/AJPH.2020.305919.

Cusick, J. (2021, March 10). Release: New polling shows strong bipartisan support for federal aid for people in need. *Center for American Progress.* https://www.americanprogress.org/press/statement/2021/03/10/496969/release-new-polling-shows-strong-bipartisan-support-federal-aid-people-need/.

Kendi, I. (2019). *How to be an antiracist* (1st ed.). New York: One World.

Manchester, J. (2018). Majority of Republicans supports 'Medicare for all,' poll finds. *The Hill.* https://thehill.com/hilltv/what-americas-thinking/412552-majority-of-republicans-say-the-support-medicare-for-all-poll.

Index

Abbott, Greg, 38
abolishment of institutionalized racism, 38
Abolition Democracy (Davis), 50
abolitionist approach to criminal legal system technology, 54
abolitionist democracy theory, 39–40
Abrams, Stacey, 147, 152
absentee ballots, 148–49, 152
academic skills, 165
achievement gaps, 160, 168
affirmative action, 8, 135
Alabama, 128
Alexander, Michelle, 74
algorithmic risk assessment tools, 52, 61–62
amendments to US Constitution, 143
American Civil Liberties Union (ACLU), 56, 150, 152
ammunition, 20, 25
Anslinger, Henry, 67
anti-Asian hate crimes, 10, 109–20, 125–26; culture and language barriers, 117–18; law enforcement training, 116–17; public awareness, 119–20; school policies, 118–19
antiracist health equity, 101–2
antiracist sentencing reform, 44–45
Ardent Cannabis, 73

arrests in marijuana-legal states, 74–75
Asian Americans. *See* anti-Asian hate crimes
Assault Weapons Ban (AWB), 20–21
ATF. *See* Bureau of Alcohol, Tobacco, Firearms, and Explosives

Baltimore City Council, 38
barriers to casting a ballot, 148–50; absentee and early voting, 148–49; mail-in ballots, 149; voter identification laws, 149–50; voting locations, 149
Baum, Dan, 68
Bell, Derrick, 165
bias (algorithmic), 9, 180
Biden, Joe, 116, 141, 153, 181
BIPOC, 92; health disadvantage, 87, 89–90, 97; racial bias, 94–95; sociocultural orientations and resources, 94; SSR and, 91; White racial majority and, 93
Black and Latinx (BLX) students, 160; achievement gaps, 168; data blindness and, 161, 168–71; decolonizing research approach, 171–72; Title I and, 161–72
Black criminality, 34, 42, 44
Black Lives Matter, 125

black market for gun. *See* illegal markets of firearm
Black-owned businesses forgivable loans, 38
Black people: cultural trauma, 36–38; high-profile deaths of, 125; homicide rate, 16; on immigration, 125–36; years of potential life lost (YPLL), 16
Black politics, 134, 136
Black Voters Matter, 152
Bloody Sunday, 145, 153
Booker, Cory, 78
Brennan Center for Justice, 142
Brotherhood of Sleeping Car Porters, 144
Brown v. Board of Education, 8, 164
budgets: marijuana, 69–70; police/policing, 35–36
bump stocks, 21
Bureau of Alcohol, Tobacco, Firearms, and Explosives (ATF), 18, 22, 25
Bureau of Justice Statistics (BJS), 18, 117
Bush, George W., 6, 146, 151
business opportunities, marijuana and, 79–80
Butler, Paul, 56

Californian, 127–28
Canadian border, 127
cannabis. *See* marijuana
Cannabis Regulation and Tax Act of 2019, 70
carceral technology, 49–63; advocacy against, 55; bureaucracy and, 55–58; historical context, 50–53; reducing digital record keeping and sharing, 58–61; refusing any new expansion, 54–55; resisting in terms of root causes, 61–62
Casa Verde Capital, 71
casting a ballot, barriers to, 148–50. *See also* voter suppression

Center on Privacy & Technology at Georgetown Law, 58
Chin, Vincent, 113
Chinese Exclusion Act, 5
Chinese Massacre of 1871, 111–12
citizenship, 148
Civil Rights Act of 1964, 112, 144–45, 164, 165
Civil Rights Act of 1968, 112
civil rights era, 182
Civil Rights Movement, 144
civil rights organizations, 144, 152
Civil War, 143, 149
Clearview AI, 53
Clinton, Bill, 146
Clinton, Hilary, 151
coalition theories, 133
Colorado, 70, 73, 75, 76, 81
colorblindness: concept, 160; data blindness and, 161, 168–71; examples, 160; as race-neutral ideology, 160; Title I and, 168–71
community-based, anti-violence programs, 25–26
Community Control Over Police Surveillance (CCOPS), 56–57
community-police relations, 27. *See also* focused deterrence
community-policing programs, 120
Congress of Racial Equality (CORE), 144
Constitution of US, 143; amendments to, 143
contractarian justice, 99
convictions, marijuana and, 73, 76, 78–80
CORE. *See* Congress of Racial Equality
coronavirus (COVID-19), 2, 4, 7, 10, 15, 72, 180; anti-Asian hate crimes, 109–20, 125–26; as "Chinese" virus, 109, 125; racializing, 109, 125
COVID-19 Hate Crimes Act in 2021, 116, 120
crime prediction software, 52

criminality, 51
criminal justice-based solutions, 80–81
Criminal Justice Dashboard of Maryland, 60
criminal justice reforms, 5
crimmigration, 6
The Crisis (Du Bois), 131
critical race theory, 160, 165, 169, 179
cultural deprivation theory, 163–64
cultural trauma, 36–38; background, 36–37; from the routine, 37–38
culture and language barriers, 117–18
culture of poverty, 88, 163–64
CureViolenc, 26

DACA. *See* Deferred Action for Childhood Arrivals
databases, 53
data blindness, 161, 168–71, 181
data-conscious leadership, 171
data minimization, 61
Davis, Angela, 50
Davis, Larry, 97–98
Dawson, Michael C., 134
deadly force, police use of, 33, 37, 39–41
death penalty, 42–43
decolonizing research techniques, 171–72
decriminalizing marijuana, 68, 69, 74, 76, 77, 80
Defense of the Negro Race-Charges Answered (White), 144
Deferred Action for Childhood Arrivals (DACA), 129, 136n1
defunding the police, 9, 33–45, 183; abolitionist democracy theory, 39–40; antiracist sentencing reform, 44–45; efforts toward, 38–40; models, 33–34
Department of Homeland Security, 59
Department of Justice, 116, 117, 126; Hate Crimes Prevention and Enforcement Initiative, 117

Departments of Education, Health and Mental Hygiene, and Homeless Services, 38
deportations, 6
De Priest, Oscar, 144
digital infrastructure, 51–52, 54, 55. *See also* carceral technology
digital record keeping and sharing, 58–61
digital surveillance, 55, 56, 59–61. *See also* carceral technology
discrepancy in sentencing patterns, 5
disenfranchisement, 144, 145
Domain Awareness System (DAS), 55
Douglas, Frederick, 91
Drug Enforcement Agency, 67
drug legislation, 5
Du Bois, W.E.B, 50, 51, 87, 131
Dynarski, M., 162

economic equity, 99
education, data blindness: neoliberal reforms, 6–7; Title I of ESEA, 10, 160–72. *See also* colorblindness
Ehrlichman, John, 68
Eighth Amendment, 41–43
electoral college, 143, 146, 147, 150, 151
Elementary and Secondary Education Act (ESEA), 6, 10, 160, 163, 166, 167
English as a Second Language (ESL), 128
English Language Learners, 167
equity: economic, 99; philosophical, 99
ethnicity, 92–94
Every Student Succeeds Act (ESSA), 167–68; due for reauthorization, 173
Everytown for Gun Safety, 20–21
exclusions, 4–5, 7, 68–69, 131, 133, 180
expungement, marijuana and, 75–76
extreme risk protection order (ERPO), 20

facial recognition technology, 9, 49, 52, 55, 57–58, 60, 62

failing schools, 6
Fair Fight, 152
Fair Housing Act, 113
Fair Labor Act, 4
farmers of color, 4
Federal Bureau of Dangerous Drugs, 67
Federal Bureau of Investigation (FBI), 112, 114
Federal Housing Administration (FHA), 4
Fifteenth Amendment, 143, 148
Fifth Amendment, 51
firearm: addressing access to, 24–25; deaths, 15; dismantling illegal markets, 22–23, 25; homicides, 15–17, 19–21; licensing policies, 18–19, 24; policies, 16–21; policing of, 23–24; suicides, 15–17, 19, 20; transactional policies for, 19–20; universal background checks, 19, 22, 25; weapons ban policies, 20–21
firearm markets, 17–18
Florida State Supreme Court, 151
Floyd, George, 9, 33, 57, 180
focused deterrence, 27
Ford, Chandra, 91
Ford, Gerald, 146
For the People Act, 141, 142, 153, 181–82
Fourth Amendment, 40, 41, 43
Fourteenth Amendment, 143, 148
Freedom of Information Act (FOIA), 59
funding accountability, Title I, 166–68
Furman v. Georgia, 43

gang, 21, 25
gang task force, 23
gaps in wealth. *See* wealth gap
Gay, Claudine, 133
Gee, Gilbert, 91
General Data Protection Regulation, 65
Geronimus, Arline, 98
gerrymandering, 141, 143, 144, 151
G.I. Bill, 4

Gideon v. Wainwright, 51, 56
Glass, Carter, 148
Goals 2000: Educate America Act of the 1990s, 167
"good moral character" clause, 73
Gore, Al, 146, 151
GPS-enabled electronic ankle monitors, 52
Graham v. Connor, 41
Grandpre, Lawrence, 78
Great American Affordability Crisis, 2
Great Depression, 164
Great Recession, 2, 72
Green Entrepreneur, 73
group identity construction, 93
gun control, 9, 180, 183; measures, 21–27; policy-oriented conversations on, 15; policy reforms, 17–21
gun deaths, 16, 17, 19. *See also* homicides; suicides
gun rights, 21
gun show loophole, 18
gun trafficking, 22
gun violence, 9, 15–28; community-based, anti-violence programs, 25–26; dismantling illegal markets, 22–23; focused deterrence, 27; homicides, 15–17, 19–21; outreach programs, 26; overview, 15–16; policy reforms and, 17–21; procedural justice, 27; racial disparities and, 16–17; recommendations for equitable reduction of, 24; red flag laws, 20, 25; suicides, 15–17, 19, 20; weapons ban policies, 20–21; years of potential life lost (YPLL), 16

handguns, 20–21
Harrington, Al, 71
hate crimes, 112–14, 125–26; data, 114–16; legislation, 112–13; standard definition of, 114. *See also* anti-Asian hate crimes

Hate Crimes Prevention and Enforcement Initiative (Department of Justice), 117
Hate Crime Statistics Act (HCSA), 113–14
Hawkins-Stafford Elementary and Secondary School Improvement Amendments, 167
Hayes, Rutherford B., 151
health: proximal predictors, 96; social determinants of, 96–97
health care, 180, 183
health disadvantage, 87–90; Theory of Fundamental Cause, 96–97
health equity, 98–100; antiracist, 101–2
health inequity, 89–90
Hernandez, José Santos Quintero, 60–61
Highway Safety Act, 60
homicides, 15–17, 19–21. *See also* gun violence
hospital-based violence intervention programs (HVIP), 26
How to be an Antiracist (Kendi), 183
Hughes, Bryan, 142
Hung, Man, 160
Huntington, Samuel, 127

identity construction: ethnic, 93; group, 93; self-perceived, 93–94
illegal immigration, 6
illegal markets of firearm, 22–23, 25
immigrant health, 87–89
immigration, 125–36; American identity and, 127–28; Black public opinion on, 125–36; competition model, 132; contextualizing, 129–32; employment, 132–33; enforcement, 5–6; illegal and legal, 134
Immigration Act of 1924, 129–30
Immigration and Customs Enforcement (ICE), 6, 60–61
impacted communities, 78–79
Improving America's Schools Act (IASA), 167
Institute of Education Sciences, 167

institutionalized racism, 38
interest convergence, 165
Intergroup Contact Theory, 100
International Association of Chiefs of Police (IACP), 117
interpersonal racism, 91
intimate partner homicide, 17
investors, 71, 73, 77
Iron Pipeline, 22

James, Sherman, 98
Jefferson, Brian, 54
Jim Crow, 74, 142, 180
job opportunities, marijuana and, 79–80
The John Henryism scale of High Effort Coping, 98
John Lewis Voting Rights Act. *See* For the People Act of 2021
Johnson, Lyndon B., 145
Johnson-Reed Act. *See* Immigration Act of 1924
Jones, Camara Phyllis, 91
Juneteenth, 179

Kainz, Kirsten, 162
Kemp, Brian P., 142, 147
Kendi, Ibram X., 183
Khan, Hamid, 57
King, Martin Luther, Jr., 112, 145
Koper, Christopher S., 20
Ku Klux Klan, 112

LACCHR. *See* Los Angeles County Commission on Human Relations
language barriers. *See* culture and language barriers
Las Vegas mass shooting of 2017, 21
Latino immigration, 134
law enforcement training on hate crime, 116–17
legalization of marijuana, 69–81; arrests, 74–75; benefitted group, 71–72; criminal justice-based solutions, 80–81; investment in impacted communities, 78–79; job

and business opportunities, 79–80; recreational use, 68, 69, 74–75, 78–79; reducing mass incarceration, 77; resentencing, expungement, and pardons, 75–76; tax revenues and budgets, 69–70
Lewis, John, 141, 145, 152, 153
licensing policies for firearm, 18–19, 24
Lindsay, Shanel, 73
linked fate, 134
loans, paycheck protection, 4
Los Angeles County Commission on Human Relations (LACCHR), 112
Los Angeles Uprisings of 1992, 126
lynchings, 126

majority/minority status distinction, 90, 100
Manchin, Joe, 142
Maori Education Movement in New Zealand, 171
Marihuana Tax Act of 1937, 67
marijuana, 9–10, 67–81; arrests in post-legalization states, 74–75; businesses and jobs, 70–74, 79–80; criminal justice-based solutions, 80–81; decriminalizing, 68, 69, 74, 76, 77, 80; impacted communities, 78–79; legalization, 69–81; mass incarceration, 77; moral panic and, 67–68; racist media reports, 67; recreational use, 68, 69, 74–75, 78–79; resentencing, expungement, and pardons, 75–76; tax revenues and budgets, 69–70
marijuana industry, 70
Marijuana Justice Act, 78
Marijuana Opportunity Reinvestment and Expungement Act (MORE Act), 79
Maryland, 60
Maryland Image Repository System (MIRS), 60
mass incarceration, 50–51
massive resistance, 8

mass shootings, 15, 16, 20–21, 180; handguns, 20–21, 24–25; Las Vegas mass shooting of 2017, 21
mass surveillance, 51–53
maternal mortality, 88
McCabe, Katherine T., 134
"The Meaning of July 4th for the Negro" (Douglas), 91
Merkley, Jeff, 141
metastatic racism, 183
Mexican border, 127
Mexican immigration, 127
Miranda v. Arizona, 51
Mizuno, Yuko, 133
MORE Act. *See* Marijuana Opportunity Reinvestment and Expungement Act
Morris, Irwin L., 133
Movement for Black Lives, 51, 62. *See also* Black Lives Matter

National Association for the Advancement of Colored People (NAACP), 126, 144, 145
National Commission on Excellence in Education, 6
National Council of Negro Women, 144
National Rifle Association, 24
National Urban League (NUL), 144, 152
National Voter Registration Day, 152
A Nation at Risk, 6, 167
native stocks, 130, 136n2
needs assessments, Title I, 166–68
New Deal, 4
New York, 76, 78–80
New York City, 39, 57; Domain Awareness System (DAS), 55
New York City Council, 38
New York City Police Department, 38
New York Times, 141, 152
Next Generation Information (NGI), 59–60
Ngai, Mae M., 136n2
Nineteenth Amendment, 143
Nixon, Richard, 67–68, 146

No Child Left Behind Act (NCLB), 6–7, 167

Obama, Barack, 146
Office for Victims of Crime (OCV), 117
Office of Community Oriented Policing Services (COPS), 117
Office of Justice Programs, 117
Operation Peacemaker Fellowship (OPF), 26
oppressive social orders, 95
Oregon, 75–76
over-policing, 23

pardons, marijuana and, 75–76
Parks, Nijeer, 49
Paycheck Protection Program, 4
Pearl Harbor, 111
Pennsylvania, 22, 72, 76, 128
People v. Hall, 111
Pew Research Center, 6, 152
philosophical equity, 99
photo ID, 149–50
police brutality, 33, 37–38, 40
Police Executive Research Forum (PERF), 117
police/policing, 22–23; budgets, 35–36; firearm, 23–24; officer-involved shootings, 23–24; racism and, 35–38; as systemically racist, 35; trauma inflicted by, 36–38; use of force, 40–44; violence and harassment, 23–24
police reform, 34
police violence, 49–50
policy reform, 179
post-civil rights reforms, 182
poverty, culture of, 88, 163–64
Powell, Adam Clayton, 164
Powers, Rebecca S., 132
procedural justice, 27
property tax revenues, 38–39
Proposition 187, 127–29
Proposition 227, 128
prosecution, marijuana and, 74, 76, 80

public awareness, hate crime and, 119–20
punishment, criminal law investigatory power as, 44; death penalty as, 42–43; just, 43; post-conviction, 43. *See also* police/policing
purging, 147

R3 (Restore, Reinvest, Renew) program, 70
race, 92–93
racial bias, 94–96; historicizing, 94; negative, 94; positive, 94; racial identifiers, 95; SWRS, 94–95, 97
racial disparities: gun violence and, 16–17; in marijuana arrests, 74–75
racial equity: designing social policies for, 7–8
racial profiling, 6, 35, 36
racial threat theory, 35–36
racism: data blindness, 161, 168–71, 181; historical roots of, 3; institutionalized, 38; as interactive multilevel phenomena, 91; interpersonal, 91; policing and, 35–38; post-civil rights reforms and, 182; social policies and, 3–8
Rainey, Joseph, 143
Rawls, John, 99
Reagan, Ronald, 68, 146
Reardon, Sean F., 160
recreational use of marijuana, 68, 69, 74–75, 78–79
red flag laws, 20, 25
redistributive social service programming, 99
redistricting, 151
Reed, David, 130
research and evaluation: data blindness and, 161, 168–71; decolonizing, 171–72
resentencing, marijuana and, 75–76
Revels, Hiram, 143
risk assessment tools, 61–62
risk score, 49

Salley, John, 71
Sandy Hook Elementary School shooting, 21
San Francisco, 76
Sarbanes, John P., 141
SB 1070 of Arizona, 6
Scholastic Aptitude Test (SAT), 167
school policies, hate crime and, 118–19
school segregation, 160
SCLC. *See* Southern Christian Leadership Conference
scofflaw dealers, 22, 25
Secure Communities, 59–60
self-defense, 22, 23
self-perceived identity construction, 93–94
sentencing: antiracist reform, 44–45; discrepancy in, 5; informed decisions, 35; modern-day reformers, 34–35
September 2001 attacks, 6
Shelby County v. Holder, 146
shootings: police-involved, 23–24; racial disparities in, 16–17
slave patrols, 35
slavery, 180
SNCC. *See* Student Nonviolent Coordinating Committee
Snoop Dogg, 71
social contracts, 99
social determinants of health, 96–97
social minorities, 99–100
Social Security Act, 4
Southern Christian Leadership Conference (SCLC), 144, 145
Soviet Union, 163
Sputnik, 163
SQF (Stop, Question, and Frisk), 23
standardized test scores, 6
Stop AAPI Hate Coalition, 115
#STOPASIANHATE, 120
Stop LAPD Spying Coalition, 57
straw purchases, 22
street-level bureaucrats, 4
street outreach programs, 26

street violence, 21
structural inequality, 90
structural racism, 3–4, 90–92
Student Nonviolent Coordinating Committee (SNCC), 144, 145
Students for Fair Admissions v. Harvard, 8
Stumpf, Juliet, 6
suicides, gun deaths, 15–17, 19, 20
supremacy, 94. *See also* White supremacy
surveillance, 50
SWRS. *See* Systemic White Racial Supremacy
systemic racism, 182
systemic structural antiracism, 100–102; health equity, 101–2
Systemic Structural Racism (SSR), 10, 87, 89–101; antiracist health equity, 101–2; public policies addressing, 100–102
Systemic White Racial Supremacy (SWRS), 94–95, 97

Targeted Universalism, 101
tax revenues from marijuana, 69–70
Taylor, Breonna, 9, 33, 42, 180
technology, 61–62
Tennessee v. Garner, 40–41
Theory of Fundamental Cause, 96–97
Theory of Justice, 99
Thirteenth Amendment, 143, 148
Thornton, Michael C., 133
Title I of ESEA, 10, 160–72; and BLX student performance, 161–63; colorblindness and, 168–71; decolonizing research techniques, 171–72; eligibility requirements, 166; funding accountability, 166–68; national development during racial unrest, 163–66; needs assessments, 166–68
transactional policies for firearm, 19–20
trauma inflicted by police/policing, 36–38. *See also* cultural trauma

Travis, Jeremy, 73
Trump, Donald, 132, 146, 151
Trump-era policies/politics, 179, 180

undocumented persons, 128
Uniform Crime Reporting (UCR) program, 114
universal background checks, 19, 22, 25
universal health insurance program, 1
urban gun violence, 15, 16
US Census, 118, 130
US Commission on Civil Rights, 113, 119
US Department of Health and Human Services, 96
US Supreme Court, 151; on death penalty, 42–43; *Furman v. Georgia*, 43; *Graham v. Connor*, 41; on just punishment, 43; *Tennessee v. Garner*, 40–41; on use of deadly force, 40–41; *Woodson v. North Carolina*, 43

Vance, Cyrus, 80
"The Veil of Ignorance" (Rawls), 99
Violent Crime Control and Law Enforcement Act, 20
voter awareness, 152
voter identification laws, 149–50; opposition to, 150; photo ID, 149–50
voter registration, 144–46; limitations, 147–48; purging, 147
voter suppression, 10, 146–53, 181; barriers to casting a ballot, 148–50; fight against, 152–53; impacting strength of voting, 150–51; limiting voters and voter registration, 147–48
voting blocs, 147, 150
voting laws, 142
voting locations, 149

voting participation, 145–46
voting reform, 10, 142, 181–82; as states' rights, 142
voting rights, 181–82
Voting Rights Act, 141, 144–47; amendments to, 146; legislative protections, 145; voting participation and, 145–46
Voting Rights Advancement Act. *See* For the People Act
voting strength, 150–51

War on crime, 5
War on drugs, 5
wealth gap, 4–5
weapons ban policies, 20–21
Weathering Hypothesis, 98
When Affirmative Action Was White (Katznelson), 4
White, George Henry, 144
White anxieties, 164
Whiteness, 127
White supremacy, 130, 134–35, 143; SWRS, 94–95, 97
White voters, 132, 142
Who Are We?: The Challenge to America's National Identity (Huntington), 127
Wilmington Race Riot, 126
Wilmington Race Riot of 1898, 126
women: intimate partner homicide, 17; killed with a gun, 17
Woodson v. North Carolina, 43
World Health Organization (WHO), 109
World War II, 111–12, 119

xenophobia, 180

years of potential life lost (YPLL), 16

About the Authors

Dr. **Niambi Carter** is an associate professor of political science at Howard University. She is the author of the award-winning book, *American While Black: African Americans, Immigration, and the Limits of Citizenship* (2019, Oxford University Press), that investigates African American public opinion on immigration. She is an expert on Race and Ethnic Politics in the United States with a particular emphasis on Black Politics, Politics, Public Opinion, and Political Behavior. Her work has appeared in the *Journal of Politics*; *Political Psychology*; *National Review of Black Politics*; the *DuBois Review*; and many others. Her next project examines US Haitian refugee policy.

Dr. **Tyrell Connor** is an associate professor in the Sociology Department at the State University of New York—New Paltz. He received his BA in psychology from Hampton University and PhD in sociology, specializing in law and society, from Purdue University. Currently, he is the director of the Criminology Concentration within the department and a member of the university's Diversity & Inclusion Council. Tyrell's research primarily focuses on the impact of race within specialized court programs. His current research qualitatively examines how community court judges and staff address race to improve outcomes for people of color. He has published research in Race and Justice, Crime and Justice, Sexual Aggression, and Social Welfare and Human Rights. Outside of the academy, Tyrell remains actively involved with the local community. He runs a biweekly group at Newark, NJ's community court with college-age formerly incarcerated men of color that focus on ways we can improve our communities and ourselves. He is also a Diversity and Equity consultant for the National Association of Drug Court Professionals where he audits drug courts around the country to suggest ways to improve racial outcomes. Additionally, he is cofounder and cohost of the Black & Highly Dangerous (BhD) podcast, which aims to bridge the gap between academia and the people by interviewing various scholars, professionals, and activists that focus on issues involving people of color.

Dr. **Michael Hudson-Vassell** is an independent researcher with a specific interest in understanding formal and informal education systems and the ways in which they can be (re)organized to cultivate the academic and personal brilliance of Black students. He has worked at various levels of education, including as a policy analyst at the state level, an institutional research associate at the community college level, and a teacher at the school district level.

Janice A. Iwama is an assistant professor in the Department of Justice, Law & Criminology at American University in Washington, DC. She received her PhD in Criminology and Justice Policy from Northeastern University. Dr. Iwama's primary research lies in exploring the intersection of race, ethnicity, immigration, and crime. With more than fifteen years of experience in research, she has worked extensively on projects involving racial disparities, gun violence, and victimization. She has previously worked with other law enforcement agencies across the country in applying statistical and analytical methods to help improve our understanding of racial disparities in stop data given recent demographic, political, and social changes. She has also collaborated with federal, state, and local agencies in developing best practices in the areas of hate crimes, gun violence, and policing. Her work on racial profiling, hate crimes, and gun violence has been highlighted in national and local news outlets.

Jalila Jefferson-Bullock is an associate professor of law at Duquesne University School of Law. She is a prison abolitionist, and her research focuses on de-emphasizing incarceration as punishment, with a particular focus on elderly and ill prisoners. She teaches Constitutional Law, Criminal Law, Criminal Procedure, and Race and American Law. She sits on the Academic Review Panel of the Pennsylvania Sentencing Commission and the Police Use of Force Committee for the Allegheny County Bar Association.

Jelani Jefferson Exum is dean and Philip J. McElroy professor of law at the University of Detroit Mercy School of Law. Her research focuses on sentencing and policing reform, as well as issues of race in the criminal justice system. The authors would like to dedicate this chapter to the numerous Black lives that have been lost to violence at the hands of police officers. It is their sincere hope that this moment generates genuine systemic change that truly embraces the value of Black lives by protecting them from state-sanctioned terror. They are grateful to Gabrielle Campbell and Alexandria Porche for their excellent research support.

J. Nicole Johnson graduated from the University of Pennsylvania in 2013 with a Master of Science in Education and is currently working toward her PhD in Organizational Leadership. As a therapist, company culture cultivator, and a leadership development facilitator, she works to support others in living the lives they desire. This intersection of professional development and job training and an individual's happiness and life satisfaction are the focus of her current studies. It is her hope that not only will our personal but also our professional lives will create an environment that allows us to not simply survive but thrive. J currently resides in Texas; however, she is a diehard Jersey girl. If her nose is not in a book, you will find her spending time with her pups, enjoying her latest Netflix binge or roaming the world.

LaTeri McFadden, PhD, is a Baltimore native. She attended Bowie State University, where she earned her Bachelor of Science degree in Child and Adolescent Studies, an interdisciplinary program. Towson University, earning a Master of Science degree in Human Resources Development and Post-Bachelor's Certification in Management & Leadership Development. Finally, she attended Capella University, where she earned a Doctor of Philosophy degree in Organization and Management with a specialization in Human Resource Management. Her research focused on the generational perspective of work-life balance and wellness in the nonprofit sector. Professionally Dr. McFadden has been a Program Manager for a Nonprofit, Senior Benefits Specialist, Leave Management Subject Matter Expert, and an Adjunct Professor. Dr. McFadden is currently involved in various community initiatives, including serving as a board member for several nonprofit organizations, Pressley Ridge of Maryland, African American Fire Fighters Historical Society, and The Be Org. In addition, Dr. McFadden is a Life Member of Sigma Gamma Rho Sorority Incorporated. Lastly, she serves as an officer for The Greater Baltimore Urban League Young Professional Auxiliary, Greater Baltimore Leadership Associations, as Vice-President of Finance. In addition, she recently completed the National Urban League Congressional Advocacy Program.

Angela S Murolo, MA, MPhil, is an instructor at Sacred Heart University College of Arts and Sciences and a doctoral candidate at John Jay College of Criminal Justice/CUNY Graduate Center. Her research interests include drug policy. She was a volunteer with the (former) Chai Project in New Brunswick, NJ, who worked to bring clean needles to the injecting community to promote safe injecting practices. Her current research investigates aging within the criminal justice system. Her dissertation research aims to generate an in-depth understanding of the aging prison population and their challenges with reentry and reintegration into society. The research also seeks to understand the parole officer's role in assisting reentry for elderly parolees. Her dissertation builds on a previous publication in the *Journal of Correctional Healthcare* which provided an overview of correctional responses to the aging prison population. This article covered topics including segregated housing, hospice, age-appropriate prison programming, health care, and geriatric parole. She has written extensively on compassionate release and geriatric parole. She currently teaches courses covering the correctional system at Sacred Heart University in Fairfield, CT.

Jay Pearson is associate professor of Public Policy at Duke University's Sanford School. Hailing from rural eastern North Carolina, Pearson is a population health scientist trained in Health Education, Health Behavior, Social Epidemiology, and Health Demography. Dr. Pearson has lived and worked in a diverse range of communities and sociocultural contexts, both in the United States and abroad. His research leverages these experiences to investigate the identity-mediated population health effects associated with the lived experience, and biological embedding of public policy decision making on majority/minority identity construction, social stratification, structural and institutional social bias.

Daphne M. Penn, PhD, is a Provost's Postdoctoral Fellow in the Department of Sociology and Population Studies Center at the University of Pennsylvania. She earned her BS in human and organizational development from Vanderbilt University, an MS in sociology from Purdue University, and her PhD in education from Harvard University. Her research focuses on the roots of racialized inequality in the United States and the politics of ethno-racial stratification within the context of demographic change. Penn's scholarly work has been supported by the Ford Foundation, the Center for American Political Studies, and the Immigration Initiative at Harvard. She has published research in *Sociology of Education*, *Sociological Studies of Children & Youth*, and *AERA Open*. In addition to her scholarly pursuits, Penn is the cohost and cofounder of the Black and Highly Dangerous podcast. She is also the founder and editor of The Ebony Tower, an online platform created to help academics of color thrive in the ivory tower.

Candice C. Robinson, PhD, is an assistant professor of sociology at the University of North Carolina-Wilmington. She received her PhD from the University of Pittsburgh. Her research agenda connects the areas of race, class, civic engagement, and social movements using mixed methods. Her case study of the National Urban League observes how participation in civic engagement overtime by the Black Middle Class supports broader social justice aims. She has published research on the Black Middle Class, Black Millennials, and the National Urban League in Issues in Race and Society: An Interdisciplinary Global Journal: Special Issue on the Global Black Middle Class; Sociological Perspectives, Sociology Compass, and Black Millennials: Identity, Ambition, and Activism. Dr. Robinson is currently working on a coauthored book manuscript titled the "Sociology of Cardi B," a book that highlights the importance of utilizing cultural icons in understanding sociological concepts for the public and our students. Dr. Robinson has committed her career to conducting interdisciplinary scholarship that acknowledges the nuances of experiences of Black people in America.

Daniel Semenza is an assistant professor in the Department of Sociology, Anthropology, and Criminal Justice at Rutgers University—Camden. Dr. Semenza is a faculty affiliate of the New Jersey Gun Violence Research Center and an external fellow with the Health Criminology Research Consortium at Saint Louis University. He research issues related to gun violence, victimization across the life course, criminal justice exposure, and community health disparities.

Dr. **Charisse Southwell** is a K–12 Title I Research Specialist, adjunct faculty with Florida Atlantic University, and an independent researcher who works with community-based organizations to use decolonized research methods in their institutional decision making. Dr. Southwell has taught courses on race and culture in education and is teaching emancipatory research inquiry to public sector researchers in South Florida. Dr. Southwell has published in outlets such as the *Journal of Teaching and Teacher Education, Equity & Excellence in Education,* and the *Journal of Faculty Development.* Currently, Dr. Southwell is working with university faculty and public sector change agents to create a research-practice partnership that will bring scientific infrastructure to local efforts that support Title I targeted populations in South Florida.

Emily Tucker is the Executive Director of the Center on Privacy & Technology at Georgetown Law, where she is also an adjunct professor of law. She manages the Center's work to expose and mitigate the impact of digital age technologies on historically marginalized communities. She also teaches classes on surveillance and civil rights at the law school. Before joining Georgetown, Emily worked for ten years as a movement lawyer, supporting grassroots groups to organize, litigate, and legislate against the criminalization and surveillance of poor communities and communities of color. She is a 2021 Soros Justice Fellow.

Brian Wade is a research fellow in the Center on Crime and Community Resilience at the School of Criminology and Criminal Justice at Northeastern University and a doctoral candidate and presidential fellow in the School of Criminal Justice at Rutgers University. His research examines gun violence, underground economies, and crime control efforts in disadvantaged, urban settings.